D0485981

PHRASE AND WORD ORIGINS

A Study of Familiar Expressions

(formerly titled: *Phrase Origins*)

BY

ALFRED H. HOLT

REVISED EDITION

DOVER PUBLICATIONS, INC.

NEW YORK

Published in Canada by General Publishing Company, Ltd., 30 Lesmill Road, Don Mills, Toronto, Ontario.
Published in the United Kingdom by Constable and Company, Ltd., 10 Orange Street, London WC 2.

This Dover edition, first published in 1961, is a revised and enlarged version of the first edition published by Thomas Y. Crowell Company in 1936 under the title *Phrase Origins.*

International Standard Book Number: 0-486-20758-7
Library of Congress Catalog Card Number: 61-2238

Manufactured in the United States of America
Dover Publications, Inc.
180 Varick Street
New York, N.Y. 10014

TO
PHILIP MARSHALL BROWN

PREFACE TO THE DOVER EDITION

THERE IS a sort of legend that, when metal became scarce in World War II, the plates of *Phrase Origins* were melted up and fired at the Japanese. And the Crowell edition soon became a collector's item, if not a Rare Book. Last summer the pathos of this situation touched the heart of President Hayward Cirker, of Dover Publications, Inc. He felt —and I was inclined to agree with him—that it was a good book, and that seekers after knowledge should not have to pay ten or twelve dollars for a two-dollar volume. Without much difficulty he prevailed on me to undertake this revised and enlarged edition. It has, in fact, been a joy to work with him on this fascinating subject.

Again I am indebted to the entire staff of the Williams College Library for their gracious and diligent assistance, especially to Wyllis Wright, Miss Juanita Terry, and, once more, Don Cary. Some others who have helped me greatly on this second venture are: Professor Tom Burns Haber of Ohio State, Margaret Ward of the Haskin Information Service, Grace Fuller of the Reference Division of the Library of Congress, Dr. Mitford Mathews of the University of Chicago, Captain W. R. Hurder of the U.S. Merchant Marine Academy, Wesley Stout and Rev. Dick Blanchard of Fort Lauderdale, Professor Hallett Smith of Cal. Tech., and a very outspoken gentleman of vast experience, Chester F. Cook, of Los Angeles.

ALFRED H. HOLT.

Fort Lauderdale, Fla.
September, 1960.

PREFACE TO THE FIRST EDITION

On the cover of his delightful and scholarly *The Romance of Words*, Dr. Weekley caused to be inscribed: "Words have ancestors, too. It's great fun to trace them." This is even truer, I believe, of phrases, as trailing a word to its source will often land you in a Gothic or Sanskrit dictionary, whereas a phrase detective may find himself plying his trade in a poolroom or railroad yard, or while listening to a radio comedian. While many single words have been included in the following list, it is usually because they are the key-words of phrases; but some are there because, when they were used in an incidental way in treating of the source of some other expression, it seemed pertinent to mention their own root-meaning; and others, frankly, are there because they seemed just too exciting to omit.

The choice of phrases for inclusion has been largely influenced by considerations of picturesque interest. Common and obvious proverbs like "Murder will out" and "The burnt child dreads the fire" do not get in, unless there is some significant dispute about date or ancestry. We have also tried to exclude comments whose only importance lay in the opportunity they offered for wisecracks; for example, we might have listed "Izzat so?" ("Is that so?") just in order to mention that *izzat* is Persian for credit or reputation. And, in that connection, the only apology that can be offered for occasional levity is that a good recipe for remembering a stodgy fact is to associate it with some ridiculous remark made by a smart aleck.

A certain type of reader, and one for whom I have the highest respect, will notice at once that we have not been entirely consistent in our use of quotation marks and italics. Our policy has been to avoid these wherever the meaning was abundantly clear without them, with the exception, of course, that foreign terms are regularly italicized. Clearness, at the expense if necessary of consistency, has therefore been our aim.

The more important books which I have consulted are listed in the bibliography. However, special mention should be made here of those on which I have relied most heavily. They are: the Oxford English

Dictionary, through its 1933 Supplement; Webster's New International Dictionary (1934); Burton Stevenson's *Home Book of Quotations* (1935); and Crowell's *Handbook for Readers and Writers* (1925).

Newcomers in the field may be puzzled by the mystic letters, "N. & Q." The frequency of their occurrence in the text suggests the desirability of something more than a cold statement that *Notes and Queries* is a unique little magazine that has been published weekly in London since November, 1849. Its original subtitle explained that it was for "Literary Men, Artists, Antiquaries, Genealogists, Etc." For seventy-four years it ran at the masthead Captain Cuttle's immortal "When found, make a note on." In 1865, the descriptive title became "For Literary Men, General Readers, Etc.," and in 1923, when the captain was dropped overboard, it was revealed that the editors were henceforth to direct their attentions chiefly to "Readers and Writers, Collectors, and Librarians." As that pretty clearly includes us all, it would be altogether ungracious in us not to keep in touch with this clearinghouse of very miscellaneous information, and to make use of its generously offered facilities.

A word in explanation of the dedication. Dr. Philip Marshall Brown, formerly professor of international law at Princeton, suggested that I make the study, and kept after me until I did. I wish also to express my thanks to President Crowell, without whose constant help and sympathetic cooperation this book would not have been possible. Others who have been of great assistance to me are: the staff of the Williams College Library, especially Miss Ethel Richmond and Mr. Donald E. Cary; Mr. Allen W. Read, of Sir William A. Craigie's dictionary staff, at the University of Chicago; Miss Mildred Keenan, of New York City; and Mr. Arthur W. Browne, of Mountain View, California.

ALFRED H. HOLT.

Williamstown, Mass.
May, 1936.

ABBREVIATIONS

(*See Bibliography for Additional Reference Books*)

OED = *Oxford English Dictionary.*
Webster = *Webster's New International Dictionary* (1934).
Stevenson = Burton Stevenson's *Home Book of Quotations.*
Crowell = Crowell's *Handbook for Readers and Writers.*
E.P. = *Oxford Dictionary of English Proverbs.*
N. & Q. = *Notes and Queries.*
B. & L. = Barrère and Leland, *Dictionary of Slang.*
EDD = *English Dialect Dictionary.*
ME = Middle English.
q.v. = "which see."
cf. = compare.
c. = *circa* (about).

PHRASE AND WORD ORIGINS

A

about the bush. See BEAT AROUND THE BUSH.

absolutism tempered by assassination. This neat stab at the Czarist government was first put in writing by Count Münster, German envoy at St. Petersburg in 1800, but he claimed to be quoting a Russian noble. It has been flattered by numerous imitations, two of the best known being: "Despotism tempered by epigrams" (pre-revolutionary France), and the Gilbertian "Despotism tempered by dynamite."

academic groves. This somewhat trite phrase is not just a bit of poetic fancy (similar to the theory that a college must always be on a hill and have ivy). *Academe* was the name of the olive grove near Athens, where Plato taught. Hence, a school of philosophy.

ace in the hole. At cards, an ace is a "one-spot"; at tennis, it is a single devastating serve that one's opponent cannot touch. Both show their descent from Latin *as*, a unit. (See DEUCE.) But in aviation, the less literal meaning of "one who excels" caused it to be applied to a pilot who had brought down five or more enemy planes.

An ace in the hole, in poker a reserve card that you alone know about, means that you have some secret reserve strength.

adage. See CAT.

adder. This word for snake originally began with *n*, but somewhere between 1300 and 1500 the *n* was attached to the article *a*, to make "an adder" out of "a nadder." The same thing happened to "a nauger," a tool for cutting a hole through the *nave* of a wheel; the ME word was *navegor*. Today it is *auger*. (See MAD.)

admirable Crichton. See CRICHTON.

admire. Students are usually filled with "admiration" (in the old sense) when they read in *Macbeth* about "most admired disorder," or in *Paradise Lost*, "Let none admire That riches grow in hell." The original meaning (*ad + mirari*, to wonder at) has been almost entirely lost, though it was used as recently as 1865 by Carlyle. The above examples are, therefore, "rather to be admired than imitated."

advice. See PUNCH'S ADVICE.

aerobatics. Americans prefer "stunt-flying" or just "stunting," perhaps because the Greekish word seems a heavy-handed sort of pun on "acrobatics." However, the coinage is reasonably sound, both roots being Greek; the literal meaning is something like "walking on air."

African golf. See DIE IS CAST.

aghast. See FLABBERGAST.

agonizing re-appraisal. See BRINKMANSHIP.

aisle. The British are only now getting accustomed to our use of *aisle* to mean the passageway in a church or theater, while we have the utmost difficulty in discovering any other useful meaning for it. It seems to represent a *section* of the auditorium, particularly if that part is set off from the rest by a row of pillars; as if we were to say, "A thousand people sat in the left aisle"—which in America would be a gross violation of the fire laws. The word is ultimately from Latin *ala*, wing or armpit. The outlandish spelling and pronunciation of *aisle* may be attributed to confusion with *isle*.

Theatrical slang, "We laid 'em in the aisles," is very similar to "We knocked 'em dead," signifying to the initiated that we were very successful.

The use of *middle-aisle* as a verb, to mean "get married" ("They middle-aisled it yesterday") is credited to Walter Winchell, Broadway correspondent.

akimbo. The Middle English form of this was *in kenebowe*, possibly from a Scandinavian word suggesting kink or bow, and thus related to *elbow*. It may also be related to "game" as in "game leg." The picture is, of course, of a determined looking matron, hands on hips, elbows protruding.

Alabama. Though Century says that "Here we rest," the translation given by Edwards, is incorrect, the name being that of an Indian chief met by De Soto, the new Webster gives a definition singularly close to the earlier, more poetical interpretation. Surely "I make a clearing" expresses in prosaic and literal form the basic idea of "Here we rest."

alabaster. See ALLEY.

Albany beef. See RABBIT.

all clear. See HIGH BALL.

alley. This "most precious of marbles" (Weekley) probably derives its name from *alabaster* (which used to be *alablaster*, perhaps by confusion with *arblaster*, a cross-bowman). The cheaper "marbles" being made of clay or terra cotta, those made of alabaster or real marble were especially prized and affectionately nicknamed "alleys," in the same way that Thomas became "Tommy."

Use the expression "He hasn't got all his marbles" with caution, if at all. It is certainly sexual in origin. The meaning is, "He's not quite all there," a half-wit. (See NUTS.)

allez fusil. See LALLAPALOOSA.

All Fools' Day. See APRIL FOOL.

all hollow. See HOLLOW.

alliances. See ENTANGLING ALLIANCES.

alligator. The passion of early etymologists for relating every discovery in story form is well illustrated here. Edwards tells an "anecdote" of early explorers pointing out the creatures and exclaiming, "There's *a lagarto*!" It is perfectly true that *alligator* comes from *el lagarto*, the lizard, which goes back to Latin *lacertus*, the fleshy part of the forearm—but any etymology in anecdote form, no matter how sound, is at first suspect in the best circles. The scientific facts that the *o* of *lagarto* became *or* in the same way that *fellow* became "feller," and that the new word took hold because it had "a literary and etymological appearance" (OED), are certainly interesting enough without being tricked up like a bedtime story.

all is lost save honor. The original of this, as Bartlett says, was "not quite so sublimely laconic": *De toutes choses ne m'est demeuré que l'honneur et la vie qui est saulve.* Perhaps the form from which the English translation was made was the Spanish: *Toto se ha perdido sino es la honra.* At any rate, it was Francis I of France who said it, in a letter to his mother. And, in the delightful words of H. G. Wells, "The salvage of honor was but temporary," inasmuch as he proceeded to break the treaty he had just signed.

all one a hundred years hence. See FIRST HUNDRED YEARS ARE THE HARDEST.

all righty. See KID.

all's right with the world. Perhaps by confusion with the town crier's "Ten o'clock and all's well," this has been persistently misquoted as "All's *well*." It is, of course, to be found in Browning's *Pippa Passes.*

all those men have their price. See PRICE.

almighty dollar. With Ben Jonson's "almightie gold" in mind, perhaps, Washington Irving coined this phrase and first used it in his "Creole Village," *Knickerbocker Magazine*, 1836. Dickens, who was a close friend of Irving's, later worked it into *Martin Chuzzlewit.*

As for *dollar*, it comes from the German *thaler*. The *Joachimsthaler* was a coin minted in Joachimsthal, *Thal* being the word for "valley."

aloof. See STARBOARD.

Amazon. It was traditionally supposed that the name for this mythological tribe of female warriors signified, in Greek, "deprived of one breast," the idea being that it interfered with archery and had to be burned off. The mildly sadistic shiver that almost anyone gets out of such a tale has unquestionably helped to popularize it. Realists believe, however, that the name is derived from some unknown word in a tongue that is perhaps extinct. Which is indefinite enough.

amber. See FLY.

Amen Corner. This has a number of different connotations. In origin, it is probably the corner at the end of Paternoster Row, where the monks, in procession to St. Paul's (London) on Corpus Christi Day, would reach the "Amen" of the Lord's Prayer. There was also Ave Maria Lane and Creed Lane. The plant of the Oxford Press is now situated on that corner, which gave that publishing house the bright idea of using the name "Amen Corner" for its advertising column in the *Saturday Review of Literature.* Other meanings given to Amen Corner, according to the context, are: the "mourners' bench" for enthusiastic penitents, in the front row of church; and the traditional "smoke-filled room," originally in the Fifth Avenue Hotel, where politicians gathered, it was said, to protect plutocratic privilege.

A later "smoke-filled room," having more to do with practical politics than with plutocratic privilege, was in Chicago's Blackstone Hotel. Out of it came the nomination of Warren G. Harding.

ampersand. This is the official name of the symbol &. It arose thus: our long-suffering ancestors had to repeat the alphabet with the occasional insertion of a *per se*, i.e., wherever the letter "by itself" made a word, as "A *per se* A," "I *per se* I." Thus the last "letter" of the alphabet was "& *per se* &," soon corrupted to "ampersand."

amuck. To run "amuck" comes from a Malay word meaning kill, and is more than two centuries old. Sometimes under the influence of opium a native would dash insanely down the street, striking with a dagger at anyone he met.

ancient and fish-like smell. Though both phrases are Shakesperean, do not imagine that reference is here made to that famous something that was rotten in the state of Denmark (from *Hamlet*). This smell occurred in *The Tempest*, and was, in short, Caliban, as Trinculo discovered.

ancient and honorable. See ARTILLERY. CRACK.

anecdotage. This happy result of a collision between *anecdote* and *dotage* has been ascribed to John Wilkes, in about 1835. It was popularized by Disraeli, who used it in the preface to his father's book (1848) and in *Lothair* (1870).

angel. Many a "big butter and egg man" has become an "angel" by taking a flyer on Broadway; in other words, by furnishing financial backing to a show or a particular actor (or actress). This application of the word may easily owe its origin to a gushiness of gratitude not unknown among chorus girls.

It is also crook slang for a male pervert, doubtless a development of "fairy" in that sense.

"Angels on horseback" are, in British usage, "delicious little morsels of oysters rolled in bacon and served on crisp toast."

Annie Oakley. In memory of a famous riflewoman (member of the Buffalo Bill troupe) who could throw a playing card into the air and shoot it as full of holes as a punched meal ticket before it landed, this means a meal ticket, and, figuratively, any complimentary ticket or newspaperman's pass.

In yacht racing, it is a ventilated spinnaker. The British having adopted the expression, the Americans (true to tradition) invented a new one for the bulging sail—and it became a "Mae West."

Webster has a fascinating triple definition for a "Mae West": (a) an inflatable lifesaving jacket; (b) a twin-turreted combat tank; (c) a two-lobed appearance in a descending parachute caused by one or more displaced suspension lines. These derivations are, frankly, obvious.

ant. See MYRMIDON.

antimacassar. A typical antimacassar—though not called that—is the little doily fastened on the back of a parlor-car chair, at the top. Macassar oil was a trade name for a greasy mid-Victorian hair tonic which did unpleasant things to upholstery, if one did anything so uncouth as to snuggle comfortably back into a chair.

ants in his pants. See BEANS.

anything for a quiet life. When Sam Weller immortalized this catch phrase, with his reference to the man "who took the sitivation at the light'ouse," it was already hoary with age, having been the title of an Elizabethan play, by Middleton.

ape. See JACKANAPES.

aphrodisiac. See OYSTER.

appeal from Philip drunk to Philip sober. Valerius Maximus tells this story of Philip of Macedon: that one of his female subjects, not satisfied with a decision of his while in his cups, appealed to the only higher court—the same man in his right mind—and won her case. Perhaps there is some remote association between this expression and the popularity of "sober as a judge."

apple cart. See UPSET THE APPLE CART.

apple of the eye. "The apple of my eye" is not a literal translation of the Old Testament Hebrew, which really means "little man in the eye," and corresponds to "babies in the eye" (one's own reflection as seen in the pupil of another person's eye). The use of it, in English, to mean something very precious to one, goes back to the 9th century. The pupil of the eye was believed to be apple-shaped, and was known to be very sensitive and therefore entitled to special protection.

apple-pie order. The cut-up apples, in a pie, are not usually, if ever, carefully arranged. "Alpha-beta order" sounds far-fetched, as a source, though some alphabet book for children may easily have begun with "A is an Apple Pie." The French *nappes-pliées*, folded linen (indisputably neat), has been suggested. I like *cap-a-pie* as well as any—the English rendering of the French "from head to foot." But it must be admitted that the origin of "apple-pie order" is still a mystery.

"Apple-pie bed" is easier: the bottom sheet is folded and tucked in (like the crust of a pie) in such a way that the victim's feet will penetrate only halfway into the bed.

April fool. Why All Fools' Day should be April first is still a matter of conjecture. The source has been variously given as: the tricky weather; the mock trial of Christ; the fruitless errand of Noah's dove; the rape of the Sabine women. Crowell prefers the explanation that when New Year's Day used to fall on March 25, the ensuing week of festivities closed with appropriate rites on April Fool's Day.

archbishop of a rogue. See SILK PURSE OUT OF A SOW'S EAR.

archie. First applied to the German anti-aircraft guns, this term soon came to include all of that type. OED gives a 1922 quotation explaining that a catch phrase from a music-hall song, "Archibald, certainly not," was the remark with which a young aviator used to greet the bursts of shrapnel that menaced his plane.

architecture is frozen music. Poet Schelling is believed to have first expressed this idea in his *Philosophy of Art.* Goethe said the same thing, about the same time (1829), as quoted in Stevenson: *Die Baukunst ist eine estarrte Musik.*

arena. See KNUCKLE-DUSTER.

Argyle. See GOD BLESS THE DUKE OF ARGYLE.

armed to the teeth. Though one is inclined to associate this with the pirates of the Spanish Main, so heavily armed that an extra knife or so had to be carried between the teeth, the expression is not common in English literature before Cobden (1849).

army. See CONTEMPTIBLE LITTLE ARMY.

artillery. Any kind of engine for discharging missiles—bows, crossbows, catapults, slings—and bean-shooters, I suppose—was originally classed as artillery. This is indicated in Crashaw's allusion to "Love's great artillery" (bow and arrow, of course). London's Honourable Artillery Company was founded as an archery club. One wonders whether the charter members of Boston's Ancient and Honorable Artillery knew that.

asbestos. See HOMERIC LAUGHTER.

asparagus. This 2nd century Latin word, from the Greek for sprout or shoot, was not a homely enough word for our 18th century ancestors. Tongue in cheek, at first, perhaps, they called it "sparrow-grass," a variant which remained in polite usage for many years. Then suddenly society concluded that it was vulgar, and dropped it.

ass. See EASEL.

assassin. Under the leadership of the Old Man of the Mountain, a band of Mohammedan hashish addicts terrorized the Near East for two centuries. The Italian *assassino* carried the idea of "hashish-eating killer" into English. Curiously, a somewhat similar origin is given for *thug* (q.v.).

assassination. See ABSOLUTISM.

athletics for the alumni. See PARK.

Atkins. See TOMMY ATKINS.

at loggerheads. See LOGGERHEADS.

at my uncle's. See UNCLE.

at sixes and sevens. See SIXES AND SEVENS.

attendance. See DANCE ATTENDANCE ON.

Atwell, Roy. See SPOONERISM.

auction. See DUTCH.

auger. See ADDER.

auk. See HALCYON DAYS.

autumn. See FALL.

Ave Maria Lane. See AMEN CORNER.

average. This ordinary looking word has a desperately complicated history. In the archaic sense of "work done for the feudal lord by the serf's oxen," it is connected with Latin *opera*, works, and French *avoir*, to have; as in the case of *chattel* (q.v.), the word for property was practically synonymous with the word for cattle. However, in its usual sense, it derives from a French *avarie*, which in turn is perhaps from the Arabic, and had originally to do with the damage to an insured ship or cargo. *Average* damage was something less than total damage; hence, the notion of the mean between two extremes. But this explanation barely scratches the surface. (See OED.)

away. See RIGHT AWAY.

awkward. See DEXTEROUS.

AWOL. See FRENCH LEAVE.

ax to grind. Both Webster and OED refer to "a story told by Benjamin Franklin," as do Brewer and Crowell. But Walsh asserts boldly that the frequent attribution to Franklin is erroneous, as the credit belongs to Charles Miner, in the *Wilkes-Barre Gleaner*, 1811. Bartlett confirms this, as does Benham, though the latter attributes it vaguely to Franklin also, without giving chapter and verse. As a matter of fact, OED's first reference is to Miner's 1811 use of the phrase, when Franklin was already twenty-one years dead. The reason for the confusion may be a mistaken identification of "Poor Robert the Scribe" (Charles Miner) with "Poor Richard" (Franklin). The source of the phrase is the parable of the boy whose work at the grindstone is so flattered by a stranger that the boy grinds the stranger's ax for him.

B

Babbitt. Though not from his most famous novel, *Main Street*, the character of Babbitt (from the novel of that name) brought to its creator, Sinclair Lewis, the distinction of being able to see, in his lifetime, "a Babbitt" used everywhere (like "a Pecksniff" or "a Shylock"). As a businessman who, in the words of the radio comedians, has traded in his ethics and his chivalry for a Buick, he has already had numerous descendants: Babbittess, Babbittian, Battittism, and Babbitry. Curiously enough, an earlier Babbitt, a real one, had given a word to the language, the name of a metal alloy he had invented.

baby kisser. While the term does not appear in *Pickwick Papers*, the idea is there, and may have been the source of this somewhat cynical term for a politician. The incident occurred at the Eatanswill election.

baccalaureate. See BACHELOR.

bachelor. This is not a very satisfactory word for an unmarried man. The only etymological excuse for it is in the idea of young which is implied in *baccalarius*, assistant on a grazing farm, and which apparently accounts, too, for Bachelor of Arts, etc. The "baccalaureate" address is related, but by a sort of pun, as if connected with *bacca lauri*, laurel berry. Webster derives *baccalarius* from *baculum*, shepherd's staff, the same word from which *bacterium* (shaped like a rod) comes.

back hand. In reading Van Brugh's play *The Mistake* (1706), tennis players are struck by the phrase, "to keep your back hand," which, an N. & Q. correspondent writes, "seems to be borrowed from the tennis court, where the principal player was backed up by others." The figurative use of it, in the play, is clearly "to help protect you from bravoes," "to prevent your being stabbed in the back." But the N. & Q. explanation does not satisfy the tennis fan. OED confirms my belief that Van Brugh had in mind the technical term for a stroke that has to be played with the racket arm stretched across the body; i.e., a stroke made on the left side of the body by a right-handed player. "I'll keep your back hand" apparently meant what a doubles player would mean today if he should say to his partner, "I'll take with my fore hand those center shots that you would otherwise have to take with your back hand." (See DEXTEROUS.)

back seat driver. Webster and OED suggest that the back seat is an inconspicuous position, one of "comparative obscurity." We have changed all that—at least in reference to motoring. It can readily be seen that the back seat driver, or autokibitzer, is just as important as the one at the wheel, for it is the one in the back seat who sees all approaching danger long before the driver does, and shouts a warning, thus enabling the driver to concentrate on such things as billboards and pretty pedestrians. In politics, a "back seat driver" is almost always a critic of the present administration.

back teeth afloat. Listed by B. & L. as meaning "drunk," this also has a less polite significance, namely, that one's bladder is uncomfortably full.

back up. See HUMP.

bacon. See BRING HOME THE BACON.

bad actor. While this might occasionally mean exactly what it says, a poor actor, it is originally cow-punchers' slang for a vicious horse, and hence a merciless gunman, a tough customer. This conception of "bad" is far indeed from what was probably its root meaning, effeminate, perverted (from the Anglo-Saxon word for hermaphrodite).

bad egg. See EGG.

badger. A number of things are to be said about this before we can reach Wisconsin. First, the name of the animal probably derives from the white *badge* on its head, rather than from French words suggesting "little corn-hoarder." It is curious, however, that in the 16th century a badger, like a cadger, was an itinerant middleman in the grain business; rhyming slang may have had something to do with the similarity in the names.

"To badger a person" is to harry him, as dogs baited badgers in that pleasant pastime of Elizabethan days.

According to OED, "Ouisconsin" was already famous for its abundance of badgers in 1833. The Indian name of the region probably meant "place of the beaver or muskrat hole." However, another explanation is that the pioneer workers in the zinc and lead mines of southern

Wisconsin, like badgers, "dug in" for the winter, living for the most part underground. Perhaps the term "diggin's" as applied to any locality is to be traced to these Wisconsin miners.

bag. A game, race, or bout which is "in the bag" is one of which the successful outcome is foreseen, usually because it has been "fixed" in advance. The metaphor is probably derived from hunting; i.e., trophies already shot and tucked away in the game bag. "On ice" carries it a little further, by putting the game in the ice-box. (See CARPET BAGGER.)

baggage. The word is found in England as early as 1550, in the sense of army supplies (the *impedimenta*, amusing word which must have given many a young student of *Cæsar* an inkling of the fun to be found in origin-tracing); and that sense, transferred to the women of the army, the camp-followers, and influenced by French *bagasse*, prostitute, may have accounted for the contemptuous word for girl or woman, as in "You little baggage"; to the Elizabethans this corresponded roughly to our 1920 "flapper," a term which ranged rather widely from those who were innocent of morals to those who were just plain innocent. As is well-known, baggage, in America, is luggage, in England. The origin of the word baggage is probably French *bague*, bundle.

baker. See PULL DEVIL, PULL BAKER.

baker's dozen. OED supports the theory that this comes from the custom of issuing thirteen loaves for every dozen to the hucksters, the extra loaf representing the middleman's only profit. Other possibilities are: (1) thirteen was a quorum for a Sabbath gathering of witches, and the early unpopularity of bakers seems to have linked them with the devil; (2) there was a heavy penalty for short weight, which could be guarded against by issuing thirteen loaves to a dozen.

bald. See BALLED UP.

balderdash. Edwards connects Nash's use of "barber's balderdash," in a 1599 play, with the froth that results when you dash balls of soap in hot water, but modern writers sternly reject the theory, at the same time offering nothing better. From "a jumbled mixture of liquors" the word came to mean frothy talk, a jumble of words.

ball. To be "on the ball" is British collegiate slang for "hitting on all six" (eight, twelve, or sixteen, if preferred)—i.e., all the cylinders of a motor firing perfectly, and hence everything functioning exactly as it should. The "ball" figure seems to be from the close and clever following of the ball, in soccer.

Our complimentary remark, "He certainly has something on the ball," signifies power and effectiveness; the allusion is to the deceptive spin given a baseball by a skilful pitcher. (See HIGHBALL. SHOOT THE BULL.)

Quaintly combining two expressions, the *Saturday Review* once said, of a chronically unlucky person, "She sure has got something on the eight-ball." (See BEHIND THE EIGHT-BALL.)

ballast. Teutonic roots signifying "back-load," "belly-load," and "bad lading" have all been suggested as possible ancestors of this word which describes the unprofitable cargo taken abroad to keep a ship right side up. Possibly the oldest form is the Scandinavian *barlast*, bare load. This word *last* is still used as a lumber measurement.

In the sense of gravel tamped around railroad ties, ballast is said to have received its name from the fact that piles of discarded ship-ballast were utilized in the construction of English railroads.

balled up. In the sense of "confused, mixed up," this may originally, as Mencken suggests, have had an improper meaning connected with the vulgar ejaculation, "Balls." But the dictionaries prefer to trace it to the forming of hard and uncomfortable balls of snow or ice under the hoofs of a horse that is drawing a sleigh. These hard lumps would make a horse flounder if not actually balk.

The word *bald* as applied to a head was formerly spelled "balled" and may have come from association with the idea of roundness and smoothness. OED, though not at all certain of this, has nothing more convincing to offer.

ball of fire. See THAMES.

balloon. See CARRY THE BANNER.

ballot. See BULLET.

balls. The three golden (or rather "gilded") balls of the pawnbroker were taken from the coat of arms of a firm of Lombard usurers, the first great money-lenders. There are three balls, it is said, because the odds are 2–1 that the article will never be redeemed. It was formerly thought that the three purses of gold given by St. Nicholas to three virgins, or the three balls on the Medici coat of arms (intended either as pills, in a punning allusion to "Medici," or as a reference to the three balls on the mace of the giant Mugello, who was killed by a Medici) had something to do with the case.

ball the jack. Weseen defines this as "to travel fast," and "to risk everything on one attempt," but gives us no help as to derivation. While either element, taken separately, may have sexual connotation, the combination seems to have none, and indeed was in polite usage as the name of a popular song and dance step, recently revived from World War I days. I have a feeling that it was originally railroad slang and had some connection with either the "high ball" (the signal to go ahead) or the rolling of the wheels.

ballyhoo. Shouted advertising in front of a circus tent, on the part of the barker or *spieler* (from German *spielen*, to play). Thus, by transference, any loud publicity. The word seems to have for its ancestor, along with British *bally* (a euphemism for *bloody*), the village of Ballyhooly, in Cork, a community noted for its brawls.

balm in Gilead. The question, "Is there no balm in Gilead?" occurs in Jeremiah 8:22 (being rendered "treacle" in Coverdale's translation). "Balm" is a contraction of "balsam," a resinous gum having soothing and healing properties. The expression "balm of Gilead" has been irreverently used to mean illicit whisky, whereas it was familiar in an earlier period (that of Charlotte Brontë) in its proper sense of comforting or soothing.

balmy. See BARMY.

bamboozle. This is still listed as slang, though Swift expressed the fear, in 1710, that it was becoming part of the language, along with such terrifying novelties as "banter" and "kidney." No origin has been found for it, except a possible gipsy word, which OED frowns on; but it may be worth noting how many words ending in *-zle*, such as *drizzle*, *fizzle*, *foozle*, *mizzle*, *pizzle*, are disreputable or unpleasant. As *bamboozle* means "to pull the wool over someone's eyes," i.e., to cheat, it may conceivably have been influenced by *confuse* and *dazzle*.

bandbox. "Just out of a bandbox" means fresh and dainty, like a party dress that has been carefully packed in a flimsy box. These boxes were originally created for the band trade; i.e., clergymen's bands, a sort of stock or necktie of the 17th century.

banjo. This is probably a negro corruption of Greco-Latin *pandura*, a stringed instrument, cognate with *mandolin*, *mandola*, and the obsolete *bandore* and *banjore*. Negroes have been specifically associated with "banjers" since as early as 1774.

The musical instrument is not related to the toy once called a *bandalore* (which Skeat "guesses" was coined from French *bande de l'aure*, "string of the breeze") and in its present incarnation known as a yo-yo.

banner. See CARRY THE BANNER.

banquet. Derived from the Italian for "little bench," this was formerly a sort of dessert (in the American sense), a sweetmeat that followed the meal, often being served in another room. Horwill points out that while the modern sense of "public dinner" is familiar on both sides of the Atlantic, Americans use the word in reference to "much less sumptuous repasts."

banshee. It is possible to prove that this word for an elf-woman, a familiar spirit that wails just before the death of some member of the family, is related to *queen* and *gynecology*! The Gaelic *bean side*, woman of the fairies, is etymologically connected with the Greek root meaning "woman."

banter. See BAMBOOZLE. CHAFF.

bantling. See BASTARD.

barber pole. The characteristic striped pole in front of a barber shop (or as our British cousins say, "hair-dressing saloon") originated in the days when a barber was also a surgeon and a dentist. If he was equipped for bleeding people (about all a surgeon ever had to do, appendicitis not having been invented) he would attach to a pole outside his door the symbol of his trade: a rag smeared with blood. The word *barber* derives from Latin *barba*, beard (*barbarian* being simply "a bearded man").

"Barber shop harmony" first arose in the days when magazines were not provided for the waiting customers, who beguiled themselves with the close harmony of "Sweet Adeline." One wonders whether a battered *Confidential* is any improvement.

bargain. "To strike a bargain" may be simply from striking or shaking hands upon its conclusion. However, Webster admits the romantic possibility that it is in imitation of *fœdus ferire*, to seal a bargain by sacrificing a victim.

barker. See BALLYHOO.

barmy. Though sometimes traced to St. Bartholomew, patron saint of the feeble-minded, this is probably from *barm*, the froth on *beer* (these two words are from the same root). From "yeast" and "ferment," as connected with this froth, come the idea of flighty or slightly insane. The American version, found also in England, is *balmy*.

barnacle. To most Americans this means just one thing: a kind of shell-fish that has to be scraped off a ship's bottom. For a Britisher life is more complicated: *barnacles* may be wild geese or *pince-nez* spectacles, as well. It was once thought that there was a tadpole-frog relationship between the goose-barnacle and the barnacle-goose (pictures of both of these may be seen in the new Webster—advt.). Suggested derivations are: from *bernake*, the ME name for the goose; from *pernacula*, suppositititious diminutive of the Latin word for mussel; and from the Old Irish *bern*, a cleft. The colloquial use to mean "spectacles" probably derives from Old French *bernicles*, an instrument of torture; hence, *barnacles* for a veterinarian's nose pincers. A correspondent of N. & Q. wrote, in 1857, "I have always thought barnacles and spectacles identical."

barn-burners. Derived from the fable of the man who burned down his barns to rid them of rats, this term of derision was applied to the radical element of the Democratic party of New York, shortly before the Civil War.

barn-stormer. The rash of red-barn theaters that breaks out, principally in the East, every summer has helped to make it intelligible why a barn-stormer should be an actor. Originally, however, the actors who appeared in barns were not fresh from Broadway triumphs but were second-rate "booth-bursters" or strolling players.

After World War I, "barn-stormer" was applied to an aviator who parked his "crate" (usually an old biplane with a Liberty motor) in a barn at some conveniently large and level pasture, and took people joy-riding at a dollar or two a shot.

barrage. In pre-World War I dictionaries this was pronounced in sturdy English style and meant about the same as a dam across a stream. But by 1914 civilization had advanced far enough to make it necessary to borrow from the French *tir de barrage* a word to express a curtain or barrier of artillery fire which would blow to bits everything in a certain area, then pick itself up and move (at a predetermined rate of speed, in the case of a "creeping barrage") to a place where more of the enemy might still be inconveniently alive.

barunduki. For some years I was convinced that Mrs. Edith Cooke of Williamstown (formerly of Superior, Wis.) was the only person in America who called a chipmunk a barunduki. It wasn't in the big Webster (still isn't) or anywhere else I could find. Still she contended that northwestern Wisconsin had 'em. Then suddenly, on Sept. 20, 1959, the *American Weekly* ran a picture of a girl in a barunduki turban and stole—and one glove!—playing a clarionet. Ben Kahn, the New York furrier responsible, writes me that the word, "as far as we know," is of Russian origin, that the animal *is* a Russian chipmunk, that the fur was very fashionable in the twenties, and that it is now enjoying a revival. I think it's about time it got into Webster. But how did it get into Wisconsin?

bashaw.

> 'Tis a very fine thing to be father-in-law
> To a very magnificent three-tailed bashaw.
> —G. Colman (the younger), *Blue Beard* (1798)

As the meter shows, this word for a Turkish official whom we now call a *pasha* was, and still is, accented on the last syllable. It probably meant "head," by derivation. By way of contrast, perhaps, the number of horse tails attached to a dignitary's standard indicated how important a head he was. Three tails was as high as they went.

basiate. See BUSS.

basilisk. Another name for the legendary cockatrice, alleged to have been hatched from a cock's egg by a serpent. Equally absurd was the death-ray from its eyes, its "killing glance." Anti-royalists should note that this ridiculous creature means, by derivation, "little king." "Basilisk" was one of the terrifying names given to early firearms; among them were "serpent" and "culverin" (from the French word for snake).

bass the lubber. See LUBBER.

bastard. Pointing out that the German *bantling* conveys the idea of having been conceived on a bench, OED derives *bastard* from French *bât*, a pack saddle, the muleteer's bed while on the road. Webster considers that the origin of the word has not been established.

bat. In the sense of stick or club, the word is connected with French *battre*, rather than with the nocturnal creature. The latter probably accounts for the slang use of *bat* for *prostitute*, one who hides out in dark recesses during the day. The expression "on a bat," meaning "on a spree or a drunk," carries also this thought, perhaps, of being out all night; it is unlikely that there is any direct allusion to the cant term for a "lady of easy virtue." (See CASEY AT THE BAT.)

bats in the belfry. See BELFRY.

battalions. See GOD IS ON THE SIDE OF THE HEAVIEST BATTALIONS.

battledore. The instrument with which you bat the shuttlecock (in the game which begat badminton) apparently derives its name from a heavy club with which clothes would be beaten or smoothed in a primitive laundry; in Provençal it was a *batedor*, in Spain a *batidor*. It is thus related to *beetle* (see under FILLIP) and to *bat*.

battle royal. Few are so fortunate (or perhaps so unfortunate) as not to know from personal experience what is meant by a battle royal. However, the fact that it originated in an elimination tournament for game-cocks, in which only the fittest survived, is not so commonly known.

bawl out. See HAUL OVER THE COALS.

bayonet. While Webster says quite confidently that the first *bayonets* were made in *Bayonne*, France, OED is not so sure, and quotes an Old French word for crossbow shaft as a possibility. What we do know is that at first they were short flat daggers, then they had a long ramrod-like handle that went down the muzzle of the musket (thus arranging it so that if an absent-minded private should fire his gun with the bayonet fixed, the results would be more disastrous to himself than to the enemy), and finally they were attached to lugs on the outside of the barrel, near the tip.

The most familiar quotation about bayonets is this, from Dean Inge: "A man may build himself a throne of bayonets, but he cannot sit on it."

bayou. Here is one of the few words on which Webster and OED are in complete disagreement. Associated with Mississippi and Louisiana, this term for a creek or marshy overflow is said by OED to be probably a corruption of French *boyau*, gut. But as long ago as 1894, W. S. Wyman, of the University of Alabama, wrote to the *Nation* (LIX, 361) criticizing this derivation and quoting from a book published in 1761 what seems conclusive evidence that bayou is from a Choctaw word meaning creek or stream. Webster accepts this and adduces *bogue* as a direct descendant of the Choctaw word, and one that is still familiar in delta country as a variant of bayou.

beachcomber. First as a sort of pun, perhaps, on "beachcomber" in the sense of a long curling wave, the term was applied to one who "combed" the beach for *flotsam and jetsam* (q.v.) that he could trade for food (or more likely drink). Hence, any vagrant, especially in the South Sea islands, who lives by plunder or begging, near a waterfront. Hence again, any beggar or *panhandler* (q.v.).

bead. See DRAW.

beadle. The pompous official satirized more than once by Victorian writers derives his name from Anglo-Saxon *beodan*, to bid or summon. This is cognate with German *bitte*, "Please"—not that a beadle always bothered to say "Please."

beagle. Virginians were at one time nicknamed "beagles," presumably because of a mutual enthusiasm for chasing foxes. The derivation of the dog's name is obscure; possibly the connection is with the French word for "open throat," in allusion to the musical barking of the "buglers," as the little hounds are sometimes called; the old French word for throat, *goule*, is cognate with gullet.

beans. "He doesn't know beans about it." Walsh says this is a sly dig at Boston's pretensions to culture—a hint that Boston knows her beans if nothing else. However, a single bean is a little thing, of no great value, and that seems to be the most plausible explanation of the phrase.

"Full of beans" is the equivalent of "full of oats," meaning high-spirited. Both are originally horsy expressions, though one seldom hears of feeding a horse beans to make him lively. A third way of suggesting squirming activity is "full of red ants," or, in the chaste and yet vigorous phraseology of General Hugh Johnson, "ants in his pants."

bear. See BULLS AND BEARS.

beard. The lilting phrase, "beard the lion in his den," meaning to defy someone on his own home grounds, is lifted entire from Scott's *Marmion*. "To beard" is "to seize by the beard."

The Shakesperean equivalent for "You get in my hair" was "Thou art ever in my beard."

beat. See DEAD BEAT.

beat all hollow. See HOLLOW.

beat around (or about) the bush. As Weekley points out, there seems to be a mixed metaphor here. Heywood uses "beating the bush" in reference to the helpers who start the fox, but the notion of going around the bush rather than plunging to the heart of it would seem to apply less well to the beaters, who make enough noise to scare the average fox from a good distance away, than to a hesitating hound. The phrase goes back at least to 1520.

Beat Generation. According to John Clellon Holmes (see *Publishers' Weekly*, Oct. 5, 1959), Jack Kerouac coined the phrase, which author Holmes then used in his novel *Go*. No bearded guitar player himself, Mr. Holmes asserts: "To the beatnik of today, I'd be the biggest square of all time."

A *beatnik* is usually an angry young man with a beard, or his somewhat promiscuous "chick" in bare feet, ragged T-shirt, and jeans. A combination of Beat Generation and a Russian suffix (as in *sputnik*, satellite, "fellow traveler"), a beatnik has been described as "sick and tired of everything but the basics: sex, booze, dope, and jazz." They also drink *espresso* coffee, play atonal music on guitars, read and write bad poetry, and furiously burn midnight oil—on the highways. (See SQUARE.)

beat it. See HOOKEY.

beat the band, beat the Dutch. Both are rather vague euphemisms for "beat hell." The first carries the idea of making enough noise to drown out a brass band, the second may be reminiscent of the wars with the Dutch, to which English owes many of its most uncomplimentary metaphors. (See DUTCH.)

bedded-down. See LAGER BEER.

Bee, B. E. See STONEWALL JACKSON.

beef-eaters. One Mrs. Markham wrote a history of England in which she defended the Yeomen of the Guard from the scandalous implication that they might be eaters of beef (suggested by their famous nickname); she dragged in a French word *buffetier* which she said meant a waiter at a sideboard—and which word-detectives have been busy declaring fictitious, ever since. The true situation is not so much that they were beef-eaters while scholars ate only mutton (as a French dictionary implies), but that the beef-eater, like the earlier "loaf-eater," was a well-fed menial, a servant who earns his "board and keep," in the American vernacular.

bee in his bonnet. In Herrick's "Mad Maiden" (1648) there was a remark about a bee in a bonnet that implied the owner of the bonnet to be slightly insane. A suggested connection, rather nebulous, is between the bee and the soul. Or it may just be the way an idea seems to buzz about in our heads. What is usually conveyed is that the person in question has a single-track mind, on which he can proceed in only one direction.

beer. See BARMY. CHRONICLE SMALL BEER. LAGER BEER.

Beersheba. See DAN TO BEERSHEBA.

beetle. See FILLIP ME WITH A THREE-MAN BEETLE.

before you can say Jack Robinson. This is the famous "Palpably Ben Trovato" phrase. Ever since Brewer thus condemned the legend that "Jacke! robys on" appeared in an old play, reference books have been repeating the "palpably *ben trovato*" without bothering to credit it to Dr. Brewer. Weekley refers jokingly to this gentleman Ben Trovato, obviously of Italian birth, who is always inventing fantastic etymologies. Other suggestions of Mr. P. B. Trovato's are: that a volatile person named Jack Robinson used to make flying visits of extraordinary brevity; and that a 19th century song by Hudson first used the phrase (it is found in Fanny Burney's *Evelina*, 1778 (E.P. to the contrary notwithstanding)). In America an equivalent expression brought in "Sam Patch," noted jumper. This indicates what I think is the true solution: that the name must be familiar to all, and easy to say. "Jack Robinson" is in the very forefront of common names in England.

beggar description. "A scene that beggars description," as Shakespeare well knew (*Antony and Cleopatra*) is one that has your powers of description down and out, and begging for help.

beg the question. A question-begging proposition is one that stacks the cards by assuming something not yet proved. For instance, a poor question for a debate would be, "Resolved, that *entangling* alliances should be avoided." "Begging the question" is a translation of *petitio principii*.

behind the ears. See CUB.

behind the eight ball. This is darky slang, of poolroom origin, meaning "out of luck." A big negro is sometimes "an oversize eight ball"—the eight being the only one that is all black. In one form of rotation pool, the balls must be taken in order except the eight, which must be pocketed last; anyone sinking the eight ball prematurely is penalized. Therefore if the eight is between you and the ball you must take next, you are out of luck. A delightful conjecture is that there is a mystical connection between this expression and the classic "blackballing" indulged in by exclusive clubs. (See BALL.)

belch. See BURP.

belfry. "Bats in the belfry," like "bee in his bonnet," which it resembles in meaning, became popular as much through its alliteration as through any great appropriateness. The idea, I suppose, is of eerie creatures flapping about in a great emptiness.

"Belfry" has nothing to do with bells, etymologically. Originally a sort of primitive "tank," a movable tower used in attacking walled cities, it evolved into a watch tower with an alarm bell. The old belfry, weapon of aggressive warfare, took its name, *berfray*, from the German for "guard-the-peace" (the Duce, the Mikado, and Soviet imperialists all would understand that) but eventually adopted the *l* of its bell, as was to be expected.

bell. See RING A BELL.

bell, book, and candle. Referring to excommunication with all the trimmings, this old phrase gave rise to the familiar medieval oath, "By book and candle!" Though *bell* comes first, the correct order is probably indicated by the directions, "Do to the book, quench the candle, ring the bell," the ceremony being ended with discords from the belfry. The earliest example in E.P. is 1300, "wid candil, boke, and bell."

belly. See BOLSTER. FUSS-BUDGET.

belly-cutting. See HARA KIRI.

bender. See ELBOW.

benedict. "A happy benedict" (also spelled "benedick") is now taken to mean, after Benedick, a character in *Much Ado about Nothing*, a newly married man who has been a long time making up his mind. There has been some confusion about it, owing to the belief that Benedict, patron saint of celibates, was meant, and that therefore a benedict was a bachelor. Fortunately, having bolstered our Shakesperean argument by adducing the nuptial benediction as an additional reason for calling a newlywed "blessed," we have concluded that a hard-boiled bachelor who finally succumbs to feminine wiles may then be called a benedict. Shakespeare probably borrowed the name and the idea from Kyd's *Spanish Tragedy*, with which he was very familiar.

benefit of clergy. For some occult reason, our medieval ancestors thought a criminal should be punished less severely if he knew how to read and write; if he did succeed in reading what was known as his "neck-verse," he went under the jurisdiction of the ecclesiastical court, where the death penalty could not be invoked for minor offenses. Based on an injunction in I Chronicles ("Do my prophets no harm") the custom reminds us of present-day diplomatic immunity from arrest. "Benefit of clergy" was extended to women in 1691, and abolished in 1827. Kipling's punning use of it in his short story (applying it to the marriage ceremony rather than to a death sentence) helped pave the way, perhaps, for the somewhat less classic titles of Octavus Roy Cohen, such as *Nuts and Reasons*, and *Scrambled Yeggs*.

benjamin. See JOSEPH.

benny. See JOSEPH.

be of good cheer. See CHEER.

Berkshire. This name of pleasant associations (derived from a kind of tree, possibly a "bare-oak") is now well-known in England as that of a superior breed of swine. It is pronounced quite differently over there, too, something like "Bark-shur."

berry. See RAZZ.

berserk. The confusion between the homonyms *bear* and *bare* has led to a dispute as to whether this originally means fighting "bare of mail," or, supernaturally, "in the form of bears," or "with a bear's skin on instead of armor." The third suggestion is approved, but any one of the three could have led to the meaning of "martial frenzy" and, of late years, "violent insanity" (an encouraging sign of the times, perhaps).

better. See NO BETTER THAN SHE SHOULD BE.

between the devil and the deep blue sea. See DEVIL.

between two stools. This old phrase, implying failure because of hesitation between two alternatives, may have arisen from a practical joke invented, no doubt, by the cavemen: a blanket covers two somewhat separated stools on which two men are sitting; they invite a third to sit between them, then suddenly rise. The only trouble with this as a source is that the trick would tend to encourage indecision and caution. A better example might be the children's game of Musical Chairs, where a moment of indecision as to which chair to try for may send you crashing to the floor "between two stools." But I am afraid this game does not date back to 1390, as the phrase does, in English, and even further back in Latin and French.

beyond the pale. Related ultimately to "paling fence," this expression conveys that some person or nation has been branded an "outlaw," outside the limits of the civilized world. The "pale" has been applied at various times, particularly in Ireland, to a section that has been brought under English domination. Kipling made *Beyond the Pale* part of our everyday vocabulary with his story of that title.

Bible belt. This invention of Mencken's was about contemporary with the once famous "monkey trial" of John Thomas Scopes for admitting that he believed in evolution (though he did not actually teach it, he told me once, as he was a mathematics instructor). As applied to that section of the South that takes Adam and Eve very literally and very seriously, the clever alliteration and contemptuous explosiveness of "Bible belt" caught the public fancy at once.

bicker. See CHEW THE RAG.

Big Bertha. See GUN.

big butter and egg man. See BUTTER AND EGG MAN.

Big Dipper. See CYNOSURE.

big shot. See MOGUL.

big squadrons. See GOD IS ON THE SIDE OF THE HEAVIEST BATTALIONS.

big time. "He's in the big time now" might mean either in the "two a day"—theatrical for an act that went on only twice daily rather than five or six times—or in the major leagues (baseball). The former probably came first, chronologically.

bilge. This slang word for nonsense or filth is short for bilge-water, the slightly used water that collects in the very bottom of a ship. OED's first quotation for the slangy use is from Hutchinson's *If Winter Comes.* The word is a variant of *bulge*, and refers (though there seems to be a slight difference between British and American usage here) to the curve connecting the flattish bottom of a big vessel with the straightish sides.

bilious. See HUMOR.

billet. See BULLET.

billiards. A delightful story is told of a pawnbroker named *Bill* who used to push three balls around with a *yard*-stick; the term "cannon" arose, says this writer, from the fact that some young clergymen (canons) became devotees of the new game. However, the scholars ignore this fable and point simply to the French *billart*, a little log, which was originally a hockey stick but evolved into the cue. *Cannon* is believed to be a corruption of *carom* (q.v.).

Billings, Josh. See JOSH.

billingsgate. See LIMEHOUSE.

billy. See HILL BILLY.

bird. "A little bird told me," meaning that I do not care to reveal the source of my information, is very old, the suggestion for it being found, perhaps, in the Koran or in the Bible (Ecclesiastes 10:20). Shakespeare and Swift both made use of the figure. The source idea, OED says, may be in the swift and noiseless flight of a bird. A fascinating guess, apparently baseless, was made by Bellenden Ker in 1837, when he cited a Dutch expression, *Er lij t'el baerd*, "I should betray another," as a likely source for "A little bird" when used as a suave synonym for "I won't tell you."

For *bird* in the sense of "Bronx cheer," see RAZZ.

bird-lime. In OED, the first definition of lime is "bird-lime" ("now only poetical"). Most of us think of lime as something white and dusty that you use in building operations, or on tennis courts. By derivation, however, it was first slimy, like mud (Latin *limus*); then sticky or viscous (the Latin word for mistletoe, *viscum*, came to mean "sticky" because bird-lime was made from it!); then it was narrowed to mean the calcium oxide we are familiar with. Weekley establishes the curious fact that the verb "lime" can mean "caulk" (fill the cracks of a boat), which comes from *calicare*, which in turn comes from *calx*, lime. If at first it seems strange that "slimy" should evolve into "sticky," just try to drive a car up a red-clay hill, and then to get the clay off your boots afterwards.

birl. See LOG-ROLLING.

biscuit. Originally this meant about the same as hard tack; it was "twice cooked" (French *bis + cuit*) so that it would keep, on a sea voyage, as Benjamin Franklin knew. No young man who marries an etymologist need expect his breakfast biscuits to be fluffy. The German *zwieback*, which we call rusk, is also "twice-baked" (*zwie* = twice, not *zwei* = two), but to call a piece of it a biscuit would simply go to prove that a translation need not be an equivalent.

biscuit-eater. See CRYING OUT LOUD.

bishop. See FOOT.

bit. The British slang for any small coin (as "threepenny bit") was transferred, in the South and West of the U.S., to the old Mexican *real*, worth 12½ cents, an amount which at one time was called a "shilling" in certain eastern states. In those regions within the Mexican sphere of influence, "quarter" is said to be almost unknown. A short-bit is ten cents, a long-bit fifteen. "Four bits" and "six bits" are common there —but people east of the Mississippi get headaches trying to compute those at 12½ cents a throw.

bite. Shifting, in its allusion, from the damaging bite of an animal to the credulous bite of a fish, the word gave birth, some years ago, to the slangy "I'll bite," meaning "I'll be the goat—go ahead with your trick." In 1897, to *bite* was to cheat.

bite off more than you can chew. See CATCH A TARTAR. IRON.

bites of a cherry. See CHERRY.

bite the dust. Homer had the idea first, but Byron and Nick Carter exploited it. In Pope's well-manicured translation of the *Iliad*, it appears as "bite the bloody sand" but in our own Bryant's version it is "bite the dust." However, it took the dime-novel (so much better known in England as the "penny-dreadful") to confer immortality on "Another redskin bit the dust."

bitter end. The less-used portion of an anchor-rope, nearest the bitts, was known as the "better" or "bitter" or "bitters" end; Captain John Smith and Defoe were familiar with such terms. Yet that does not prove that the popular "to the bitter end" has a nautical origin. There is a verse in Proverbs: "her end is bitter as wormwood." No doubt the two ideas helped each other into immortality.

blab. See GAFF.

black art. This appropriate sounding name for the art of divination, or necromancy, is all a mistake, based on a faulty identification of *necro* with *niger*, black. Then, too, necromancy, divination through a study of corpses (the Greek root *necro-*, as in necrologist, revealing that a dead body will be found somewhere in the vicinity—and strengthening our conviction that the study of words is as thrilling as a mystery story) necromancy, I repeat, had perforce something dark and secret about it that made the association with black a very natural one.

blackguard. We need not turn to braggart or *blagaart* (Dutch) for a source. The original form was undoubtedly "black guard," but it is not known whether it was first used of a body of menial servants who did the dirty work on the big estates, or of a guard of soldiers at Westminster, or of the shoe-shine artists who invaded military centers just before parade time. The first is the most convincing.

black magic. See HOODOO.

blackmail. This term for "hush-money," a bribe paid someone to keep a disgraceful secret, is quite unrelated to either armor or letters. *Mail* in this sense is a 16th century Scotch word for rent or tribute. The Middle English word from which it came was akin to the Anglo-Saxon *maethel*, meeting, and thus to *moot* (q.v.). "Black mail," paid in grain, meat, or the lowest coin, was distinct from "white mail," paid in silver.

black man in the closet. See NIGGER IN THE WOODPILE.

Black Maria. In 1924, Black Maria, London's horse van for female prisoners, made its last trip, being replaced by a motor. The British police van was introduced in 1838. It may have been christened after a negress of Boston who used to help gather the prisoners, but this has not been proved. Another name for the paddy-wagon is said to be Blue Liz.

During World War I, the German high explosive shell that released a heavy black smoke was dubbed, among other things, the Black Maria.

blanket. To be born "on the wrong side of the blanket" is a rather silly way (used in *Humphrey Clinker*, 1771) of expressing illegitimacy.

blarney. Today's dictionaries do not bother with the story that the village of Blarney, near Cork, being besieged in 1602, delayed its surrender by cajolery and soft speeches until help came. However, it is recognized as a fact that there has long been in the castle wall at that village a stone difficult of access which people undertake to kiss, the tradition being that if you succeed you will be granted the power of lying with a straight face.

blatherskite. When analyzed, this word appears to be more than a little physiological in origin: *blathra,* to talk nonsense, is related to *bladder,* and *skite,* excrement, bears a resemblance to its cousin, one of our best-known taboo words. Both are from the Norse via Scotland. The first element has given birth to "blithering," the second, apparently, to "skate," as in "cheap skate." A British definition for *blatherskite* is "the ruddy duck," which sounds like John Bull profanity but is clearly enough an authentic bird.

blessed word. See MESOPOTAMIA.

bless you. See GOD BLESS YOU.

blighty. This word for England or home, which swept into popularity during World War I, as descriptive of a wound serious enough to entitle its proud possessor to a trip home, was well known to Anglo-Indians before the 1914 calamity, though the first OED quotation is dated 1915. It is from a Hindustani word, *wilayet* or *bilati,* meaning "a distant country," hence England.

blind man's buff. See HOODWINK.

blizzard. OED cites *blow, blast, blister, bluster,* to indicate the onomatopœic possibilities. Another possible connection is with *blitzen,* used as an exclamation by the Germans. The word came into general use in 1880–1881, but it has been found in the Middle West, in the sense of a blinding snowstorm, as early as 1870. An earlier use, in the sense of a retort or a blow, was already obsolete.

block. See CHIP.

bloody. English word-historians are frankly at a loss to account for their prejudice against this useful adjective, which for 200 years was perfectly respectable. Vigorously rejecting as possible sources such profane or indelicate suggestions as "By 'r Lady" and certain phenomena connected with menstruation, our cousins fall feebly back on the "bloods," the aristocratic rowdies, of a century or so ago, who undoubtedly did occasionally get "bloody drunk," "drunk as bloods." Accepting this as a plausible origin, and understanding the popularity of "bloody" as a graphic and even terrifying word, I still see no reason why it should ever have been printed "b - - - - y," unless it *is* remotely sexual, as many think.

bloody warriors. See WALLFLOWER.

bloomer. For some reason, Mrs. Amelia Jenks Bloomer has denied inventing or wearing the first bloomers (in about 1850). But they have been irretrievably pinned on her. Webster even has a sketch of her in costume, a smock nearly concealing a pair of baseball pants that are too long for her; she looks like a stratosphere balloon with two hot-dogs peeping out at the bottom. Since shorts took the place of bloomers for girl athletes, the word has saved itself from obsolescence by attaching itself to underdrawers more or less close fitting.

"Blooming," in British slang usage, is apparently a euphemism for "bloody." And "bloomer" in the sense of *faux pas* is probably a collision form of "blooming error." It may have originated among the Australian convicts.

blow. In Aesop's fable the satyr's breath could either warm or cool as he desired—so "blow hot and cold" is supposed to be a symbol of inconsistency, of vacillating between the two sides of a question. However, we do blow our soup to cool it, and our hands to warm them, the catch being that our breath may be either cooler or warmer than the object blown on.

"The wind blew great guns" is expressive and need not be stared at over-critically. It seems to refer to the thunderous noise of a howling wind. Dibdin used it in the early 1800's, and it is also, to many, unforgettably associated with *David Copperfield.*

blow the gaff. See GAFF.

blue. That this is the color of approaching death explains perhaps the connotation of despondency and despair (as in *blue devils*, the *blues*, and possibly, too, the *blue laws*). But the fact that in blazonry it represented chastity is not easily reconciled with the idea of "indecent," which was suggested in the movie, *The Little Colonel*, when Shirley Temple asked for "a blue story" (i.e., everything in it blue) but Lionel Barrymore did not know any "blue" stories suitable for her ears. "Blueness" in this sense was used by Carlyle, and is probably connected with *bibliothèque bleu*, indecent books. Theatrical slang preserves this meaning in "blue gag." Perhaps the blue of burning sulphur has some remote bearing on the situation.

Blue Liz. See BLACK MARIA.

Blue Peter. When a blue flag with a white square snaps at the masthead of a vessel, it is her way of saying, "Well, I must be leaving." In the British signal code, the flag stands for "P," but there is no proof that it was intended as the initial of French *partir*, to depart. Webster says that the flag was called the "blue repeater," soon telescoped into "blue Peter."

bluestocking. This nickname for the sort of woman who, in the opinion of Rousseau, "will remain a spinster as long as there are sensible men on earth," originated in the informality of a gentleman named Stillingfleet, who wore blue worsted stockings to a gathering of literary women instead of the more formal black silks. Though I have heard a University of Chicago professor caution the coeds against becoming "well-informed women" if they want to attract men, OED says that the old prejudice against women who show a taste for learning is breaking down, and that as a result the contemptuous word "blue-stocking" is obsolescent. Anyway, it dies at a ripe old age, over 200.

blurb. Defined by its inventor, Gelett Burgess, as "a sound like a publisher," this word filled a need, for it mysteriously describes your fed-up feeling after reading a dust-cover panegyric of the more violent type. Can it be that it is a glorious blend of "blurt," "burp," and "bi-carb"? It was coined in about 1914, but did not "make" the OED until 1924 (the first quotation); and the editors of the Supplement still thought (in 1933) that "blurb" was a waif-word without a history.

B. O. A strenuous advertising campaign on the part of a soap company has persuaded us that this means "body odor." But to theatrical people it conveys just one thing: box-office. It can also stand for branch office, board of ordnance, brought over, bad order, and bachelor of oratory.

bobby. Sir Robert Peel was primarily responsible for the establishment of the Irish Constabulary, during his term as secretary for Ireland (1812–1818), and later for the reorganization of the London police, through the New Metropolitan Police Act of 1828. "Peeler," as a nickname for his men, came into almost immediate use (1817) but "bobby" apparently did not creep into print before 1851. The latter appears to have a permanent place in the language.

bobtail flush. See FOURFLUSH.

Boche. Popularized by the propaganda hatreds of war, this old word for "cabbage-head," used occasionally in France from 1860 on, is probably short for *caboche*, of which we have an 1889 definition: "wooden-head," or *rake* (q.v.). Since early in World War I, of course, it has meant a German.

bogey. "The bogey-man" (sometimes "boogy-man") whose sole function seems to be to scare children into behaving themselves, is apparently related to *bug* and *bugaboo* (q.v.). Scattered through a number of languages there seems to be a root similar to "bug" or "puck" which connotes something supernatural. About the earliest English word for specter was *bogle*, from which our *boggle* comes (the conception being that of a horse shying).

"The Bogey Man" was a popular song of about 1890. And from it, we are told, arose the golf term, "bogey," meaning to the Britisher, somewhat the same as "par," the number of strokes that a really good player ought to take for the hole; the difference is that "par" is primarily determined by the number of yards, while "bogey" may be altered by circumstances, such as weather or modesty. In American usage, "bogey" is one stroke more than par. It used to be always "Colonel Bogey," in tribute to the fictitious gentleman against whom one of the pioneers in this kind of golf, thinking of the above-mentioned song, used to say he was playing.

"Bogie," to a railroad man, is likely to mean the free-swivelling truck to which the "ponies," the small wheels under the front end of a locomotive, are attached. It comes from a name, of unknown origin, applied by coal miners to a low truck for heavy hauling.

bogus. Warning us first against "bogus" etymologies (and then proceeding to spell the hero's name two different ways, *Willard* and *Millard*), OED throws its influence back of an ex-Vermonter's story of a counterfeiting machine that was dubbed a "bogus" in Ohio in 1827; and then connects this with *tantrabogus*, a Vermont word for "bogey-man." It is true that most references to *bogus* have to do with counterfeit money. Another story works in Borghese, a swindler of about 1835. A third, which I like better than either, cites a Scotch gipsy word for counterfeit coin, *boghus*. Mencken suspects a French origin; possibly *bagasse* or *bogue*.

Bohn. See BONE UP ON.

boloney. Well representing the American pronunciation of *bologna*, the comparatively indestructible sausage, this slang term was about contemporary with "banana oil" in the sense of "nonsense, bunkum." Its origin is unknown but its history is bound up with Al Smith's. He it was who (to quote Stevenson) remarked, on being asked to lay a brick at a cornerstone ceremony, "Nothing doing. That's just 'boloney.' Everybody knows I can't lay bricks." Again, when President F. D. R. sent up a trial balloon about a commodity dollar, adjusted with reference to the general price level, Al Smith punctured it almost single-handed with his sarcastic "boloney dollar." (See SHOOT THE BULL.)

bolster. Related to *belly* (from the root sense of "swell" or "puff up") and to *poltroon* (q.v.), this means, strictly speaking, a long cushion. To bolster a theory is to strengthen or support it as if by propping it with cushions.

bolt. In the phrase "bolt upright," *bolt* means simply "straight as an arrow" (a bolt was an arrow with a bullet-like knob). "He has shot his bolt" is from this word for arrow, not from the bolt of a door, which, in fact, is connected with the "straight" idea in this same source word; as is *bolt* of cloth, from its long narrow shape. The verb *bolt*, suggesting speed, and the noun of *thunderbolt*, are also derived, it is believed, from the flight of an arrow. Thus the idea of "straight" and that of "fast" go down through the centuries until they culminate in that triumph of civilization, the joke about the seasick person who should have bolted his food. It may be a surprise that "a bolt from the blue," meaning a complete surprise, is not very old (Butler, 1911). "A bolt out of the blue" was listed by OED (1888) but not dated. Stevenson found it in Carlyle's *French Revolution*, 1837.

bolter. See MUGWUMP.

bone. "I have a bone to pick with you" largely succeeded "a crow to pluck" in the sense of "I am displeased with you about something." The "crow" business was Elizabethan, and lasted pretty well through Dickens's time. Neither is easy to explain, but the notion of two dogs with a "bone of contention" between them is probably suggested in the one case. Two dogs with but a single bone to pick are not likely to remain friends long.

To "make no bones" about a thing goes back to the early 1500's. In a version of the Abraham and Isaac story one writer said, "Abraham made no manier bones ne stickyng." In the sense of "raise no difficulties," the phrase may refer either to finding no bones in the soup, or to making no attempt to influence the actions of the dice in a game of "rolling the bones." Collegians of the seventies and eighties used the expression "bone up on" to mean "study hard" but spelled it "Bohn," for those were the "trots" that enabled our ancestors to learn so much Greek and Latin. (See FUNNY BONE.)

bonehead. Though the adjective *boneheaded*, in the sense of "stupid," has been spotted as early as 1903, it appears that Fred Merkle's famous failure to touch second base, in 1908, was the occasion for the popularizing of the term "bonehead play," as Stevenson gives the credit to a sporting-page story mentioned by Sullivan in *Our Times*. The first date for *bonehead* in OED is 1913, *Seven Keys to Baldpate*.

bonfire. Fantastic explanations have been proposed. But if the original spelling, "bonefire," had been retained, some good printer's ink would have been saved. Skeat and OED agree that the source, back in heathen times, was a rousing fire of bones. In Picardy there is an equivalent, *fu d'os*, that corroborates this interestingly.

bonnet. See BEE IN HIS BONNET.

boo. See RAZZ.

booboisie. This is Mencken's word, amusingly parallel to *bourgeoisie*, for the uncivilized and illiterate who persecute evolutionists and believe in storks and Santa Claus. Webster, not convinced of its permanent importance, goes only as far as "boobery." "Booby," as a spiritless fool, goes back at least to Young (author of *Night Thoughts*), and is from Spanish *bobo*, which may derive from Latin, *balbus*, stammering.

A "booby hatch" (or hutch, or hack, or hut) was originally a small cover for a companionway on a vessel; hence, a sleigh or wagon with a removable hood, something like the dome-shaped roof that can be slid over the open cockpit of certain airplanes. The transference of "booby hatch" to mean insane asylum seems to be due entirely to the powerful associations of the word *booby*.

boodle. See KIT AND CABOODLE.

book. See BELL, BOOK, AND CANDLE.

books. "Am I out of your books?" or "in your bad books" or "in your black book" all mean about the same as "not in your books," from *Much Ado about Nothing*; i.e., not on your list of friends. Brewer says that in the good old days a single sheet or list could be classified as a book.

boom. In the sense of a violent upward trend, as in business or in the popularity of some candidate for public office, this may have been derived from the suddenness and the rush of a cannon shot; or the booming along of a river, or of a ship under full sail; or the boom of thunder, with its gradually increasing intensity. Or all of these may have helped the good work along. Perhaps the booming of explosives in mining operations should be added to this list, as the date of origin is about 1875, and the locality suspiciously close to mining country.

How long ago did Clancy first "lower the boom"? It means, of course, to get rough with somebody, to knock people down or about. But what kind of boom was the original Clancy familiar with? Surely not a microphone boom or a sonic boom, though perhaps it should be said that if those Air Force boys lower their sonic booms much farther we won't have any picture windows left. While the Head of the Archive of Folk Song of the Library of Congress could find me no reference to this Clancy earlier than 1947, and is not inclined to consider the song "a folk product," I have been assured by a number of mature individuals, mainly from the New York area, that Clancy used to lower the boom when they were children. One clinched it, I thought, by adding, "There were about twenty verses." On certain sailing vessels a boom can be raised and lowered, but the early Clancys were more at home on the docks or in heavy construction work than on boats. It is my guess, therefore, that the idea of "conking" somebody with a boom arose from crane or steam-shovel operations, and that Clancy most likely was a stevedore!

boondoggle. Daniel Boone's dog need not apply; it is a popular etymology of the barefaced sort. Secondly, I reject my own explanation, concocted before I saw *The Literary Digest* of June 1, 1935; namely, that *boon* is something you get free, and that *doggle* is rhyming slang for *boggle*—thus, that *boondoggling* is doing something rather badly that is hardly worth doing at all. However, it is now clear that Mr. Walter

Link of Rochester gave his son's Boy Scout neck-strap, a plaited thong or lanyard, that curious name. And in all probability Mr. Link, in his boyhood, had picked up the word from a playmate of Scotch descent, because EDD unquestionably recognizes *boondoggle* as a Scottish word for a marble that you obtain as a gift, without having worked for it. The strange thing is that the word Mr. Link thought he had coined should have this connotation in reference to New Deal relief work for unemployed.

booshwah, bushwa. Webster says this is a corruption of *bodewash*, which means bosh or trash, and derives from *bois de vache*, "cow's wood" or dried dung (compare "buffalo chips," used in frontier days for firewood). It is only a coincidence, perhaps, that the disreputable ejaculation, "bullshit," is used in exactly the same way as "bushwa." (See POPPYCOCK. SHOOT THE BULL.)

boost. This "ugly word" (says an N. & Q. correspondent) was current in England from 1300 on, died an unlamented death, then was revived as American slang. This may well be true, as EDD lists a *boose*, energy, and a *poose*, push. OED does not mention them as possible sources. Webster does recognize them now, but rather spoils it by saying "Origin uncertain." The basic idea is "energy" and "push," all right.

boot. See CABOOSE.

boot-jack. See GIN.

bootlegger. Though this word was supposed to become obsolete with repeal of Prohibition, there is evidence that the species may have survived after all. A New York publication explained in 1890 that the name derived from the liquor smuggler's practice of concealing a bottle in his boot top.

bootlick. See CURRY FAVOR.

boots and saddles. By folk etymology, the French cavalry command (now practically obsolete) "*Boute selle!*" ("Put saddle!") became "boot and saddle" in England, and "boots and saddles" here—the bugle call most familiar to the cavalryman (unless it was the mess call).

booze. This very old word somehow has never quite risen above barroom levels. To "bouse" meant, in the 14th century, to drink deep. It may have come from the Dutch *buyzen*, to tipple, or *buise*, a drinking vessel; and these may go back to Hindustani, *booza*, drink, which has descendants in almost any language. When "bouse" or "booze" became general in the 16th century, it was thieves' cant.

boozy. See WOOZY.

bo-peep. Americans associate this with the little shepherdess of the nursery rhyme, not with the game of "peek-a-boo," which OED describes in loving detail under "bo-peep"—not even giving "peek-a-boo" as a variant, though "keek-a-boo" is listed. The traditional scariness of "boo" (see BUGABOO) makes the game much more exciting when played under American rules.

In the days before backless bathing suits, when even a wee glimpse of feminine underwear was deemed a great treat, "peek-a-boo" shirt-waists had quite a vogue. They consisted chiefly of tiny holes.

Borghese. See BOGUS.

born on the wrong side of the blanket. See BLANKET.

bosh. From a Turkish word meaning "nothing, empty, worthless." Popularized about 1825 by Morier's books about Turkish life.

boss. There was something about the sound of "master" that bothered the early American democrat, so he adopted the Dutch synonym for it, *baas*. Washington Irving used it, as "boss," in 1806. When it got back to England, in fairly recent times, few realized (as Weekley points out) that it had crossed the Atlantic twice to get from Holland to England. In Dutch the word had at one time meant "uncle," and is supposed to be related to Old High German *basa*, aunt. It has no connection with "boss" in the sense of protuberance (as in "emboss").

bottoms up. See MUD.

boulster lecture. See CURTAIN LECTURE.

bounce. See FLY A KITE.

Bountiful. See LADY BOUNTIFUL.

bow. See DRAW. TWO STRINGS TO HIS BOW.

bowels of compassion. Just as the liver was considered the seat of courage, the bowels were considered the headquarters for mercy, pity, kindness. It is a Biblical idea (Genesis, Colossians, I John), but Shakespeare, Congreve, and William Penn all made effective use of it.

Another figurative sense in which it appears is as in this sentence: "Far into the bowels of the land have we marched."

bower. In the game of euchre, the right bower is the *knave* of trumps; and *knave* closely parallels in meaning the German word for farmer or peasant, *Bauer*, from which this *bower* comes. *Bowery* is also a relative as it comes from the Dutch word for countryseat or farm—which helps account for the fact that the ancient and honorable Bowery Savings Bank has little or nothing to do with bums.

bowl of cherries. See CHERRY.

boycott. In 1880, in County Mayo, Ireland, Captain Boycott, agent of an estate, became unpopular with the tenants, but the landlord declined to remove him. Thereupon the tenants devised for him a sort of ostracism or excommunication. Within six years, English papers were printing the new word without a capital letter.

bozo. This word for fellow or man is southwestern in origin, and hence doubtless has Mexican ancestors. However, Webster specifies *bozal*, a nose hitch. Yet in the cow-country *mozo* is familiar as a man of all work, being simply the Spanish for "young man." With the word *'bo* (for hobo) in mind, and a cold in the head, what more simple than to change *mozo* (pronounced with the Mexican *s*, not the Spanish *th*) into *bozo*? An interesting sidelight here is the relationship between *mozo* and *mousse* (pronounced "moose"). Though Webster gives this as British nautical slang for a boy serving an officers' mess, OED fails to list the word *mousse* in this sense. The housewife knows it, of course, as a frozen dessert concocted without elbow-grease.

Bradford. See GRACE OF GOD.

braggadocio. Those who pride themselves on pronouncing this with the Italian sneeze, as in *'cello*, should be told that it is not an Italian word, but was simply invented by Spenser as the name for one of the characters in *The Faerie Queen*, one who personified vain boasting. Spenser probably called it either "sheeo" or "keeo." We might therefore say that the word is an Italian body built on a "brag" chassis.

brainstorm. This "highly American compound," as Mencken calls it, is now good legal English for a temporary fit of insanity, and has been used with marked success in murder trials (for example, in the Thaw case). According to Weseen, it is also collegiate slang for "a sudden thought, especially if considered brilliant," but this ironical use is infrequent.

Brain Trust. In Lindley's book, *The Roosevelt Revolution*, James M. Kieran is credited with first applying the nickname "Brain Trust" to F. D. R.'s professorial advisers.

brake. Dickens has something about the noise made by a six-horse break (*Pickwick Papers* II, xxi). This was either a large carriage frame with no body, used for "breaking" or training horses, or a pleasure vehicle for a half-dozen passengers. It may also be spelled "brake," and while the origin is apparently the sense of "break" mentioned above (as we have in the slang "broncho-busting"), the idea of restraining or retarding may have entered in. The whole problem of *brake* and *break* is a vexing one. The device by means of which people endeavor, not always with conspicuous success, to tame their speeding automobiles should perhaps be spelled "break." Then again, it may be from Dutch *braeke*, the nose ring of an ox. It is probably an application of brake in the older "lever" or "curb" sense. And now who wants to account for *brake* as meaning bush or thicket?

branch. See OLIVE BRANCH.

brand new. Not from the clearly distinguished *brand* of the maker, nor from the perhaps appetizing appearance of a bucket of *bran* (a common corruption), but from the same source as fire-*brand*, which is cognate with *burn*. The Germans have a word for it, *funkelnagelneu*, spark-nail-new; and the French, *tout battant neuf*, fresh from the anvil. Shakespeare called it "fire-new," in *Twelfth Night*.

brass. See DOUBLE IN BRASS.

brass knuckles. See KNUCKLE-DUSTER.

brass tacks. "To get down to brass tacks" means to get down to business. But it is not clear why. It would be if the brass tack were the best kind of tack, but the fact seems to be that there is no such thing as a solid brass tack. Brass-headed tacks, yes. But we all know what an expensive nuisance those decorative little nails are. They are, however, used in upholstery, so that a possible source of the expression may be in the thought of putting the finishing touches on a project. Unfortunately, the phrase usually implies a beginning of serious business rather than a topping off.

OED lists "tin tacks" as a variant of this expression. Both of the supporting quotations are from George Bernard Shaw. (See also TALK TURKEY.)

brawl. In the modern slang sense of "party," usually a "dancing party," this may easily be a survival from the British dance of that name, resembling a cotillion, and descended probably from French *branler*, to shake. Thus the brawl would seem to be a distant cousin of the shimmy.

bread-basket. See CODGER. UPSET THE APPLE CART.

break. "To get the breaks" means to have good luck, but "to make a break" still suggests a *faux pas*. Though the dictionaries indicate that a break may be either favorable or unfavorable, the trend seems to have been from bad to good: in 1883 a break was usually bad; about 1914, the phrase "even break" was popular (as in F. P. A.'s well-known "The best you get is an even break"); and today only a gag-writer would connect a "break" with anything so unpleasant as being "broke." The notion seems to be a change in the luck, a break in the monotony, an opportunity. And there's a cheerful sound about the word opportunity.

breathing. See CLOSER IS HE THAN BREATHING.

breech-clout. See CLOUT.

brewing in the air. See SMELL.

bric à brac. Thackeray, who to a large extent popularized this, wrote it as one word and without the accent. Littré theorizes that in origin the expression is very much like "by hook or by crook," but other French dictionaries say bluntly, "*Onomatopée*." These echoic possibilities are interestingly paralleled in our equivalent "knick-knacks." Whistler, in *The Gentle Art of Making Enemies*, uses the term in an ingenious blizzard of alliteration: "a bewilderment of bric-à-brac and brummagem." (See BRUMMAGEM.)

brick. "He is a regular brick," Stevenson suggests, may go back to Aristotle's definition of a happy man as "a faultless cube." A brick is, of course, solid, four-square, reliable, honest (faces being alike, though decidedly plain). These do not serve OED as clues, however; his only hunch is that there is something energetic about the loud crash that accompanies the dumping of a load of bricks. We do have from this the phrase, "come down like a ton of bricks" which is phonetically much better than the British "a thousand of bricks," though this is *technically* correct as bricks are not sold by the ton. However, the characteristic qualities of an individual brick seem to offer more hopeful possibilities. (See SQUARE.)

bridal. Perhaps one reason people get drunk at weddings is a subconscious awareness that "bridal" comes from "bride-ale." By analogy with such words as betrothal and espousal, the *ale* was softened to *al*. As a matter of fact, however, not since 1300 has the sense of "ale" been actually important in the rather charming word "bridal."

bridegroom. You may think that, etymologically, this is just a stable boy getting married. Unfortunately, from the point of view of good clean fun, it was originally *brydguma*, bride-man, and only later got mixed up with the boy that took care of the horses. A Chinese student of mine once stated that the opposite of *pride* was *pridegloom*.

bring down the house. This was used as early as 1754 of demonstrative applause that, in the words of OED, "threatens or suggests the downfall of the building." "Raise the roof" is very similar.

bring home the bacon. Though Partridge dates this only from 1925, and Weseen gives it as cowboy slang, it would be foolhardy to deny any connection with the famous Dunmow Flitch. In the 12th century a custom began of awarding a side of bacon as a prize for connubial felicity. The couple that could swear they had not quarrelled for twelve months, or at any time "wished they were single again" (in the words of the ballad), came home with the bacon. Today the expression means, of course, "to come back with a victory."

brinkmanship. John Foster Dulles, sacrificially dedicated Secretary of State (see DEDICATED), is to be credited with "massive retaliation" (*Foreign Affairs*, April, 1954) and "agonizing re-appraisal" (NATO meeting, Dec., 1954). But he is only indirectly to blame for *brinkmanship*. Soon after the Shepley article in *Life* (Jan. 16, 1956) describing Dulles's skill in "walking to the brink of war" and teetering there, somebody (probably Adlai Stevenson, with an assist from the oneupmanship man, Stephen Potter) dubbed it "brinkmanship." Gov.

Stevenson is not quite willing to take the credit, if credit there be. He writes me: "I cannot claim authorship of *brinkmanship*. I am not sure, however, whether I read it or heard it or dreamed it up. . . . I am reasonably sure that I did not invent it." He did send me a copy of his Hartford speech (Feb. 25, 1956) in which he said: "We hear the Secretary of State boasting of his Brinksmanship" [*sic*].

broad. In 1897 this was slang for a playing card. Since 1920 it has meant a girl, especially one whose code of ethics has broadened to the vanishing point. In other words, a "broad" is seldom narrow.

broken on the wheel. See ROUÉ.

bromide. OED stubbed its toe on Gelett Burgess's *blurb* (q.v.) but did better on this, locating its source as an essay, "Bromidioms," in *Smart Set* for April, 1906. As in the well-known hangover dispeller, bromoseltzer, the basic notion of bromide is a sedative; hence, a person who uses worn-out expressions that bore rather than stimulate. Apparently the reason why its opposite, proposed in the same article, "sulfite," never caught on was that the specifications were too high; we're all of us just bromides, more or less of the time, so sulfite, being superfluous, died a-borning.

Bronx cheer. See RAZZ.

broomstick. See JUMP.

Brother Jonathan. Authorities believe that Governor Jonathan Trumbull of Connecticut was the original for this nickname that was soon largely replaced by "Uncle Sam." The story is that George Washington, short of ammunition, announced, "We must consult Brother Jonathan." The expression first appeared in print about 1816.

brow. See FAN MY BROW.

brown study. "He is in a brown study" is not very complimentary. It means nearly the same as wool-gathering, and is even older. As its source, authorities prefer the color *brown*, in the sense of "gloomy," to the notion of a wrinkled or thoughtful *brow*.

"To do a thing up brown" goes back at least to *Pickwick Papers*, and is probably from the appearance of well-done meat.

brummagem. As applied to counterfeit or tawdry articles, this word unquestionably points an accusing finger at Birmingham, as it represents an ancient local pronunciation for the name of the town and confirms the fact that counterfeiting was not unknown there, nor was, later, the manufacture of cheap shoddy merchandise, such as imitation jewelry and "phony" watches. If there is, however, any tendency on the part of purists to insist on the correct pronunciation of "Birmingham" in reference to dishonest craftmanship, I have no doubt that the Birmingham Rotary Club is industriously combating it.

bub, bubby. See GRUB.

bubble-and-squeak. A British culinary triumph: meat and greens, fried together. They have been bubbling and squeaking, during the process, since 1785 at least.

buccaneer. This rousing word for a pirate goes back to a West Indian barbecue. The *buccan* (taken into French as *boucan*) was a wooden grid for roasting wild oxen and boars. The French hunters of San Domingo, tiring perhaps of their pig-sticking, decided to employ their talents more profitably, on the high seas.

buck. "To pass the buck" is to evade a job or a responsibility by shunting it on someone else. While a "buck" is, for some unknown reason, a dollar, and while a sawbuck is a framework on which you saw firewood, the buck which one passes derives from the game of poker, being somewhat similar to the "I pass" of bridge. It may be the scapegoat idea, or have some connection with the old slang phrase for gambling, "bucking the tiger."

"Let George do it," or "Leave it to George" is another way of expressing buckpassing. A translation of *Laissez faire à Georges* (Georges d'Amboise, prime minister to Louis XII, c. 1500), the saying was revived in England in reference to Lloyd George. At Williams College it was the venerable motto of an enterprising pants-presser.

bucket. See KICK THE BUCKET.

bucket shop. Thornton connected the broker's shop in which dealings in small lots were transacted with the earlier gin-shops in which small quantities of liquor were sold. But OED accepts the explanation given in a Leeds paper, in 1886, that on slack days at the Chicago Board of Trade some members of the smaller-fry curb market downstairs would be brought up to the trading floor in an elevator or "bucket."

buckle down to work. This figurative use of *buckle* actually goes back to the days of armor.

budget. See FUSS-BUDGET.

buff. "In the buff" means stripped not only to the waist, but, in a word, stripped. Related to *buffalo*, buff signifies a thick skin or leather. The color is supposed to be that of a tanned skin.

A "buff" (back in the days of Mayor LaGuardia) was simply a person who liked to go to fires and help when permitted. Nowadays it appears to mean an enthusiast or "fan" of any sort. Nobody seems to know why.

bug. "BUG BREAKS FLIGHT OF MISS EARHART." This front page headline from the revered *New York Times* would cause a gasp if transferred to a British sheet, because there it would mean, not just the garden-variety of insect that might find its way into any aviatrix's eye, but—horror of horrors—a bedbug. A half-century ago a Briton named Bugg so disapproved of his name that he asked permission to change it to Norfolk-Howard, two of the most aristocratic names on the island; whereupon his countrymen (who lack a sense of humor, you know) took to calling bedbugs "Norfolk-Howards."

The connection between this entomological "bug" and the "bug" of "bugaboo" is not clear, though it has been conjectured. There is a characteristically unpronounceable Welsh word, *bwg*, which means a ghost, and which is doubtless related to the "bug" in the "Bug Bible," so-called because of the reference, in the 91st Psalm, to not being "afraid of any bugges by night." Shakespeare has, in *King Henry VI*, Part III, Act V, sc. ii, "Warwick was a bug that fear'd us all," meaning, in the vernacular, a holy terror ("fear'd" meaning "frightened," in this case). (See BOGEY, and BUGABOO.)

bugaboo. An effort has been made to prove that this is an old Irish war-cry. Mencken, on the other hand, thinks it an American invention. What is pretty sure is that it is related to "bugbear," and thus to *bogey* and *bug* (q.v.). The "boo" part of it is reminiscent of the old phrase for "You're yellow": "You dare not say 'bo' to a goose." There is not, we hasten to add, much foundation for the claim that this man "Boh" was a fierce Gothic general.

bugger. Meaning originally a Bulgarian, this word was applied (by people who did not like Bulgarians) to heretics and later to sodomites. In 1897 thieves were using it to mean nothing more disreputable than a pickpocket, but the classic sense of "pervert" is still commonly understood today.

bug in a rug. See SNUG AS A BUG IN A RUG.

build-up. *New Yorker* fans will remember the Arno cartoon of the chorus girl in the taxi with her white-mustached escort, whom she is reproving with "What? No build-up?" This is theatrical slang for "preparation," as in the constructing of a reputation by carefully linked publicity releases.

bulge. See FUSS-BUDGET.

bull. See COCK AND BULL STORY. SHOOT THE BULL. SMELL (a rat).

bulldoze. British dictionaries spell this Americanism with an *s* and toy with the possibility of a connection with a dose of medicine. Thornton, accurate historian of the American language, uses a consistent *z*. The statement made by B. & L., that the characteristic organ of a bull furnished the tough whip with which bulldozing was carried on, is followed by Hyamson in his less specific explanation, that the term means to threaten or bully, with a strip of hide. OED's statement that a bull-pizzle was often used as "an instrument of flagellation" tends to confirm this.

bullet. "Every bullet has its billet" was attributed by Sterne and Wesley to William III, and there is no reason to doubt that he said something of the sort. Meaning "an assigned destination" (as of sleeping quarters for soldiers "billeted" on a town), *billet* is actually related to *bullet*, through *bull*, an edict. (See SHOOT THE BULL. CLICK.)

Another word related to these two is *ballot*, used by Abraham Lincoln in his famous reference to appealing "from the ballot to the bullet."

bulley (bully) beef. OED appears to favor a derivation implying "made from an old bull" over that meaning "boiled" (from French *bouilli*, an expression that is said to have often been printed on tinned-beef labels). I believe that Webster is right in accepting the latter theory.

The curiously contradictory meanings of *bully*—"excellent," and "a cruel braggart"—can be accounted for, perhaps, on the ground of a throw-back, on the part of the complimentary ejaculation, to the original meaning of "lover." This apparently passed from the sense of "gallant" into that of "hired ruffian" (as Italian *bravo* did) and thence easily into the conception of a fellow who picks on people not his own size.

bull pen. In addition to the literal meaning, Webster mentions "barracks in a lumber camp" and "an inclosure for prisoners in time of riot" as cant or colloquial senses. OED added something about an Indiana schoolboy game, but was evidently not yet aware of our expression in reference to the inclosure near a baseball diamond, often in full view of the stands and the players, where a new pitcher warms up before replacing a teammate who has gotten himself into a bad hole.

bulls and bears. Just as there were bootleggers before Prohibition, there were bears before the great depression—long before. The origin, which has been satisfactorily ascribed to the fable of the man who sold the skin before he caught the bear, was about the time of the South Sea Bubble financial scandal in England (1720); this is borne out by the fact that the brokers who gambled on a falling market were early known as "bear-skin jobbers."

The "bulls" may have taken their name from the pleasant habit those animals have of tossing things with their horns—things that go up, but also come down.

bull session. See SHOOT THE BULL.

bum. This old word for what Mencken thought fit to call "an unmentionable part of the body," the buttocks, has never reached great popularity in this country. It may be simply a contraction of "bottom," though OED implies that no one ever thought of calling his seat his "bottom" before the eighteenth century, and that therefore the older *bum* must be onomatopœic or have something to do with a protuberance or swelling.

"Cherry bum," a nickname for hussars wearing red trousers, is an almost literal translation of the French equivalent, *culs rouges*, even to the flavor of impropriety that hangs about the words *bum* and *cul*.

Though Britons have sometimes accounted for their expression "bum bailiff" by relating it to "bound bailiff," the parallel phrases, *pousse cul*, in France, and "one jump ahead of the sheriff," in America, suggest a more homely origin than "bound."

Certain boats used in English harbors for removing filth from vessels are known as "bumboats." While Webster, with great politeness, postulates a Low German word for a boat hewn from a tree trunk (thus related to the boom of a ship), OED says frankly that "bumboat" apparently comes from the slang term, "bum."

Our phrase "on the bum" is probably just the opposite of "top," though the noun *bum* may be related to the German *Bummler*, loafer, and *Bummelzug*, slow train. Jerome K. Jerome once used the term "on the bummel."

The American slang equivalent of British "bum shaver," a short coat (*rase cul* in French), is probably "fanny cooler."

bump. To be as stolid and dumb as a log is an obvious figure of speech. Evidently "bump on a log" is just an intensive form of it. Or perhaps imagination could carry us a little further: considering that it is rather hard to be on friendly terms with such a person, we might point out that a bumpy log makes an even more uncomfortable seat than an ordinary log.

"Bump off" is an entirely satisfactory metaphor for "kill." It has the nonchalance of gangland when confronted with death, and yet there is in it the element of surprise and the sound of a gun. The figure is probably that of being suddenly pushed over some sort of precipice.

bumper. British authorities allude to "a *thumping* glassful" in an attempt to explain this word for a drinking vessel that is full to the brim. This strikes me as more far-fetched than a reference to French *bombard*, a tankard, admitted by Webster to be a possibility. Some have seen a "fancied connection" (as Skeat says) with French *bomber*, to bulge, and English *bump*, as a full glass of wine bellies out at the top.

A natural derivative is the adjective *bumper*, used of crops, for instance, to mean "overflowing."

buncombe. See BUNK.

bunk. For a time in the 19th century this was the equivalent of the later "scram." But the established meaning derives from Buncombe

County, North Carolina. Felix Walker, orating in the 16th Congress, explained his particular brand of claptrap as being directed only at his constituents in Buncombe County. B. & L. point out that an earlier use of "bunkum" in New England was laudatory, being apparently derived from French-Canadian, "*Il est bon comme ça.*" (See HOKUM.)

bunky. See COMRADE.

burl. See LOG-ROLLING.

burn. "That burns me up," meaning "That makes me furious" or "That gripes me" (an ugly figure, in allusion to the agony of gas-cramps), is a modern twist to the ancient and obvious association of anger with fire. "Burn" has also been used, intransitively, with regard to sexual passion, and, transitively, to mean infect someone with sores, especially of a venereal character. OED said (in 1888) that this last usage, which was Shakesperean, was then obsolete, but B. & L. record something quite similar in their 1897 study of slang.

burn your candle at both ends. See CANDLE.

burp. This ingenious synonym for "belch" is fully as expressive, and deserves a place in the dictionaries. It is indeed an unusually good illustration of onomatopœia.

bury the hatchet. Before smoking the peace-pipe, the Indians buried their tomahawks, covering up all signs of hostility. It meant, "Let's call it quits."

bush. See BEAT AROUND THE BUSH.

bushwa. See BOOSHWAH.

bushwhacker. This was much the same as a *jay-hawker* (q.v.), only much easier to explain. The earliest bushwhackers were riverboat men who warped their boats upstream by seizing overhanging brush at the bow and marching to the stern with it, then returning to the bow for a new hold. During the Civil War the term was transferred to guerrillas who lived in the woods, beating through the bushes on their surprise raids. There is no need of turning to the Dutch for the source of *bush* and *whack*. They come from good old English roots.

buss. Meaning a rude or playful kiss (Webster), this was originally imitative, primarily, though there is a distant family relationship with French *baiser*, to kiss. Which reminds me that when you bookish people get tired of "osculate" (from the Latin for "little mouth") you can "basiate" for a while (a 1623 word for kiss). (See KILTER.)

B. & L. made what appears to be an amusing mistake when they listed "buss" as meaning "break," in the colloquial expression, "I'll buss your head." Surely this was just a darky mispronunciation of "bust," short for "burst."

butt. See FAG.

butter and egg man. George Kaufman's play thus entitled (1925) gave added currency to this Broadway name for a wealthy spender usually lacking in artistic appreciation. Texas Guinan, night club proprietress, had a story, quite likely true, of such a man who dazzled even her accustomed eyes but would identify himself only as a big dairy producer. This may be the origin. (See ANGEL.)

butters no parsnips. See CUT.

butter won't melt in her mouth. Meaning very prim and cool, the opposite of "hot and bothered," this goes back to 1530, according to E.P. The word *demure* is usually thought of as an integral part of the proverb. Thackeray used the expression, in *Pendennis*, in reference to a girl who was "smiling and languishing."

button. Pugilistic slang for the point of the chin, this sense is recent enough not to have found conservative recognition. It derives, I suppose, from our somewhat childish faith that when we press an electric button something is bound to happen.

buzz saw. See MONKEY.

by heart. See HEART.

by hook or crook. See HOOK OR CROOK.

by jingo. See JINGOISM.

C

cabal. It is hard to make people believe that this word for an intriguing clique antedated the Charles II Ministry, and that the Clifford-Ashley-Buckingham-Arlington-Lauderdale combination was a pure coincidence. It comes, however, from Jewish *cabala*, an occult theosophy, full of hidden mysteries. The fact is that the "cabal cabinet" was made up of two separate cliques that were diametrically opposed to each other on the question of war against Holland.

caboodle. See KIT AND CABOODLE.

caboose. Derived apparently from a Dutch word of obscure origin, this was taken over by American railroad men from sea service (a deck house in which cooking was done). They applied it, as all of us know, to the squatty little car (usually red) at the tail end of a freight train, where the conductor and the rear-end brakeman make their headquarters. Someone who was struck by the resemblance of the cupola, from which a look-out is kept on the train ahead, to a small house rising above the level of a ship's deck, may have given the American car (unknown in England) this nickname. A new application of the word, in the Southwest, to a cowhide attached under a wagon and used as a receptacle for stray pieces of wood, etc., is amusingly reminiscent of the *boot* of an English stagecoach.

cad. From *cadet*, the younger son who had to seek his own fortune. Before going into the golf business, the Scotch "cadie" or "cawdy" was either a disreputable unemployed sedan-chair bearer, or a blackguard errand boy. This accounts for the Oxford version, now become general, of a low, vulgar fellow. An early use of *cad* for an unbooked coach-passenger on whom the driver made a personal profit was transferred to the conductor of an omnibus—a term familiar to Dickens. This, says OED, is obsolete; yet, curiously enough, Weseen finds it meaning, among the crooks, a railroad conductor or baggage-man. It is more probable that the old cockney word for omnibus conductor has seeped through into our underworld, than that the high-hat Oxford slang has come to be attached to those impolite train-officials (that is, impolite to the gentlemen riding the rails or the blind baggage).

cadet. See CAD.

cadger. See BADGER. CODGER.

Cadmean victory. Same as Pyrrhic victory: one in which the winner suffers as much as the loser—"One more such victory and we are lost" (Pyrrhus). "Cadmean" refers to the dragon's teeth sowed by Cadmus, which sprouted up into armed men; as was to be expected, they promptly started a fight. I am reminded of the prophecy that the Italians would lose the Italo-Ethiopian war because the one named first always loses; e.g., Spanish-American war, Russo-Japanese war, and the two World Wars (in which everyone lost).

cady, cadey. This old slang word for a hat has been preserved in some parts of the Middle West as a specific word for a derby. It was probably of cockney origin, and was familiar to the music hall audiences of late 19th century England.

Cæsar's wife must be above suspicion. He didn't believe her guilty of infidelity, but his vanity demanded a divorce if any crack-pot so much as suspected her. One may gather that he didn't love her excessively. Plutarch and Suetonius tell the story.

cage. See CODGER.

cahoots. OED dislikes the derivation from *cohorte*, given in some American dictionaries, and admits the likelihood that it comes from *cahute*, cabin or hut, which fits in with the idea of a partnership of no very respectable sort. Though Clédat's French Etymological Dictionary says the origin of *cahute* is unknown, others connect it with the Dutch *kajuit*, cabin. An illustration of the fascination of word-study is found here: a contributor to N. & Q. says that Cotgrave, in 1632, listed *cahute* as an English word for little house, as well as *cahuette*; and that the latter was another name for *luette*, the old name for the game of jack-straws! And this brings us back around the circle to the expression, to knock something (such as a little pile of sticks) "out of cahoots."

Cain. See CURSE OF CAIN.

cake. "To take the cake," meaning "to win the prize," is unquestionably of negro origin, as far as the United States is concerned. At a cakewalk, a cake was given as a prize to the one who could "strut his stuff" the best. This effort to invent fancy ways of walking accounts for some of the goofy steps of a tap-dancer's routine.

However, instances of cakes being used for prizes can be found not only in mid-Victorian England, but clear back in classical times.

cake. See JOHNNY CAKE. LET THEM EAT CAKE.

calaboose. Strangely parallel with *hoosegow* (q.v.), this variously spelled word for jail came into Louisiana French from Spanish *calabozo*, dungeon, early in the last century.

calculate. Long stigmatized as a disgusting Americanism (in the sense of "guess" or "reckon"), early examples of the same thing have been found in England. The colloquialism is not, of course, in good usage anywhere. The word itself has an interesting derivation: pebbles (*calculi*) were used by the ancient Romans in voting and in figuring their gambling losses.

Caledvwlch. See EXCALIBUR.

calories. See CAUDLE LECTURE.

camera. See COMRADE.

canard. The French expression, "to half-sell a duck" (i.e., to cheat a buyer) is usually given as the source, *canard* being the word for duck. Then there was the hoax-story of the thirty ducks who ate each other up—which probably helped popularize the idiomatic use of canard to mean a false story. A shameless punster has defined a canard as something "one *canardly* believe." (See COCK AND BULL STORY.)

candid friend. See DEFEND ME FROM MY FRIENDS.

candle.

> My candle burns at both ends;
> It will not last the night;
> But ah, my foes, and oh, my friends—
> It gives a lovely light!
> —Edna St. Vincent Millay

Obviously the idea is to live extravagantly, to waste one's resources, both financial and physical. Smollett was one of the first to use the phrase in English (1749); it was a direct translation of Lesage's "*brûloient la chandelle par les deux bouts*," but in that case it pictured two servants as robbing their master from two directions at the same time.

"He can't hold a candle to you" means "He is greatly inferior to you," the idea deriving from the menial job of link-boy, before the day of street lights or gas-lighting in theaters.

A slightly different use is the cry of the Merchant of Venice, "Must I hold a candle to my shame?" It envisions a man forced to assist thus in his own humiliation (especially, in French usage, in an amorous intrigue of some sort).

"The game isn't worth the candle" simply translates the French proverb (found in Montaigne), "*Le jeu ne vaut pas la chandelle.*" The idea is that such low stakes are being played for that no one will win enough to pay for the lights.

candle. See BELL, BOOK, AND CANDLE.

Candlemas Day. See GROUND-HOG DAY.

cannon. See BILLIARDS. CAROM.

cannon-fodder. Shakespeare had the right idea when he spoke of men as "food for powder" (*Henry IV*, Part I). Though no one has been able to pin the expression on the 1914–1918 Germans, it seems to be a direct translation of *Kanonenfutter*, and has thus been, unfairly perhaps, attributed to Boche frightfulness.

cantankerous. Thornton says this is possibly an Americanism, though the early quotations are English (OED's first is 1772, while his first American is not till 1854). However, Read cites *cantankerous* in a 1789 list of provincial Americanisms. Tucker gives *rantankerous* as a variant, but *cant* seems to have outdistanced *rant* in the survival-of-the-fittest race, perhaps through some vague association with the baleful word "cancer." Other valuable sound-implications in the word which bear out the meaning of "quarrelsome" are to be found in "shan't" and "anger."

can't take it. See TAKE IT.

Canuck. B. & L. think this is at least part Indian, Hyamson suggests a British name, *Connaught*, as a source, and Mencken gives the French some credit. The most logical theory connects *Canada* with an Algonquin ending. Thornton shows that for some time it was popular to begin it with a *K*, though the earliest instance begins with a *C*.

cap. "She set her cap at him" means apparently about what it says: she adjusted her cap at the most fetching angle, to win her man.

A variant of "thinking cap" is "considering cap." The reference in both, perhaps, is to the cap put on by the judge before pronouncing sentence—formerly in all cases, now only for the death sentence. (See FEATHER IN HIS CAP.)

capacity. See GENIUS.

cap-a-pie. See APPLE-PIE ORDER.

capital, capitalist. See CHATTELS.

card. Shakespeare and Dryden were familiar with the application of "card" to a person in various senses: a "sure" card, or "good," or "rum" (queer), or "knowing"—or just alone, to mean a "character," an *original* (as the French say). All were suggested apparently by the opportune or amusing appearance of cards at certain critical stages of the game.

That a future event is "in (or on) the cards," meaning sure to happen, is a phrase borrowed from the fortune teller's "patter."

cardinal. It is fairly simple to connect the Latin word for "hinge" with the flaming red bird that adorns the lithographed stationery of the St. Louis National League baseball club. In the first place, Latin *cardo* (unrelated to the Greek word for "heart" that we have preserved in *cardiac*) was the ancestor of the cardinals of the Roman Catholic Church, because on them *hinged* the election of the Pope. These cardinals had red hats. So when a bird was discovered to have plumage that matched these hats, it was dubbed a cardinal bird. And the St. Louis "Cardinals" took the colorful bird as their symbol, just as Chicago took the bear cub and Detroit the tiger.

carom. Also spelled *carrom* and further curiously corrupted to *cannon*, this billiard term for the striking of two object balls with the cue ball is short for *carambole*, the French equivalent, which they also call, similarly, *canon*. (See BILLIARDS.)

carpet. "On the carpet" has two distinct meanings. The French *sur le tapis*, on the table-cover (related to *tapestry*), means "up for consideration"; and when the English translated this they used "on the carpet" because the noun at that time meant table-cover. But inasmuch as most of the work of councils is transacted on the table and not on the floor, it is likely that only the second sense of "on the carpet" will survive: namely, "up for reprimand." As early as 1823, "walk the carpet" meant to get a reprimand. The basic notion seems to be, at least among railroad men, that the boss's *sanctum sanctorum*, unlike the outer offices, usually boasts a carpet. An intensive form of the saying is "on the big green carpet."

carpetbagger. The carpetbag, a Victorian institution, was usually red, and was practically inevitable to (a) travelers, and (b) plumbers. So when unscrupulous Northerners moved South after the Civil War, to win the hearts of the negroes and control the elections, they took with them their worldly possessions in these bags made of carpet material rolled up. The name "carpetbagger," which Webster shows was previously applied to embezzling bankers, was attached to these political adventurers without losing any of its stench.

carrier pigeon. See STOOL PIGEON.

carrot-top. Ever since 1696, people have gone to the colorful carrot in search of a simile for red hair. This particular form is however comparatively recent.

carry the banner. "To carry the banner," or "the balloon," or "to fly the flag," are recent expressions connected with unemployment and with walking the streets all night. A study of these reveals, first, that the "balloon" is the blanket roll of the unfortunate wanderer; second, that "flag-fallen" suggests "unemployment" because a theater's flag is hauled in when the theater is closed; and, third, that in the nineties the fees for meals and lodging at the newsboy homes were called "banners," for reasons unknown. All this does not get us much closer to an explanation of "carry the banner." The term does actually appear in Wyclif (14th century) and, strangely enough, in association with mendicants who are feigning poverty; but Skeat believes the phrase is equivalent there to "bear the bell," in reference to the leadership of a flock by its bellwether.

cart. See UPSET THE APPLE CART.

cart before the horse. This is an old proverb in almost any language. The French and Latin versions drag in some oxen. The German characteristically inverts things and puts "the horses behind the wagon." If you analyze our word *preposterous*, you will see that a similar idea is conveyed (i.e., *pre* + *post*, before the behind).

Casey at the bat. *Familiar Quotations* (Wesleyan) and *The New York Times* of May 12, 1935, agree in emphatic identification of E. L. Thayer, Harvard '88 (president of "Lampy" for three years) as the author of this immortal poem. The hero, Daniel M. Casey, was still able, in 1935, to grasp a bat and pose for the AP photographer. The poem first appeared in *The San Francisco Examiner* in 1888, and was popularized by De Wolf Hopper.

cast. See DIE IS CAST.

castle in Spain. This is the French equivalent (*château en Espagne*) of our own "castle in the air." The French may have started using it in the 11th century in reference to the fact that the Moors were in control in Spain, and that any Frenchman who boasted that he had a castle there was a bad person to leave alone with one's marriageable daughter. Most adventurers from the Spanish border of those days were experienced liars.

casual. The noun, meaning an unattached vagrant, was a natural development of the adjective, which already had this connotation in 1860. In 1897 (B. & L.), the noun was slang, but the new Webster lists it as in good usage. The military sense of "a soldier detached from his outfit" should also be noted.

cat. The phrase, "the poor cat i' the adage" (from *Macbeth*), has survived, whereas the adage itself—something about a lazy cat that wanted a fish but couldn't bear to get its feet wet—was dead and buried long ago. Parallel proverbs used to be found in French and in German.

The legend about "Dick Whittington's cat" seems to have no foundation in fact. At any rate, he did not make his fortune by means of the cat. Some have dragged in the French word *achat*, meaning barter, to explain the presence of a *cat* in the story. (See KILKENNY CATS. RAIN CATS AND DOGS. ROOM TO SWING A CAT.)

catadoupe. See RAIN CATS AND DOGS.

catamount. See CATAWAMPUS.

catawampus, cattywampus. Word scientists shake their heads over this ridiculous coinage that is said to mean fierce and also askew. In the first instance, its formation may have been influenced by *catamount*, a wild cat (literally, "cat of the mountain"); in the second, the connection seems to be with *catercornered* (see KITTYCORNER).

catch a crab. Whether you catch the blade of your oar in the water on the way back (in an attempt to "feather" it), or miss the water entirely on the pulling stroke, the effect is the same—you sprawl on your back in the bottom of the boat like a crab. Webster mentions both possibilities, but OED, as an authority on rowing, calls the second "an improper use." In any case, we need not go to Venice and the phrase *pigliar il granchio*, implying "to make a mistake," though the Italian expression does literally mean "catch the crab."

catch a Tartar. This means "to bite off more than you can chew," because, it seems, an Irishman once captured a ferocious Turk—who would neither go back to camp with his captor, nor permit the Irishman to go alone.

catercorner. See KITTYCORNER.

cat o' nine tails. See ROOM TO SWING A CAT.

cat out of the bag. See PIG IN A POKE.

caucus. OED has given this up as a bad job (for the present anyway) and I shall of course follow suit. Eliminating the wild guesses that (1) it was from a Latin word for drinking vessel, friend, or servant, and (2) that it was derived from the *corkers* in a bottling plant—we find two theories supported by about equal evidence, with a slight edge in favor of *cawcawwassoughes*, as Captain John Smith spelled it. He also referred to an Indian word for captain, *caucorouse*, later common in Virginia as *cockarouse*. This Indian term, spelled by Mencken "kaw-kaw-asu," connoted "elder," or "one who advises." It was not uncommon for early clubs to adopt Indian names (as Tammany Hall did). However, there may have been a "caulkers' club," among the shipbuilders and repairers of Boston, that met at the "calk-house" and that became the original caucus. Many authorities favor this second theory. But wise men like Skeat say "Origin obscure." The new Webster, slightly more daring, calls it "probably Algonquian."

caudal appendage. See COWARD.

caudle lecture. One Job Caudle was on the receiving end of the curtain lectures described by Douglas Jerrold in 1846. The name was no doubt chosen in allusion to the warm drink, containing wine or ale, which was served to invalids, and especially to mothers after the birth of a child, and to their visitors. The word is related to *calories* (from Latin *calor*, heat). (See CURTAIN LECTURE.)

caul. See MASCOT.

cauliflower. See KALE.

cauliflower ear. Webster implies that this apt description of a pugilist's badly battered ear is in good medical usage. Etymologically, *cauliflower* means "flowered cabbage," being identical with French *chou-fleur*.

cavalcade. See MOTORCADE.

caviar to the general. This expression, now commonplace, meaning something for which you have to cultivate a taste, does not imply, as some may think, that high military officials are unfamiliar with caviar. The word "public" must be understood after "general." The source is *Hamlet*.

cawbawn. This is given to illustrate, or rather caricature, the sort of thing that is constantly happening in the study of words. The word was listed by B. & L. as Australian native slang for "big." If I were to state confidently that the American *car-barn* (now used chiefly for housing motorbusses) derives its name from the Australian, I should be making myself only a little more ridiculous than some of my predecessors in this fascinating field.

cha. See HOT CHA.

chafe. See CHAFF.

chaff. In the sense of "kid" or "banter," this colloquial verb may be related to the actively unpleasant *chafe* (from Latin *calfacere*, to make warm). But Webster, taking it less seriously, as idle jesting, associates it with "the chaff which the wind driveth away." Suggestions based on the piling of chaff at the door of a man who beats his wife are romantic but unsubstantial.

chamber. See COMRADE.

Cham of Literature. See GRUB STREET.

Chance. See TINKER TO EVERS TO CHANCE.

chaps. Other things being equal, a provincial English word is a less logical source for these fringed leather overalls of the cowboy than a Mexican word. Such a word is *chaparejos*. The provincial English word suggested by B. & L. was *shap*, meaning tight-laced or shapely.

charge it. See CUFF.

Charing Cross. See CHORE.

charivari. See SHIVAREE.

charwoman. See CHORE.

chary. See CHORE.

chaser. See GRAIN OF SALT.

chattels. "Goods and chattels" is an illustration of the sonorous repetition that we have learned to associate with legal documents—the reason being, it is said, that lawyers used to be paid *by the word*. If so, English was admirably fitted to be the language of lawyers, as we have been collecting stray synonyms from different languages, all through the ages. But as for *chattels*; it is historically the equivalent of *cattle* and of *capital*, all three having descended from Latin *caput*, head. In short, a *capitalist* was one who owned *cattle*—that was virtually what was meant by "property."

chauvinism. See JINGOISM.

cheap skate. See PIKER.

check. Amos and Andy's old catch-phrase, "check and double check," would I think, have been understood in the 17th century, as the check-mark was already in use to mean "compared and found correct." Some modern school-teachers use the ✓ to mean wrong instead of right, on the cynical theory that there are always more things wrong than right, and that the *two* strokes of an *x* make it a time-waster. Historically, however, teachers are not justified in "checking" the answers that are wrong. The word comes ultimately from Persian *shah*, king. Also coming from it is the word for a bank-draft, spelled *cheque* in England; the notion seems to be that of checking or controlling the bank account, though it has not been my experience that when my account was out of control it helped matters any to write more checks. (See FLY A KITE.)

Two colloquialisms meaning "to die" use the word *check*, both apparently borrowed from the poker table. "To pass in your checks" and "to check out" probably refer to turning in one's chips on leaving the game, though the latter is now constantly used of the departure of hotel guests, after paying their bills, and may not derive from the card game at all.

cheek. See DAMASK CHEEK.

cheer. By derivation, "What cheer?" does not mean "What have you to cheer about?" but rather "What sort of face are you wearing today?" It comes from late Latin *cara*, face. Strictly, "cheerful face" means "face full of face." On the other hand, "Be of good cheer" is not redundant, as it would be if *cheer* meant what most of us have always thought it meant, namely, "good spirits." In any case, it must be admitted that *cheer* now means "gaiety," and that "cheerful face" is perfectly good English.

cheetah. See CHIT.

cheque. See CHECK.

cherry. The popular song of some years ago, about life's being just a bowl of cherries, may be said to have honorable ancestry: in the early 15th century, Gower and Occleve ("oak-cliff") were wont to compare life to a cherry-fair—"This lyf, my sone, is but a chirie-faire"—a rather wild jollification over the sale of the fruit in the orchards. By association with red lips, and perhaps with French *chérie*, dear, the cherry has long been a more or less intimate symbol of Venus. The word is a false singular; deriving from French *cheris* (modern *cerise*), it should, like *pease*, have kept its *s* in the singular.

The fussy and argumentative person who "makes three bites of a cherry" originally made three "bits" (*morceaux*), in Rabelais. The 1708 translation had it as "bits," but in 1737 it was "bites." Inasmuch as the meaning was not perceptibly changed, the second really was an improvement.

chestnut. The authorities have somewhat grudgingly accepted as plausible the explanation that the source of this term for a stale joke was an 1816 play, *The Broken Sword*, by William Dimond (not "Dillon," as in the 1898 Brewer). The comic captain, telling an old favorite story of his, varies it slightly by mentioning a *cork-tree* in place of a chestnut, whereupon he is reminded that "it was always a chestnut before." (See MAROON.)

chew the rag. Originally, it would seem, army slang for grumble or grouse (about 1885), this has come to mean to argue or talk at great length, and hence just to chat or reminisce. An instructive parallel is Princeton slang, "bicker," in the sense of a talk-fest between old friends. "Chew the fat," once equivalent to "chew the rag," has kept its grouchy connotation—and incidentally has lost in popularity. "Chew the cud" is of course a different thing; the picture is that of the pensive cow, ruminating (literally). "Chew out" means to bawl out, to reprimand severely.

As for the source of this "rag," there may be some connection with the *rag* signifying "razz" or criticize. Someone has also noted with interest that a sulky child often chews its handkerchief, or failing that, its shirt collar or apron.

chicken. See FLAPPER. MOTHER CAREY'S CHICKENS.

chicken feed. American slang for small change (pennies, nickels, dimes), this has not yet found adequate recognition in OED. The basic idea is not, I suspect, that chicken feed is inexpensive, but that morsels of food must be small if a chicken is to negotiate them.

child. See SPARE THE ROD AND SPOIL THE CHILD.

child is father of the man. Wordsworth's poetical paradox is from "My Heart Leaps Up." The meaning of this, and similar quotations, seems to be that "men are but children grown-up," or, with a slight difference, "Just as the twig is bent, the tree's inclined" (Pope). Milton's version was:

> The childhood shows the man,
> As morning shows the day
> —*Paradise Regained*

children. See KILTER.

chin. See LEAD WITH YOUR CHIN.

China orange. See DOLLARS TO DOUGHNUTS.

chinch-bug. Derived from Italian *cimice*, this was once a household word, in England, for a sort of louse "with a disgusting smell" (according to OED). Becoming obsolete in England, it survived in this country as an insect "very destructive to wheat and other grasses" (Webster).

Chinee. See MARQUEE.

chip. "Chip in," meaning to make a contribution, is from the poker chips, representing money, that each player puts into the "pot," thus betting on the value of his hand.

"Chipper," vivacious, might conceivably be from *chipmunk* (an Algonquin word)—cf. "lively as a chipmunk"—but the dictionaries, for geographical and chronological reasons, no doubt, say it is derived from English dialect forms akin to *chirrup* and *pert*, with a little onomatopœia thrown in.

Completely out of line with the above word, a slang "chippy," defined by B. & L. as "unwell," has fortunately died the death. Rising from its ashes, the same word is found in the new Webster to mean a "pick-up," a street-girl willing to go places and do things with a man to whom she has not been formally introduced.

"A chip off the old block" is, obviously enough, a child who resembles its parents. It is unlikely that the allusion is either to the wood of the family tree, or the block-headedness of somebody's father. E.P.'s first date is 1627.

Since very early days, ships' carpenters have answered to no other name than "Chips."

The origin of "chip on his shoulder" in the sense of quarrelsome seems to be simply a silly challenge: "knock it off if you dare." Of course to do that you had to get within reach of the other's fists. The source is American, of about 1840. (See SPICK AND SPAN.)

chipmunk. See BARUNDUKI.

chirrup. See CHIP.

chisel. This, and *chiseler*, were given fresh currency by the NRA boys, but the words are over a hundred years old, in the sense of cheat, "cut one out" of something. The figurative connection with a carpenter's chisel is clear. Though the French *ciseler* is a probable ancestor of *chisel*, the French do not use it in the Hugh Johnsonian sense.

chit. Lacking acceptable telephone service, the British in India and China had their *chit-coolies*, who trotted about with little notes. A chit is also an I.O.U., or a slip that you sign when you want something charged to your account. People are usually surprised to learn that this Oriental institution, like *tiffin* (q.v.), takes its name from English dialect. It is believed to be short for *chitty* (OED quotation, 1798), and derived ultimately from Sanskrit *citra*, marked, akin to *cheetah*, a leopard.

"A little *chit* of a thing" is, according to Weekley, cognate with *kitten.*

choice. See HOBSON'S CHOICE.

choke. See GUN.

choleric. See HUMOR.

chop-chop. This pidgin term for "fast" (rapid) is apparently related to the "chop" of chopsticks (Oriental substitute for the fork) in the same way that Cantonese *faai*, fast, is a cousin of *faai-tsz*, chopsticks. This second *faai* does not actually mean "fast," because the character, though similar to that signifying "fast," has a bamboo "radical" (root symbol)—chopsticks often being made of bamboo. Webster's assertion that "chop-chop" is the Cantonese pronunciation of Mandarin *kuai-kuai* is incorrect. The Canton ricksha coolie understands you if you say "chop-chop" but thinks you are talking English; his compatriots say *faai-ti*, "faster." The "kap-kap" invoked by B. & L., and others, was perhaps at one time the Amoy or Foochow rendering of *kuai*.

"Chop-house," for Chinese custom house, derives from Hindu *chap*, a stamp. This is used also in "first chop," first rate.

The American dish, *chop-suey*, a tasty *mélange* served in Chinese restaurants and elsewhere, was apparently invented by a hash-minded Chinese in this country. The name may possibly mean "pick up the pieces."

chore. The noun *char* disappeared long ago in England, only to turn up on this side of the Atlantic, in 1820, as *chore*. By derivation it is "an occasional job," working "by the day" (related to French *jour*). It survived in England in *charwoman*, which is now familiar in this country. "Chary" is not a relative, but belongs to the "care" family.

Charing Cross, in London, is a puzzler. It is not from *chère reine*, dear queen, but it may be from the surname Cerring. The possible connection with *char* is this: Edward I, returning to London with the body of his late queen, erected a cross at each of his *periodical* stops en route.

chortle. Lewis Carroll's portmanteau word, from *Through the Looking Glass* (1872). It was probably *chuckle + snort*, as that's about what it means, though B. & L. say "howl."

chow. Whether the East Indian relish known as "chow-chow" is related to the Cantonese word pronounced much like "chow" and meaning "fried," is not clear. But it is clear that when Mark Twain spoke of eating "chow-chow with chopsticks," he meant *chau min*, fried noodles. With so excellent a source at hand, surely it is unnecessary to invoke, as OED does, "the edible dog of China," the chow, to account for our slang word for food.

Christian. See RICE CHRISTIAN.

Christianity. See MUSCULAR CHRISTIANITY.

chronicle small beer. Found in *Othello* this means to talk about, or to be busy about, matters of small importance. "Small" beer was "weak" beer.

chukker. Also spelled "chucker," this Anglo-Indian word for a period of a polo game first appeared in print in about 1900. It derives from Sanskrit *cakra*, which is—and here is a good exercise in Grimm's Law for you—the source of English *wheel*.

chump. Meaning a short, thick lump of wood used (in Webster's phraseology) as an "end-piece," this so obviously means the *head* of somebody you don't like that it hardly needs explaining. "Off your chump" signifies, therefore, out of your head. By transference, then, a *chump* (akin to *chunk*) is a blockhead. Mencken says we adopted it from the argot of Essex.

churl. See CURMUDGEON.

cimarron. See MAROON.

cinch. While it is no easy task to tighten the cinch of a saddle, and no sure thing that the saddle will stay on the top of the horse, especially if he knows the trick every young horse should know, of taking a mighty breath and holding it until the cinching process is completed, it is nevertheless true that "a cinch" in the sense of an easy task or a sure thing is derived from Latin *cingula*, through Spanish *cincha*. The idea seems to be to have a tight grip on something, to have the situation well in hand. The intensive, "lead pipe cinch," makes no sense whatever, but there is something euphonious and conclusive about it.

circle. See SQUARE THE CIRCLE.

city editor. If a Britisher, looking for Wall Street, New York, should accost you at Broadway and 42nd Street and ask you the way to the City, think nothing of it. For in London, the commercial center alone, within the ancient boundaries, is known as the City; and the City Editor of a newspaper is in charge of the financial columns. A New York city editor, as was once said, is not a man, but a large office with a battery of telephones—the department to which all local news is reported.

clam humper. See CRAW THUMPER.

Clancy lowered the boom. See BOOM.

claptrap. Literally, a line, or scene, or gesture, deliberately planned to "catch clap," to bring applause. Thus, high-sounding nonsense. It goes back to 1727, and was a device with which David Garrick was not wholly unfamiliar.

claw me, claw thee. See LOG-ROLLING.

claw thumper. See CRAW THUMPER.

clean as a whistle. See WHISTLE.

clean dirt. See HIT THE DIRT.

clef des champs. See KEY OF THE STREET.

clergy. See BENEFIT OF CLERGY.

cliché. A stereotyped phrase—like "intrepid aviator"—that seems to flow as naturally from a linotype as ETAOIN SHRDLU does when the machine goes temperamental. *Cliché* is the French name for a stereotype plate. The word was first used in the figurative sense as early as 1892.

click. In pragmatic terms, a thing that "clicks" is true; i.e., it works. A theater act that "clicks," or "rings a bell" (q.v.), is a success. The figure is perhaps from the steady ticking of a clock, or of the valves of a motor "clicking" on all the cylinders (see BALL). Apparently from the sense of an accidental meeting as pat as if it had been planned, the term came to mean "to meet a bullet" (see BULLET) or death in any form. OED gives Wodehouse most of the credit for arousing the English, in 1922, to the usefulness and beauty of *click*.

climacteric. The "grand climacteric" is a superstition based on the magic numbers 7 and 9, the product of which gives the fatal year, 63. If you live through your 63rd year—in other words, if you pass the *climax*—you may live to a ripe old age. Superstition aside, a doctor informs me that this is literally true, inasmuch as a person who is slated to die of certain heart ailments, for instance, will almost certainly do so before he reaches 63. *Climacteric,* alone, may have reference to the menopause, or change of life, in women.

clink. The wide-spread popularity of this cant word for "jail" cannot be entirely explained by reference to the famous prison in Southwark known to British crooks as "the clink." In the first place, why was it called that, and, in the second, why did Americans adopt it so enthusiastically—unless there was in both countries a strong sense of the appropriateness of "clink" as the name for a domicile characterized by the "clank" of chains or the "clang" of an iron door?

closed shop. See SHOP.

closer than breathing.

> Closer is He than breathing.
> And nearer than hands and feet.

People usually write to N. & Q. or the *Times Book Review* about this after they have exhausted themselves trying to find it in the Bible. It is from Tennyson's "The Higher Pantheism."

close-stool. See CUCKING STOOL.

clothes-horse. See EASEL.

clout. (See also DIAPER.) Meaning not only a rag, as in *breech-clout,* but also a blow, this is at least six centuries old. The connection between the two is not clear. Possibly we can find a clue in the fact that a white rag was customarily hung on the target in long-range archery. A shot that hit the *clout* might have been acclaimed with "A clout!" just as baseball fans used to yell "What a clout!" when one of Babe Ruth's sailed over the fence.

coach. He must have been a brave man who first announced that *coach* is from Kucs, a village in Hungary; surely no one believed him. But now no one doubts.

The tutoring coach preceded the athletic coach by about forty years. In 1848, Clough used the word, the notion back of it being that a tutor, like a stage-coach, aided your progress. By 1885 the word had been transferred to athletics; but the baseball and football mentors of those early days, at Williams College anyway, were called "coachers"; before 1900 the *r* was dropped, though the men who coach behind first and third base are still referred to as the "coachers." At least, so says Webster.

On the railroads of 1880, *coach* usually meant "sleeping-car." Today, "no coaches" (i.e., no *day*-coaches) means "sleepers only."

The automobile that you have to take apart in order to get people into the rear seat used to be called a coach. Now "two-door sedan" is favored. (*Sedan* is said to come, via *sedan-chair*, from the French city of Sedan.)

coal. The French version of our "coals to Newcastle" proverb is "to take water to the river." Newcastle was, of course, one of England's greatest coal ports. The saying was already common before 1600.

B. &. L. give "to take one's coals in" as a euphemism for contracting a venereal disease. It is interesting that "to catch a cold" is sometimes used by Americans who do not wish, for one reason or another, to employ the term gonorrhea; but connection with "coals" is less plausible than with the dangerously common belief that this disease is no more serious than an ordinary cold.

coal. See KALE.

coals. See HAUL OVER THE COALS.

coaster brake. See FREEWHEELING.

coat. See JOSEPH. SANDWICH. TURN-COAT.

cobalt. See KOBOLD.

cock and bull story. The fact that Webster explains this as a "canard" (another barnyard character) is worth noting. Someone who hated to be bothered with bedtime stories, idle tales, moralistic fables—from Chaunticleer to Mickey Mouse—was probably the first (back about 1600) to dub an elaborate lie a "cock and bull story." While both *cock* and *bull* have phallic significance, the phrase seems never to have presupposed obscenity.

cockarouse. See CAUCUS.

cockatrice. See BASILISK.

cocked hat. See KNOCK GALLEY WEST.

cock-horse. While this has been used, within the present century, to mean an additional horse for getting a heavy load up a hill (like the "helper-engine" in railroading), the traditional meaning is, briefly, Daddy's foot, or any other bit of household equipment on which Baby can bounce, horseback fashion. As most modern babies are in the predicament of the Broadway sophisticate who was keen to see a Lady Godiva act because he had not seen a horse in seven years, the problem of teaching the baby how to play horse is becoming more and more complex. The only explanation of "cock," here, seems to be that the foot is cocked up to keep its daring rider from *coming a cropper* (q.v.).

cock of the walk. The "walk" is the correct technical term for the game-cock's enclosure, where he is the undisputed boss and can be as "cocky" as he pleases.

cock-sure. This originally meant *perfectly* safe or sure, rather than pert and cocky. Shakespeare thought of it as deriving from the sureness of the cock on a firelock—though why the old firearm should have been deemed even likely to go off is no longer clear. OED sees a possibility in the action of turning a stop-cock, to keep liquor securely in a barrel until wanted. The pomposity of the rooster certainly fits better with the later use of "cock-sure" than with the earlier. Hyamson notes that a third sense, that of "lecherous," is now obsolete. In a way, that's unfortunate, as we could have explained that one.

cocktail. The daughter of King Axolotl VIII of Mexico is said to have invented the mixture. Her name was Xochitl or Coctel. A number of other sources have been suggested by P. B. Trovato (see BEFORE YOU CAN SAY JACK ROBINSON).

codger. In Scotland, *cadger* has long been understood to mean a peddler, of grain, perhaps, or fish, with his goods in panniers ("breadbaskets," related to French *pain*) on a pony. It is derived from *cage*, in the sense of wicker basket. When business was poor, the wandering merchant evidently condescended sometimes to beg; hence, the connotation of tramp or beggar. By an easy shift, *cadger* could have become *codger*, but in the process the derogatory implication seems to have been replaced by a humorous or even affectionate one. Thus to greet a friend with "You old codger" or "You old bum" is a much better way of expressing your regard for him than to kiss him on both cheeks.

coil. Curious that "when we have shuffled off this mortal coil" (*Hamlet*) should be so popular as to be trite, when few have any idea what this *coil* means, and why! It seems to have been Elizabethan slang for bustle or turmoil, and may, like the ordinary *coil*, derive from French *cueillir*, encounter (Latin *collegere*, to collect), though OED does not approve. Over-zealous attempts to give the word Scotch or Irish ancestors have, in this one case, broken down OED's policy of judicial reserve, even to the use of an exclamation point, an almost unheard-of departure from tranquillity. The historic outburst is as follows: "Gaelic or Irish words do not enter English through the air, with phonetic change on the way!"

cold. See BLOW. FROST. GET. KNOCK GALLEY WEST.

cold as hell. See DRINK LIKE A FISH.

cold deck. In draw poker, the deck of cards that is in use is thought of as warm, while one that has been stacked in a certain order beforehand, waiting to be secretly substituted, is of course cold. Thus, to be "cold decked" is to be cheated. It dates back almost to the riotous days of the forty-niners.

cold feet. To have cold feet is somehow satisfactorily expressive of cowardice. The thought seems to be that when the circulation is poor and the blood leaves the extremities, a certain lack of enthusiasm results. The hearing of suspicious noises downstairs, on a winter night, almost invariably brings on an attack of cold feet. Then, too, our teeth chatter with fright as well as with cold; in fact, shivers and chills have always been pictured as accompanying terror.

cole, cole-slaw. See KALE.

colyumist. This spelling, and presumably pronunciation, is technically wrong, but may stick; certainly the genius who runs a "colyum" deserves to be singled out from ordinary writers. Incidentally, *column* has a number of interesting relatives: *colonel* (from "column of troops"); *hill* (through Latin *collis*); *excelsior* (akin to *celsus*, exalted). *Excelsior* was a trade-name, chosen in 1868 (perhaps in tribute to the popularity of Longfellow's poem), for mattress-stuffing.

come a cropper. While there is reason to associate this with the end of a horse over which one sometimes slides en route to the ground, the dictionaries prefer "neck and crop" (meaning, for some reason, "the whole business") as a source. Being linked with "neck," this "crop' would seem to be the same as "craw" (see STICK IN ONE'S CRAW), though a case might be made for "crop" as meaning a riding-whip.

come home. See COW.

come out at the little end of the horn. See HORN.

come up to scratch. See UP.

comfort. See DUTCH.

comfortable word. See MESOPOTAMIA.

comparisons are odorous. This was Dogberry's slightly daft variation of a saying that was already tottering with age at the time of *Much Ado about Nothing.* The first to introduce "Comparisons are odious" to the English audience was probably Lydgate, in 1430. Cervantes, who by some twist of fate died in the same year as Shakespeare, used the Spanish equivalent of the "odious" expression in *Don Quixote.*

complete frost. See FROST.

comrade. Akin to *camera* and *chamber*, the original of this word was a Spanish military term for chums who sleep in the same bedroom, our 1917 equivalent being "bunky." The seemingly harmless "let's just be comrades" must therefore be used with discretion. Then, too, you might be mistaken for a Communist.

In camera means "in secret," and the first picture-taking camera was a *camera obscura*, a dark box. Kodak is a trade-name, invented for the Eastman Company.

concede an edge. See EDGE.

concert. See DUTCH.

confab. This is short for *confabulation*, which itself sounds like slang to most people, but is in reality formed logically from Latin *confabulari*, "to tell fables together," hence, a conference. The unabridged form has been found in print all the way from Richardson's *Pamela* to the end of the 19th century.

confidence man. Often shortened to "con man," this term for a plausible swindler derives from his characteristic request for a deposit in advance, "to show your confidence in him." This type of trick was the "confidence game." One of the earliest uses of the expression was an 1866 assertion that President Jeff Davis, of the Confederacy, was surrounded with confidence men. (See PANHANDLER.)

confusion worse confounded. The striking thing about this well-known bit from *Paradise Lost* is the fact that both words suggest "to pour together," "to mix up." In fact, *confusion* is the noun for both *confuse* and *confound*.

conjugal. As the sour-visaged opponents of marriage have frequently pointed out, *conjugal* means "yoked together," and that is supposed to imply a sort of slavery. But it also connotes a degree of coöperation and pulling together. If anybody cares, related words are *syzygy* and *zeugma*.

conk. OED suggests a Russian origin for this aviation term, meaning the stalling of a motor. It is old British slang for nose or face; there is also a cancerous disease of pine trees, known to lumbermen as "conk"; but it is hard to trace any connection between the three uses of the word.

conniption fit. Mencken says this word for a tantrum was an American invention, and our research does indicate that the thing had no parents whatever. In this sense of hysterical rage, it has been in use since 1833.

considering cap. See CAP.

consistency is a jewel. This popular saying, as Bartlett remarks, "just growed." In 1867, a wag gave phrase-tracers a thrill—and later a headache—by publishing some faked ballads, in one of which this proverb appeared, appropriately disguised, of course, in archaic spelling.

Other famous *mots* about consistency are Emerson's, "A foolish consistency is the hobgoblin of little minds" (folks sometimes find it convenient to omit "a foolish") and Holmes's, "Don't be consistent but be simply true."

contagion. Strictly, there is a difference (which Webster brings out very clearly) between this and *infection.* By derivation, there must be *contact*, direct or indirect, with the sufferer if a *contagious* illness is to spread; but an infection, which is a germ disease, is not always transmitted by touch; many germ diseases can be transmitted only by inoculation or some other special method. In other words, an *infectious* ailment may or may not be *contagious.*

contempt. See FAMILIARITY BREEDS CONTEMPT.

contemptible little army. Former Kaiser Wilhelm asserts that he never said this of the British regular army, and the fact seems to be that it *was* "two other men"—both of them British propagandists. True, the very invasion of Belgium is an indication that he didn't think much of the British army, and it is possible that he actually said so, some years before the war; but the "army order" of 1914 in which the words appeared was almost certainly a British invention—and a valuable one, as was the nickname, "Old Contemptibles."

continental. "I don't give a continental" originated in the debased currency of Revolution days. The intensive form of it, "a continental damn," has been explained (apparently for the benefit of pious folk who liked the expression but abhorred profanity) as deriving from DAM (*damnatus*) stamped across the face of counterfeit continental money, than which nothing could have been much damneder. The same thing has been attempted with "tinker's damn" and the Duke of Wellington's "twopenny damn" (q.v.).

cook your goose. The story about the goose that was hung out in derision by the inhabitants of a besieged medieval town—whereupon the mighty Eric burned the town, thus "cooking the goose"—is ignored by the dictionary people today. However, there is no other satisfactory explanation of this phrase in the sense of "put an end to," or ruin. OED's first quotation is 1851.

cootie. This war-time word for a louse, as distinguished from a flea, may be, as Webster suggests, a diminutive of *cute*. But since the field is still wide open, we may be permitted to guess that there is some tenuous connection between it and the provincial English *cooty* (from *coot*, meaning ankle), "having legs clad with feathers."

cop. This, and "copper," for policeman, are by no means recent slang. They are found at least as long ago as 1892 (Thomas Terrell's play, *Lady Delmar*). It is more likely that they are descended from Latin *capere*, to seize, than that they are from gipsy *kap*, or from *copperhead*, in the sense of "secret foe." It is interesting but not important that *copro-* is a learned prefix signifying "dung."

"A fly cop" means, to a Britisher, a clever policeman or detective, but this use of "fly" has never caught on in America, and we should be inclined to connect "a fly cop" with a motorcycle or airplane. (See also HEFT.)

copperhead. From the poisonous snake with the copper-colored head, this was transferred to the Indians, first, then to the Dutch, then (1862) to the Northerners who favored the South in the Civil War. In each case it derived from the idea of secret treachery. The last sense (which originated in a Democratic convention in Cincinnati) is still the standard.

corduroy. "Doctors disagree" on this one. No one denies that it looks suspiciously like the French for "king's cords," nor that this might have made a very good trade name for the kind of corded cloth with which we are familiar. Webster lets it go at "probably for French *corde du roi*"; but OED, basing its contention on the fact that in a French list of various kinds of cloth there appeared the English word "king's cordes" (indicating that, in 1807 anyway, there was no good French equivalent), hesitates to say that the French originated the word *corduroy*, or the cloth. The British suggestion is the surname Corderoy as a possible source. In any event, we make a picturesque use of the word in this country in a figurative sense. Roadbuilders, confronted with swampy ground, used to make a foundation—and a very poor one —for their road by laying logs crosswise. This was a "corduroy road."

The original cloth seems to have been basically silk, to live up to its regal associations. But our modern corduroy, though admirably suited, by reason of its warmth and toughness, for sports clothes, is made of much cheaper material.

corker. In 1897, this slang word was just changing its significance from "imbecile" to "remarkable." And this isn't far off the track today. While it is not, certainly, in allusion to "corked" wine (wine that tastes of the cork), there seems to be no advantage in going into the "caulking" field; sticking to *cork*, therefore, we see possibilities in the atmosphere of finality that surrounds the act of plugging in a cork; it's a settler, or, as Joe Penner used to say, you "can't get over it." A "corker" is something, or someone, conclusive—a "knockout."

corn. See MAIZE.

corned. In the sense of "drunk" this goes back to 1785, and is probably older than the similar "pickled"; both are apparently connected with the poetical concept so beautifully expressed in the ballad, "Just pickle my bones in alcohol." "Corned beef" has been preserved by the use of salt, not alcohol, but the idea is perhaps the same. It is unlikely that either word is indebted for its existence to American corn-whisky.

coronach. See HURLY-BURLY.

coroner. See CROWN.

corposant. See SAINT ELMO'S FIRE.

corsair. The old Italian explanation that this word for pirate came from "Corsican" has been shown to have been a bit of propaganda. Latin *cursus*, course or voyage, became Italian *corso*, a chase; hence, a corsair (or *hussar*, Greek transliteration of the same word) was "one who gives chase." Later, of course, *hussar* was dressed up in a nice bright uniform and put on a cavalry horse.

Cortez. See STOUT CORTEZ.

cotton. To cotton to a person is to be attracted or attached to him. The simplest thing is to follow Webster in relating this phrase to the tendency of cotton to stick to clothing. OED is not convinced, and mentions some distressingly technical phases of cloth manufacturing as possible sources. An N. & Q. correspondent suggests these other possibilities: *kowtow*; French *côte*, side; and the fact that there is a slang verb "to cotton" that means to perform the act of coition. The popularity of "Cotton Club" as a name for a night club is probably due in part to the intimation of harmony and friendliness, but chiefly to the "Dixie" atmosphere.

cotton-gin. See GIN.

count. See DOWN FOR THE COUNT.

courage. See DUTCH. GENEVA COURAGE.

court plaster. The origin is so simple that some people miss it. The ladies of the French *court* pasted black beauty spots on their faces (no doubt, occasionally, to hide a pimple or blemish); sometimes they went to the ridiculous extreme of using representations of ships under full sail, or of chateaux.

cousin-german. See DUTCH.

cove. See KOBOLD.

Coventry. "To send to Coventry" is to ostracize. The town of Coventry, long a military center, is probably alluded to here, either because it was a Cromwell stronghold to which Oliver sent Royalist prisoners, or because, a century or so later, the women of the town, disliking soldiers for one reason or another, ostracized any girl who spoke to one (*ostracize* is cognate with *oyster* and refers to the shell used in voting the dread sentence). It is unlikely that either "quarantine" or Covent (i.e., Convent) Garden is involved in this "Coventry" expression.

cow. "Till the cows come home" is usually taken to mean a long, long time, on the theory that cows cannot be depended on to come home without being driven. An 1875 variation adds "in the morning," making it a still less likely eventuality. In Australia, it may mean "till my ship comes in" (i.e., "till I come into my fortune"). On the other hand, the old popular song used as a radio theme-song by a milk-products company implied little more than that "boy meets girl" at that particular moment, "by the old barn gate."

"Everyone to their liking, as the old woman said when she kissed her cow." This expression, which was put into the mouth of a hillbilly girl in a play as recently as 1925, appeared in a popular song about a hundred years earlier, and goes back to this classic, dated 1562: "Every man as he loveth, quoth the good man, whan he kyst his coowe." It tends further to strengthen the case of those who find backwoods Americans talking Elizabethan English.

coward. The one thing sure is that this does not mean "cow-hearted." It is known that it is akin to *caudal* (as in the *cliché*, "caudal appendage"), but whether the first coward simply "turned tail" or put his tail between his legs is uncertain. Webster *plumps* (q.v.) for the latter, while OED propounds a third theory, that the original coward may have been Coart, the timid hare in one of the early Reynard fables. The thought is that the rabbit's conspicuous white tail and the Latin *cauda*, tail, would have been mutually helpful in the development of the new word.

cowboy. Just as John Bull was beginning to grasp the idea that by "drugstore" we mean "chemist's shop," we floored him again by adding "cowboy" to "drugstore" and telling him the whole ghastly combination meant "soda-jerk." That is, attendant at a soda-fountain. He is usually believed to be a bit of a ladies' man, so that perhaps the allusion in "drugstore cowboy" is ironical, along the line that the handsome young concocter of milk-shakes is a kind of inhibited he-man. And then, of course there is a remote connection between milk-shakes and cows. Incidentally, "drugstore cowboys" was also applied to the young men who hung around drugstores instead of poolrooms as they had a better chance of meeting girls there.

Readers of Fenimore Cooper need hardly be reminded that there is another sense of *cowboy* in addition to that of "herder." During the Revolution, Westchester County suffered heavily at the hands of Tory marauders who were dubbed "cowboys."

cowcumber. Sairy Gamp's pronunciation of *cucumber* (which is a fruit rather than a vegetable, the dictionaries say) was quite the thing in 1800, the other being deemed bookish, but, some years before *Martin Chuzzlewit* appeared, "cowcumber" had become vulgar and for some reason the immortal Sarah failed to restore it to respectability.

cowpuncher. See PUNCH.

cozen. The simplest thing here is, with Webster, to accept this as an Elizabethan pun on *cousin*; i.e., to cheat by pretending to be a close relative. OED says this presents spelling difficulties, but finds fault, as well, with Weekley's Italian word, *cozzone*, for horse dealer or "craftie knave," though it is well known that the word for horse-trader in a number of languages has come, rightly or wrongly, to mean a swindler. In fine, OED is inclined to be unclubable, in this particular instance.

crab. See CATCH A CRAB.

crack. A crack train is one that has been "cracked up," in the old sense of "boasted about," not of course in the aviation sense of "wrecked." The latter appears to be fairly recent (earliest quotation in OED is 1922) and is self-explanatory; the former is obscure in origin, possibly to be traced to Latin *crepare*, to boast. Curiously enough, to make a crack about somebody (short for *wise-crack*, q.v.) is to be the reverse of complimentary.

Though "crack of doom" may refer to Gabriel's trumpet, the crack is more likely the opening blast of the celestial cannon and other fireworks that are to accompany the celebration of Judgment Day. The phrase is found in *Macbeth*, and also in Emerson's *The American Scholar*: "Let him not quit his belief that a popgun is a popgun, though the ancient and honorable of the earth affirm it to be the crack of doom."

cracker box set on a raft. See MONITOR.

cradle-books. See INCUNABULA.

cramp. See CRIMP.

crane. See DERRICK. PIG IRON.

cranky. The basic meaning of *crank* is crooked (as in the dangerous old automobile crank). This idea of distortion or eccentricity ("off-centeredness"), influenced no doubt by German *krank*, ill, led to the colloquial sense of "full of whims and crotchets."

crap-game. This dice game probably takes its name from a French expression for the lowest throw at dice, rather than from the vulgar word for excrement. There may be some connection with *crab-apple*, or with *crapaud*, the French word for toad (an old nickname for a Frenchman). No relationship has been traced between the latter and a French word for dirt or filth, which apparently comes from Dutch *Krappe*, scraps. The history of this word *crap* in the sense of dung is hard to trace because the dictionaries are squeamish about recognizing this meaning of it; however, Webster lists an old slang definition of it as sediment, dregs, or money; also of the verb as meaning to hang on the gallows. It is only a coincidence, no doubt, that the word *crapulous* implies a state of diarrhea brought on by drunkenness.

crate. The old biplane with the maze of struts and wires certainly justified the nickname of "crate" more than the slick flying fish of today's air lines. It used to be said, you know, that the mechanics would release a pigeon between the wings of one of the early planes; if the bird succeeded in escaping, they would know there was a wire broken. Applied to such a plane, or to an old car, the term derives from the ricketiness of a crate, its sides being open for ventilation. It comes ultimately from Latin *cratis*, a wicker framework, and is related to *grate* and to Dutch *krat*, basket.

craw. See SAND. STICK IN ONE'S CRAW.

craw thumpers. This old term for natives of Maryland originates in the fact that Roman Catholics played a prominent part in the early history of the state. It is an irreverent name for one who beats his breast at confession. Evidently this nickname displeases many, as two authorities vouch for these variants: "claw thumper" and "clam humper"!

crazy. See FUNNY BONE. HIPPED.

Cream City. Said to have originated in the prevalence of cream-colored brick houses there, this nickname for Milwaukee may easily have another significance, for Wisconsin is the leading dairying state in the country. By way of illustration, the neighboring county of Waukesha has more Guernsey cows than the whole Isle of Guernsey.

cream it. See LATHER.

Creed Lane. See AMEN CORNER.

crib. Deriving it, perhaps, from the sense of "basket," 18th century thieves employed this word to mean pilfer. Then, about 1840, schoolboys began to apply it to the stealing of other people's work. Though a century old the practice is not unheard of today, and it looks as if the word *crib* might live a while yet.

Crichton. The Admirable Crichton was Scotland's ideal gentleman —traveler, lover, intellectual giant, duelist—of about the time of Shakespeare. "All-perfect, finish'd to the finger nail," as Tennyson has described him, he perished in Italy when a vengeful rat (according to somewhat biased sources) ran a sword into his back. When Barrie wanted to write a play about the perfect butler on the much touted desert island, he named his dramatic fantasy *The Admirable Crichton* (1903). But it was altogether a different Crichton.

crimp. "To put a crimp in something" and "to cramp someone's style" are both related, probably, to *crumple* and to Teutonic *krimpen*, to pinch, wrinkle, make uneven. The development of the sense of "to thwart or block" (found first in about 1896) is logical enough. The noun *crimp*, meaning, in polite phraseology, an employment agent—the kind that shanghais seamen for short-handed ships—may owe some part of its popularity, if not its origin, to its being a perfect rhyme for "pimp."

crisis. Hippocrates, the great father of medicine, taught that diseases ebb and flow like the tides, and that there are certain moments, usually connected with the mystic number seven and its multiples, when one's "ability to judge" the future course of the illness is the greatest. These are the *crises*, from Latin *cernere*, to decide. It can be shown that *crinoline* is akin to *crisis*, as *crinis*, hair, derives also from *cernere*, in some obscure fashion, and hair was used to stiffen crinoline, to make it "stand up."

crocodile tears. No one will vouch for this contribution to science except dear old nature-faker Mandeville (c. 1400). This gravel-worm (literal translation of *crocodile*) was accused not only of enticing victims by his heart-rending moans but of hypocritically shedding tears while he enjoyed his meal.

crook. See HOOK OR CROOK.

crooked sea. See GRAMERCY PARK.

crooker. See ELBOW.

cropper. See COME A CROPPER.

cross. See DOUBLE CROSS. STICKS.

crossroads. See DIRTY WORK AT THE CROSSROADS.

cross the Rubicon. See DIE IS CAST.

crow. Crows make amusing pets, but not good eating—which is probably the concept behind "eat crow," American political slang (but much older than that in origin) for the humiliating process of having to eat one's words or change one's editorial policy. It has been used by as recent a writer as Carl Sandburg.

"I have a crow to pluck with you" (see BONE) was an Elizabethan figure for "I have something to complain of, about you." Plucking a crow is, I suppose, no more distasteful a job than plucking a chicken, but the difference lies in what you have left when you're finished.

Crow. See JIM CROW.

crown. This slang verb for "hit on top of the head" arises, not from the regal crown in any way, but from the word meaning the top of the head, though of course the relation is close. Other interesting connections are with *coroner* (originally the representative of the *crown*) and with *curve*, because of the circular shape of a crown.

crummy. Originally spelled "crumby," this word meant (by contrast with "crusty,") good, handsome, buxom. Just how it came to mean lousy, dirty, by 1897, is thus far a mystery. The best guess is that as the word "crumb," representing the main or best part of the bread, went out of fashion, only the idea of "messy" (associated with the particles of bread left on or under the table after eating) remained. It seems possible that the revival of the slang word in its uncomplimentary sense may have had a remote connection with a one-time craze for the boyish figure in women, i.e., away from the buxom or "crumby."

crush. See MASHER.

cry havoc. The 1933 book of this title by Beverley Nichols called attention to Shakespeare's stirring "Cry 'havoc,' and let slip the dogs of war" (*Julius Cæsar*). Though *havoc* may be related to Welsh *hafog*, devastation, or to Anglo-Saxon *havoc*, hawk, Skeat and OED derive it from French *havot*, as the French have the same term, *crier havot*, meaning that the army may now start pillaging, or even massacring without quarter.

crying out loud. Like "son of a biscuit-eater" (for "bitch"), "For crying out loud!" is unquestionably a euphemism. People think you are going to say "For Christ's sake." It was coined, I believe, in the 1920's.

cub. Pliny, Montaigne, Shakespeare, and others accepted the marvelous legend that at birth a bear cub was just a ball of flesh and fur that had to be "licked into shape." The half-licked cub was therefore only "half-baked," "not dry behind the ears." This may be the origin of *lick* in the sense of beat or defeat: instead of shaping the unformed child with your tongue you caress him with a stick, the well-known rod which should not be spared.

The reason why the fable gained such currency was doubtless that Mama Bear is notoriously bashful about having strangers present at her *accouchement*. Some debunker would have risen much earlier if kittens, for instance, had been in question.

cucking-stool. "Ducking-stool" was discovered to be a very pat euphemism for the ugly chair in which scolds and other nuisances were bound in preparation for ducking in a pond. The chair, at first often a close-stool (its name being derived from *cuck*, excrement), was attached at the end of a long pole similar to a well sweep. Blackstone, much revered as a legal authority, objected in 1769 to the primitive name's having been corrupted to "ducking-stool." Another old name for the thing was "gumble-stool," perhaps related to "grumble."

cuckoo. The word *cuckold*, meaning a husband whose wife has been unfaithful, comes plausibly from the cuckoo, which, scorning to build a home of its own, eats up other birds' eggs and lays its own in their place. Why such a bird should be considered the symbol of stupidity is somewhat difficult to discover. The quotations in Stevenson are about evenly divided between high praise of the cuckoo's song and resentment over its habits. The modern sense of "goofy," crazy, may be either from the silly monotony of its cry, or, by transfer of meaning, from the attempt made by the Wise Men of Gotham to preserve the summer by fencing in the cuckoo.

cucumber. See COWCUMBER.

cud. See CHEW THE RAG.

cuff. "On the cuff" must surely go back at least to the days of stiff detachable cuffs, because today's soft ones offer only mediocre facilities for bookkeeping. But only Weseen and Partridge (1950) list it with its correct meaning, "on credit." Instead of "Charge it," the English say, "Put it down," and should find it altogether natural to add "on the cuff."

culverin. See BASILISK.

cum grano salis. See GRAIN OF SALT.

cumshaw. To the honor of the Cantonese beggars, this Chinese equivalent of "Brother, can you spare a dime?" did not originate in Canton. But they know the word. It appears to mean "grateful thanks," in the Amoy dialect.

curfew. Simply *couvre feu*, put out the fires for the night. The primary purpose seems to have been to prevent conflagrations. The earliest spelling noted in English by Skeat is *coeverfeu.*

curlicue. Webster thinks this is just *curly + cue* (from the French *queue*, tail). Certainly "twisting tail" describes pretty well what we mean by a curlicue. The word has been in print since 1844.

curmudgeon. The origin of this word for a grouchy, "churl-minded" person (and it may be related to *churl*) is uncertain. But all who enjoy "a harmless smile" (Todd) or, as we should express it, good clean fun should know about Dr. Ash's gorgeous blunder. Someone sent Dr. Johnson the suggestion that *curmudgeon* might be from *cœur méchant* (bad heart), and the great lexicographer mentioned the theory thus in his book: "*cœur méchant*, Fr. an unknown correspondent." His successor, Dr. Ash, whose French was evidently a little rusty, copied this for his dictionary, blandly explaining that *cœur* meant "unknown" and *méchant* "correspondent."

curry favor. The Old French *estriller fauvel*, to curry a chestnut horse, came into English as "curry favel," which was soon changed, through sound associations, to "curry favor." The meaning is to win someone's favor by bootlicking subservience. It is equivalent to "hand-shaking" and "sucking about."

curse of Cain. Cain was condemned, in Biblical terms, to be "a fugitive and a vagabond" whom nobody was to kill, because he had the mark of Cain upon him. And thus rose the legend that he was never to die, never to stop, never to reach home. One of the first to use the exact words, "the curse of Cain," was Hood, in *The Dream of Eugene Aram* (1829).

curtain lecture. This institution, not yet obsolete, derives its name from the curtains on a four-poster bed, behind which the erring husband would listen (or not, as the case might be) to his wife's nightly sermon. Variants are: a *caudle lecture* (q.v.); boulster lecture (title of a 17th century play).

curve. See CROWN.

customer. See TOUGH.

cut. Evidently derived from the harvesting of ice—a job that must be done at top speed while weather conditions are favorable—"That cuts no ice" means "That's no use," or "That cannot change the situation." Mencken would prefer it to "That butters no parsnips," if the "ice" figure had not been overworked.

The verb "to cut up" and the adjectival "cut-up" have very different meanings: "to cut up" (intransitive) is to show off, to behave badly; to be cut-up is to be dejected. The former is conceivably from the sort of showy dance-step that Mr. Fezziwig performed so deftly; the latter clearly enough refers to the wounding of one's feelings by a sharp sorrow.

To "cut" liquor is to adulterate it, perhaps because you thus "cut down" the amount of real booze required.

The "cut of his jib," meaning "facial expression," has sometimes been connected with a word for "lower lip" (of horse or human). But the nautical explanation is better: that the shape of a vessel's jib sail often revealed what sort of craft it was. The exclamation "I don't like the cut of her jib!" appears therefore in every well-conducted pirate story.

"Cut and run" means "to make a hasty departure," because any emergency is a serious one in which a ship has to cut the cable to its anchor instead of waiting to haul it up.

cymbal. See HUMP.

cynosure. "The cynosure of neighboring eyes" derives from the Greek for "dog's tail"—because that's the name of an important constellation, the Big Dipper. "Cynic" is easier to account for, being a direct descendant of the word for dog.

D

daft. See DUFFER.

dam. See CONTINENTAL. TINKER'S DAMN.

damask cheek. While paying indirect tribute to Damascus embroidery, this is really just another way of saying "rosy cheek," as it means blush-colored, like a damask rose. Or to be, with Webster, coldly technical: "red in hue, of medium saturation and medium brilliance."

damn. See TINKER'S DAMN. TWOPENNY DAMN.

dance attendance on. While Hyamson repeats Brewer's story about the bride whom custom required to dance, on her wedding day, with all who asked her, no matter how obnoxious to her, the more conservative dictionaries either offer no explanation or allude to "kicking one's heels" in an antechamber while waiting for some officious person who is constantly "in conference."

dander. There seems to be an increasing belief that this word, which was commonly used through the Victorian era instead of *dandruff*, may have been used in that sense in "get your dander up," get angry. If so, the picture is a ludicrous one, of a wrathful man "tearing his hair" and rather scattering dandruff in the process. Other conjectures have been: from a West Indian word meaning "ferment"; from a dialect form meaning "spark" or "shiner," which leads an N. & Q. fan to connect the *dander* phrase with "knock the spots (i.e., sparks) off"; a Scotch "danders," hot cinders; and perhaps the furthest fetched, a telescoped form of "damned anger." Partridge suggests Romany *dander*, to bite.

dandruff. See DANDER.

Dan to Beersheba. Judges 20:1 is the source of "from Dan to Beersheba." It was popularized by Laurence Sterne. Though it represented only the 150 miles from one end of the Holy Land to the other, the implication then was "all over the known world," and we have gallantly preserved the fiction to this day.

dark horse. Bombaugh tells a vivacious story about one Sam Flynn, from Tennessee, whose coal black horse looked like just an ordinary plug but won plenty of races, and plenty of bets, for his owner. However, scholars ignore the fable. Thornton indicates by his silence his belief that the phrase is not of American origin. The first recorded use of it in this sense is in Disraeli's *The Young Duke*; the passage is worded in such a way that the reader knows something more subtle than the mere color of the horse is intended.

Davy Jones's locker. Century says, rather loftily, "Many guesses have been made." OED declines to guess, but does accept *duppy* as a West Indian word for ghost. Webster and others give "duffy" as a variant of this, and "duffy Jonah" as the original of Davy Jones. The locker is, of course, the seaman's chest, and the whole phrase, to go to Davy Jones's locker, signifies to go to the bottom of the sea, to drown. (See MOTHER CAREY'S CHICKENS.)

dead as a door nail. Though this has been traced clear back to 1350, conscientious philologists have to admit, as Dickens did, that they can see no particular reason why it should be a *door* nail and not a coffin nail, for instance. In the absence of any other theory, I incline to the one that the door nail may once have been the specific name for the one on whose head the knocker kept banging until life (if any) surely must have departed. Ordinary nails are, in fact, not used in the building of doors. It is possible that in its original use the phrase may have implied being as dead as something that had never existed.

dead beat. In the sense of exhausted, almost dead, this goes back to 1821. And the substantive sense of tramp or sponger may have arisen soon afterwards, as it is found in print in 1875, the idea being, doubtless, that when you're down and out your ethics are bound to get a little shaky. The dead-beat escapement of a watch gets its name from a physics term for a beat which does not recoil. Which appears to mean, but probably doesn't, that the watch (like some I have known) ticks once and then stops.

dead, for a ducat. Hamlet's exclamation as he kills Polonius, pretending to mistake him for a rat, as he no doubt was. It seems to mean, "I'll wager a ducat that I get him."

deadhead. Lowell used the word, in the sense described below, as early as 1853. Theatrical and railroad people agree that it means one who gets a free seat or free ride. Bombaugh tells of the discovery, in Pompeii, of little ivory skulls that were used as free passes into the ancient theater. Another application of it is to one who drinks at others' expense.

Lumbermen speak of a log which does not float buoyantly as a deadhead.

deadlock. See HOLY DEADLOCK.

dead pan. This contemporary term for a poker-face comedian (i.e., expressionless) cannot be derived, we contend, from Elizabeth Barrett Browning's poem, "The Dead Pan," whose theme is "Great Pan is dead!" Since 1833, at least, "pan" has been used to mean mouth or face, presumably because (in the words of Webster) it is "broad, shallow, and often open." "To pan," meaning to scold, may be remotely connected with the "pan" of a tamping bar, the head on which a sledge hammer can be struck.

dead stick landing. This is an aviation term for a type of competition at air races. The plane must be landed with the motor shut off. Though an aviator usually means the *joy stick* (q.v.) when he says "stick," in this case (the editor of *Aviation* assured me) the propeller is referred to. It would, obviously, be impossible to make a conventional landing if the lever operating the controls were "dead."

debunk. (See BUNK.) OED's first quotation for this useful word is from the *New York Evening Post*'s announcement, in 1927, that it had engaged W. E. Woodward, author of a novel entitled *Bunk*, to write "debunking" articles for the paper. The purpose is to peel off the bark of legend surrounding the lives of important people; the danger is, of course, that in the process some important slabs of truth may be sliced off and lost.

deck. See COLD DECK.

deck out. See DICKEY.

dedicated. How did we ever, prior to about 1950, get along without this word? Hardly an hour passes that we don't hear or read about somebody—running the gamut from the Messiah to Hoffa, from a prima-donna to a taxi-driver—who is "dedicated." Down with "dedicated"! Can't we make-do with *devoted* or *faithful* or something, for a while anyway? (But see BRINKMANSHIP.)

deep blue sea. See DEVIL.

defend me from my friends. The idea goes back, Stevenson says, to about 870. Maréchal Villars expressed it best, to Louis XIV, when he added, "I can defend myself from my enemies." Canning, in England, desired to be saved from the "candid friend." While recognizing the fact that well-meaning friends can do you a good deal of damage (the classic example being Mr. Winkle, in Bardell vs. Pickwick), the incurable optimist would still rather have friends than enemies.

deliberate. See WITH ALL DELIBERATE SPEED.

Denmark. See ANCIENT AND FISH-LIKE SMELL.

derrick. Originally spelled *Derick*, this Dutch name is identical with Dietrich, Theodoric, and Dirk. Logically enough, it came to mean a gallows and then a crane because it was the name of a famous hangman of about 1600, at Tyburn.

derring-do. This fine old trumpet-blast of chivalry is a fake. Through "a chain of misunderstandings and errors" (OED), complicated by one misprint, our "desperate deeds of derring-do" (*Ruddigore*) claims descent from Lydgate's simple phrase meaning "daring to do." Lydgate was imitating something in Chaucer, Spenser took it from Lydgate, adding that it meant "manhood and chevalrie," and Sir Walter Scott kept the ball rolling. But when you come right down to it, "dare to do" is a man-sized challenge for anyone; pseudo-archaism or not, "derring-do" packs a thrill.

description. See BEGGAR DESCRIPTION.

despisery. See FAMILIARITY BREEDS CONTEMPT.

despotism. See ABSOLUTISM.

dessert. Generations of Americans have been puzzled by this passage in *A Christmas Carol*: "They had just had dinner; and with the dessert upon the table, were clustered round the fire, by lamplight." No American child can understand why the banquet board should be abandoned by the feasters before the dessert has been polished off. The explanation is simple: that the British say "the sweet course" where we say "dessert," whereas by the latter the British mean the bowls of fruit and nuts and raisins. By derivation, the *last* course should be the dessert (French *desservir*, to clear the table). Horwill adds the curious fact that the British use "dessert spoons" in dealing with puddings and ices—the American "dessert."

desuetude. See INNOCUOUS DESUETUDE.

desultory. From Latin *desultor*, one who leaps down, or leaps from horse to horse—a circus stunt. Thus the word connotes "inconstant," passing from one to another.

deuce. Just as *ace* signifies "one," *deuce* in most of its senses is related to "two." It is the lowest throw in dice, the lowest card in the pack; in tennis, it is a tied score after which it takes two *successive* points to win. Various libidinous demons have been uncovered to account for the exclamation "The deuce!" but it seems likely, from the fact that the Germans use "*Das Daus*" in the same way (i.e., as an exclamation and in reference to the game of dice), that bad luck at dice had more to do with making *deuce* nearly synonymous with *devil* than any heathen deities whatsoever. Here too, I think, we may look for the origin of that quaint superstition about two-dollar bills.

deux sous. See TWOPENNY DAMN.

devil. In the days of ignorance and superstition, the growth of the term "printer's devil" may have been influenced not only by the inky blackness of the printer's small assistant, but also by the notion of occult mystery long associated with the art. Again, Aldus, pioneer Venetian printer, had as helper a black slave, somewhat unusual in those days and capable of inspiring a measure of dread. It is significant that in the 1683 quotation that speaks of the way these printer's devils "black and bedaub themselves," they are referred to as "spirits." However, the dirtiness was the essential factor.

"Between the devil and the deep blue sea," an obvious metaphor, is possibly an allusion to the herd of swine possessed by the legion of devils (Matthew 8:32). The "deep blue sea" in the story was that of Galilee, not the Dead Sea, which is used in a 1690 version of the saying. (See DEUCE. DICKENS. PULL DEVIL, PULL BAKER.)

devil to pay. See PAY.

dexterous, sinister, awkward. "Right-handed," "left-handed," "back-handed." The first therefore suggests skill, the second bad luck, or treachery, the third the clumsiness of a misfit, "using the wrong hand." Curiously enough, the Teutonic word *awkward* has never developed the sense of ill-omened or hypocritical that attaches to both Latin *sinister* and English *left*, as in "over the left (shoulder)" signifying "I don't mean what I just said." It would seem that "left-wingers" (i.e., radicals) ought to be insuperably handicapped by the damaging contrast between "right" and "left" that has been solidly built into our language from the beginning.

diaper. This flowery euphemism for what our remote ancestors called a baby's "clout" is typical of the silly lengths people will go to avoid soiling their lips with an indelicate word—only to find that the new word has suddenly begun to bring the blush of shame to the maiden cheek. (See MANURE.) In the original Greek, diaper meant either pure white cloth or white cloth figured with costly embroidery. The French *diapré*, according to Brewer, signified "cloth variegated with flowers." As for the theory connecting the word with the town of Ypres, OED sums up the situation well by calling it "a gratuitous guess."

dice. See DIE IS CAST.

dickens. Many are surprised on hearing someone say pompously, "In the words of Shakespeare, 'What the dickens!'" But it's to be found in *Merry Wives of Windsor*. Our hard-boiled friends, Webster and OED, after considering well the host of suggestions connecting this word with "devilkins," or Nicholas Machiavelli, or "nicks" (Scandinavian water-devils), or Old Nick—spoil all the fun by growling, "Probably a diminutive of Dick (from Richard) and used as a euphemism for devil simply because they both begin with *d*." (See HARRY.)

dickey (dicky). Our ordinary use of this to mean false shirt front (also child's bib, in England), has been found by OED as early as 1881, and pretty clearly comes from German *decken*, to cover, with which "deck out" but not "decorate" are allied. Other uses of *dickey* apparently have to be related to the cozy nickname *Dick*, for Richard; "dickey bird," for canaries and such, is an instance. Whether that will account for the little seat at the rear of a carriage—transferred, as was natural, to the rumble seat of a roadster—or whether we must postulate some ancester of "doo-hickey" (a what-you-may-call-it) is a question. *Rumble seat*, which, somewhat surprisingly, goes back hand-in-hand with *dickey* almost to 1800, is certainly more appropriate, in its allusion to the rumble of the rear wheels, than is "dickey." Unfortunately I have found no proof of the antiquity of "doo-hickey."

"Dicker" is derived, not from the idea of covering up or cheating, but, oddly enough, from Latin *decem*, ten—symbolizing figures used in bargaining.

Dick Whittington's cat. See CAT.

die. See EAT, DRINK, AND BE MERRY. ROOT.

die in the last ditch. See DITCH.

die is cast. Suetonius says that Cæsar's words were "*Jacta alea est*," "The dice have been thrown," as he crossed the Rubicon. Though *die* can mean various other things, including a form or pattern used in metal work, it is here one of the galloping ivories used in African golf. Mussolini, no mean hand himself at crossing Rubicons, caused a monument to be erected at the spot where Cæsar invaded Italy.

dies but never surrenders. This flamboyant boast about the French Guard was attributed to General Cambronne, who was taken prisoner at Waterloo. When he denied it, pointing out that the Guard, speaking generally, had not died and had surrendered, it transpired that the phrase had been invented two days after the battle, by one Rougemont. A similar remark was made about Zachary Taylor by one of his men when the Americans were summoned by Santa Ana to lay down their arms: "General Taylor never surrenders." (See NUTS.)

die young. See GOOD DIE YOUNG.

diggings. Used since the earliest days of places where mining operations were going on, "diggin's" did not develop the sense of quarters or lodgings until the 19th century. There is a strong impression that this use arose first either in the lead mines near Galena, Wisconsin (where two other well-known colloquialisms, *badger* and *sucker*, may have sprung up), or in the "forty-niner" territory of California.

Dimmesdale. The symbolic meaning of Hawthorne's name for the sensitive and sinning minister of *The Scarlet Letter* was deepened for me by the discovery of this quotation from More's *Confutation* (1532): "Tindal will nedes dampne us all into Dymminges dale." The combination of "dimness" and a valley of shadows fitted in well with the novelist's purpose. And he was perfectly capable of taking his suggestion for the name from that ancient source. It was not too outlandish, either, for there is a "Dinsdale" listed in Savage's *Genealogical Dictionary of New England*.

dimmock. Though this can be found in a number of slang dictionaries, it is not recognized by Webster or OED. It is said to be still in use, meaning money, and to be derived from *dime*.

dine with Duke Humphrey. It was really unfair to Duke Humphrey that after his death this came to mean "go without dinner." While he was alive many almsmen enjoyed the hospitality of his table;

after the castastrophe, the phrase connoted to these men (often voluntary prisoners in the cathedral precincts, to avoid being arrested for debt), "Now that Duke Humphrey is dead, I don't dine"—the more so because he was supposed to be buried there, in old St. Paul's (though in reality his tomb was at St. Albans). The expression was popular with the Elizabethans but is found as recently as in *Martin Chuzzlewit*.

dirt. See HIT THE DIRT.

dirty work at the crossroads. According to Stevenson, the first recorded use of this phrase which means anything from intrigue to assault and battery, was by Walter Melville, in *No Wedding Bells for Him*. A correspondent of N. & Q. agrees that the phrase is to be traced to one of Melville's melodramas, music-hall sketches of the eighties, one of which was entitled, "A Girl's Cross Roads." Mr. Melville is not, however, positive that he made use anywhere of the "dirty work" phrase. Knowledge of the somber custom of burying suicides at crossroads, with stakes through their hearts, probably contributed to the effectiveness of the expression.

dish of tea. This is neither modern British slang, nor an American burlesque of it. Between 1662 and 1862, OED links *dish* with tea, coffee, chocolate, and aquavitae (see WHISKY). It seems that a small *bowl* without a handle could also be called, more or less indiscriminately, a *dish* or a *cup*.

ditch. The famous defiance, "I will die in the last ditch," was said by Hume, in his *History of England*, to have been uttered by William III, later of the William-and-Mary combination. He gave it as a sure recipe for never having to see his country's ruin.

dive. Used as a noun, this slang word for a "joint," a low resort, dates back to about 1880. The word "low" used in defining it indicates in part the figure back of *dive*; but more important was the underground location of most of these beer-cellars and gambling dens. It is unlikely that the colloquial verb *dive*, meaning to plunge one's fork into a large pot, played any part in the history of this other *dive*.

divine right of kings. Based on the Old Testament doctrine that "God's anointed" get their right to rule straight from God, this dogma was played for all it was worth by the Stuart kings. Inasmuch as the king's power derived from God alone, it was unlimited; the subjects had no rights, and the king could do no wrong; and neither he nor his heirs could forfeit their right to rule. A nice little arrangement, on the whole. But the British have not always taken it lying down. Pope, for instance, referred to it pleasantly as "The right divine of Kings to govern wrong." He put a little protective camouflage on the phrase by surrounding it with quotation marks, but it was probably his own idea.

divorce. See CÆSAR'S WIFE MUST BE ABOVE SUSPICION.

Dixie Land. Southerners apparently object to the unsubstantiated tale that the island of Manhattan was once a sort of paradise for slaves, who looked back with longing on their kind owner (a Mr. Dixie) who had had to "sell them south." Some authorities inclined to the Mason-*Dixon* line as the source, but Webster (1934) proposed with some confidence a theory that was new to me; namely, that a New Orleans bank used to issue a $10 bill with the French word for ten, *dix*, prominently displayed. Associating Dix, and gradually Dixie, with the joyous sensation of possessing ten dollars in New Orleans, Southerners presumably came to think of Dixie as a pleasant sort of name for the South in general.

do as the Romans do. See ROME.

do a thing up brown. See BROWN.

doctor. As a verb meaning to adulterate, as with chemicals or raw alcohol, there is nothing new about this. Even so up-to-date an expression as "The fugitive had his face doctored by a plastic surgeon" had its counterpart in 1774, when the verb was used of "cozeners" disguising their appearance. The idea is, perhaps, that a doctor is of no particular use unless he can alter your condition in some way, for better or for worse.

In certain parts of the tropics, a cool breeze which springs up in the afternoons is referred to as the "doctor," no doubt from the cheery exclamation, "Here comes the doctor," that usually suggests relief, even if there be mustard plasters or castor oil along the way.

An American gesture of resignation is "You're the doctor," meaning "Go ahead, tell me what to do and I'll do it."

Doctor Fell.

> I do not love thee, Dr. Fell,
> The reason why I cannot tell.

This was Tom Brown's ingenious version of a Latin couplet assigned to him by Dean Fell of Oxford, who, we are told in all seriousness, threatened to expel the boy if he failed to supply a satisfactory translation. The dean showed a commendable sense of humor in accepting the young rascal's paraphrase. The date was about 1650.

dodger. In the Artful Dodger sense, of tricky or slippery, this one is easy enough. The Brooklyn (now Los Angeles) Dodgers were originally the Trolley Dodgers. (Does anybody remember what a trolley car was like?) But the real problem is why an advertising circular, a hand bill, should have been, since 1884, a dodger. Can it have been from the similiarity in appearance to the hard-baked corn cake of that name, or from the way the boys distributing the circulars dodge in and out, from one doorway to another?

dog. See GO TO THE DOGS. PUT ON THE DOG. RAIN CATS AND DOGS.

dog's nose. See HAIR.

dog's tail. See CYNOSURE.

dog that bit you. See HAIR.

dogy. (Rhymes with *logy* or *bogy*.) This measly little hero of a lugubrious song popular at the nadir of the depression doesn't even have an origin. Since 1903 it has been a familiar name for a motherless, no 'count calf, a sort of fag end. Perhaps this is a clue, as there is a Dutch word, *dagje*, meaning a small bit of rope.

doldrums. Byron was one of the first to use "in the doldrums" of a ship becalmed near the equator. The word seems to have been formed from the adjective *dull* as a sort of contrasting running-mate for *tantrum* (origin unascertained, but related to dialect form *antrim*, also meaning fit of anger). Figuratively, then, the doldrums are similar to the lonely blues, the condition of being bored to tears.

dollar. See ALMIGHTY DOLLAR.

dollars to doughnuts. The equivalent British figure for a sure thing, a bet with overwhelming odds in your favor, is "Lombard Street to a China orange" (dating from about 1830). Overlooking the fact that the latter is somewhat more obscure (Lombard Street symbolizes the banking district, but no one seems to know why the China orange was chosen, unless it was in reference to the diminutive *kumquat*, the Cantonese word for "gold orange"), we must still admit, I think, the superiority of the alliterative American phrase.

don't let poor Nelly starve. See NELL.

doo-hickey. See DICKEY.

doom. See CRACK OF DOOM.

dope. Though cursed with a multiplicity of uses in American slang, the little word seems to be traceable in almost every sense to Dutch *doop* (pronounced "dope"), a thick liquid or sauce. Opium, when heated, flows sluggishly, hence the word dope was applied to opium derivatives and thus to simpletons or dupes (as far back as 1897) who act as if stupefied with drugs. On the other hand, a drug used to stimulate a horse before a race may be "dope," and thus, perhaps, to "dope" a race meant to have secret advance knowledge as to its outcome. "Give me all the dope," meaning the inside information or the gossip, seems to be from this source. Closest of all to the Dutch original is the familiar "dope" used on the wings of airplanes to shrink the fabric so that it will be taut.

Dora. See DUMB DORA.

do right by our Nell. See NELL.

dory. See HUNKY-DORY.

do things. See GO PLACES AND DO THINGS.

double cross. "On the cross" is given by B. & L. as meaning the opposite of "on the square." "To cross up" a person is still to cheat or disappoint him in some way. Strictly, therefore, a "double cross" implies a cheater cheated. An early form of it seems to have been "to put on the double-double," explained by B. & L. as meaning, in racing circles, to cheat a crook who thinks he has a race safely "fixed." The expression "double-dealing" does not, of course, connote *double* dishonesty.

double in brass. This is dance-orchestra slang meaning to be able to play a horn in addition to your own instrument. Thus, to be versatile, or, still more broadly, to get income from two sources (Weseen).

It may have originated in the theatrical world. To mount a parade announcing a production, it was sometimes necessary to put actors or stagehands into band uniforms and let them pretend to blow a horn.

double life. See TWO-TIMER.

doublet. See DUST HIS JACKET.

double-time. See TWO-TIMER.

dough. See DUFFER.

doughboy. Since about 1867 American infantrymen have been dubbed doughboys. Mencken (1923) thought it was because the pipe-clay that was used to whiten the uniforms caused them to become soggy and doughlike in the rain. But it is generally believed that the name derived from the resemblance between the large brass buttons of their uniforms and the dumplings of that day that were called "doughboys."

Partridge (1937) made an amusing mistake on this. Professing to quote Thornton and OED (Sup.), he described them as "globular glass buttons," whereas both of these sources unmistakably say *brass*. The tongue twister tripped him, no doubt. But in any case what soldier, before the invention of shatter-proof glass, would stand for large *glass* buttons?

doughnuts. See DOLLARS TO DOUGHNUTS.

down and out. See DOWN FOR THE COUNT.

down cold. See GET.

down for the count. This word count was not recognized by OED until the Supplement came out; the first quotation is dated 1913 ("take the count"), the reference being to the ten seconds allowed a prize-fighter to get back on his feet after having been knocked down. If he is unable to stand then, he is "down and out," an expression often used figuratively. The famous "long count" was not an unfair one. No doubt it saved Gene Tunney. But the one time heavyweight champion, one of the coolest and brainiest boxers who ever pulled on a glove, knew what he was doing; he remembered what the excited Dempsey forgot: that the count could not begin until the other man had returned to his corner.

down in the mouth. See KEEP.

down on (upon). When Bob Sawyer exclaimed to Mr. Winkle, "You don't mean to say you weren't down upon me!" (*Pickwick Papers*, Vol. II, Chapter X) he was using a Briticism which is rather astonishingly omitted from Webster; i.e., in the sense of "being wise to" or "aware of." Conversely, the nearest OED gets to our use of "down on" to mean "bearing a grudge" is in "to have a down on," to dislike.

dozen. See BAKER'S DOZEN.

drag a red herring across the trail. See RED.

drakes. See DUCKS AND DRAKES.

draw. "To draw a bead on," meaning to take aim, refers to the bead-like appearance of the front sight of the old muskets. The idea was to bring the rear sight and the bead in line with the target.

Meaning to exaggerate, or even, less diplomatically, to lie, "draw the long bow" goes back apparently to the tales of Robin Hood and his men, and the wonderful feats they performed with their *artillery* (q.v.). The phrase parallels, therefore, our more modern "tell a fish story."

"Draw it mild," a figure taken from the tap-room, contrasts with "Draw it strong." Thackeray was one of the first to use "draw it mild." The transferred use of it is "Be moderate; keep within the truth; don't overstate."

drawn. "Hanged, drawn, and quartered" differed radically, authorities believe, from "drawn, hanged, and quartered." In the first case, the corpse of the executed person was "drawn," just as a fowl is "drawn" or eviscerated today; then it was torn to pieces, often by horses. In the cases where "drawn" comes first, the reference is probably to the condemned man's being dragged through the streets behind a cart on his way to the gallows.

dress. "Dressing the house," is theatrical argot for selling the tickets in such a way that a small audience will go a long way toward making the "house" seem comfortably filled. Thus the nakedness of large blocks of empty seats is decently covered.

Derived from this theatrical use of "house" is our "full house" (OED gives a quotation indicating that the British invert this to "House Full") used of a hall where the S.R.O. sign ("standing room only") has been hung out, and figuratively in any case of obvious overcrowding. It also means, in poker, three of a kind and a pair, as three kings and two tens.

A "dressing-down," the dictionaries hint, is equivalent to a "trimming," in the sense of a severe scolding. The conception seems to be that of making the recipient more presentable.

drink. See EAT, DRINK, AND BE MERRY.

drink like a fish. While this is listed as an "idiotism" by Vizetelly, it is still in constant use (somewhat like the ridiculous "cold as hell"). In spite of the fact, mentioned by Brewer, that many fish swim with their mouths open, it is fairly certain that fish do not drink much water, intentionally. Stevenson appears, at this point, to have stolen a march on OED, as the latter's first quotation for this is 1837, while Stevenson found it in Shirley's play, *The Triumph of Beauty*, 1646.

drive like a Jehu. See JEHU.

drizzle. See MIZZLE.

drop. "He's ready to fight at the drop of a hat" is surely familiar to all good Americans. Yet Webster does not bother to account for it, and OED leaves it out altogether. It sounds a bit Irish to me. Anyway it comes, presumably, from the use of this simple signal at the beginning of a fight, though another possibility is that it parallels "take off your coat" or "roll up your sleeves" or "spit on your hands" as intimations that hostilities are about to start.

"To get the drop on somebody" means to be covering him with your gun so that he does not dare to reach for his own. On the old Colt double-action revolver (introduced in 1835), the cocking of the hammer by the thumb was best done by holding the muzzle up, then *dropping* it smartly into firing position.

A 1915 quotation in OED reveals that "drop" was then the new underworld name for a "fence," receiver of stolen goods. A place, I suppose, where you could drop anything "hot" you might happen to have.

drug on the market. If you say "Ph.D.'s are a drug on the market," you mean about the same as "The woods are full of them." This *drug* is perhaps from the French *drogue*, meaning rubbish.

drugstore. See COWBOY.

Dryasdust. Himself a zealous antiquarian, Sir Walter Scott was entitled to have a little fun with the more prosy members of that tribe. "Dr. Dryasdust," dull and bookish research man whom Scott invented, also makes memorable appearances in the works of Carlyle and of William James, symbolizing the sort of writer that they certainly were not.

dry behind the ears. See CUB.

ducat. The source of this as a slang word for "ticket" is probably two-fold: they sound a little alike; and a slight confusion may have arisen in the minds of the less highly educated as to just what a ducat was anyway. The word itself is related to duchy and duke, being applied to a coin issued by the "duchy" of Sicily in early days. The word *ducatus* which appeared in the inscription on the coin should not be credited as the source, but it may, says OED, have contributed to spread the name. (See DEAD, FOR A DUCAT.)

duck. See CANARD. LAME DUCK.

ducking-stool. See CUCKING-STOOL.

ducks and drakes. All of us have tried skipping flat stones across the surface of a pond, but I imagine that few Americans know that that is called "playing ducks and drakes" (from the efforts of the birds to take off from the water); or that the expression which means "play fast and loose" or "squander recklessly" comes from the magnificent possibility that some wastrel might use coins of the realm instead of pebbles. The history of the phrase starts in about 1585.

Another exciting game, duck on a rock, introduces in some localities the name *drake* again, this time as the larger rock on which the stone called the *duck* rests.

duck's egg. See GOOSE.

duck soup. Why this should carry the meaning of "easy task," any more than chicken soup or turkey soup—or hard-boiled eggs, for that matter—is somewhat of a mystery. It is at any rate easier to say; it clicks more trippingly from the tongue than either chicken soup or turkey soup. And, once you have the remains of a duck dinner, it certainly is easy to cram them into a pan, pour some water over them, and light the gas. Probably, too, the endearing "ducky" (obsolete term, by the way, for a woman's breast), helped the new "duck soup" along the road to popularity.

dud. In the sense of a shell that fails to explode, and hence a "flop," a counterfeit, a "flat tire,"—in short, a failure—this was in use (in all but the first sense), as long ago as 1897, and, as a matter of fact, is listed by EDD as meaning a soft, spiritless person, an item substantiated by OED's 1825 example, "a soft dud," a term of contempt derived perhaps from an obsolete word for scarecrow. Though it was not apparently influenced by *duds*, clothes, its World War I popularity may have been enhanced by its similarity to *thud*; when a dud landed it must have been quite a comfort to hear a thud instead of a heart-rending crash.

dude wrangler. Though *dude* is not supposed to be American in origin, one of the two earliest references (1883), is from our own (if I may be permitted a local allusion) *North Adams Transcript.* Its origin is not known, but it may be connected, because of its "fine clothes" connotation, with *duds*, which may in turn be from a Scotch word for "rag." In cowboy usage the dudes are the tourists from the East whom the dude wrangler takes care of, just as the horse wrangler is in charge of a string of horses. As for the etymology of *wrangler*, it seems nearly as ridiculous to derive it from the noun meaning "an angry dispute" as from the British word for "an honor man placed in the first class in the mathematical tripos."

duffer. Meaning an awkward fool (but again, like *codger* and *bum*, often used affectionately), this may be from an Anglo-Saxon *daffe*, a fool, or English slang for a peddler of sham jewelry, or possibly from the *duff* of *plum-duff*, i.e., *dough*, thought of as a soft spongy substance.

Daft is probably related in some way; and *daft*, like *silly* (q.v.), has had a somewhat fantastic history. At first suggesting mildness, gentleness, it passed through the stages of dumbness and imbecility to actual insanity.

Duke Humphrey. See DINE WITH DUKE HUMPHREY.

Duke of Argyle. See GOD BLESS THE DUKE OF ARGYLE.

Dulles, John Foster. See BRINKMANSHIP.

dumb cluck. See STOOGE. ZANY.

dumb Dora. This has no connection with Great Britain's "Defense of the Realm Act." But can it go back to David Copperfield's child wife?

dunk. This word, born of the fatal attraction between a doughnut and a cup of coffee, comes from German *tunken*, to dip.

Dunmow Flitch. See BRING HOME THE BACON.

dust. See BITE THE DUST.

dust his jacket. We need hardly invoke the ancient word "dust" that meant (without reference to any cloud of dust) strike or hit, in order to account for this not very serious threat to thrash somebody. Carpets have been beaten since before 1690, I dare say. A variant that would be an improvement, because of alliteration, if the other word for jacket had not been so careless as to drift into obsolescence, is "dust his doublet." I heard the 20th century version of the old jest over the radio a while back. It was something about a six-year old, threatened with having his pants dusted for him, urging his father not to do anything old-fashioned, but to use the vacuum cleaner.

dustman. See SAND.

Dutch. Webster has several columns of expressions utilizing the word *Dutch.* The derogatory ones, of which there are plenty, can for the most part be traced to the bitter hostilities of the 17th century. Here are a few: *Dutch courage*—pot valor; *Dutch comfort*—"things could be worse"; *Dutch treat*—everyone in a party pays his own way; *Dutch auction*—the auctioneer names a top price, then comes down till he gets a bid; *Dutch feast*—one at which the host gets drunk before the guests; *Dutch concert*—drunken, discordant uproar; *in Dutch*—"in wrong," out of favor; *talk like a Dutch uncle*—to reprove smartly.

All but the last are fairly obvious. The suggestion that a Dutch uncle and a cousin-german (an "own-cousin," from whom a degree of frankness might be expected) have possibly some facetious connection is far-fetched. But by putting "reverse English" on the theory that uncles are generally indulgent, we discover that a Dutch uncle is very severe. (See also BEAT THE BAND.)

E

ear. See CAULIFLOWER EAR. CUB. SILK PURSE OUT OF A SOW'S EAR. TIN EAR.

earmark. Clear back in the 16th century, English farmers used to slit or notch the ears of their sheep or cattle as an identifying mark. But the phrase "to earmark money for a particular purpose," is still deemed colloquial by Webster, though OED finds it in respectable use with this meaning in 1890.

earwigging. This is given in Weseen as general slang for "eaves-dropping," but the orthodox use of it is rather to whisper into other ears gossip or flattery; to attempt to influence by insinuations or private talk. At one time, an earwigging was a rebuke in private, and thus clergymen were nicknamed "earwigs." The ancestor of the word was Anglo-Saxon *ear-wicga*, an insect that allegedly had a passion for crawling into your ear.

easel. As in the case of *clothes-horse*, a beast of burden has given his name to a stand or rack; in this case it is the patient *ass* (Dutch *ezel*, German *Esel*, Latin *asinus*) who bears the artist's canvas for him while he works. Many a temperamental painter must have made bitter jokes about this.

East River. See GRAMERCY PARK.

easy. See HONORS ARE EASY.

eat cake. See LET THEM EAT CAKE.

eat crow. See CROW.

eat, drink, and be merry, for tomorrow ye die. This precise form is not found in the Bible. In Ecclesiastes and Luke, the death is omitted; in Isaiah and I Corinthians, the merriment. Brewer and Crowell imply that Plutarch, in describing the Egyptian custom of introducing a skeleton at their feasts, used a similar phrase; however, the passage in the *Moralia* ("Dinner of the Seven Wise Men") suggests rather that the bringing in of the mummy or skeleton was intended to act as a wet blanket.

eavesdrop. In the old days, one could apparently learn much about what went on inside a house by standing under the eaves and listening; hence, to listen in, intentionally and treacherously, on business not your own. Note, by the way, that *eaves* is singular; the plural would have to be *eaveses*.

eccentric. See CRANKY. HUMOR.

edge. OED couples an 1896 sense of "having a grudge against" (obviously derived from a "sharp temper") with a 1929 American quotation signifying "have an advantage over"—and is seemingly satisfied that the first explains the second. I confess I don't see why "Princeton's team is conceded an edge" should mean "has a better chance to win," unless the figure is shifted to that, say, of two articles of clothing such as a skirt and a petticoat; if the *edge* of the latter shows, it may be said to have the advantage of the skirt.

More difficulty arises over the word as applied to intoxication: "have an edge on." It may be either from the notion of being unusually "edgy" or quarrelsome in your cups, or from that of seeming to be in fine fettle, like a newly sharpened ax or knife.

editor. See CITY EDITOR.

egg. It was not necessary to dig up Thomas Egg, American criminal, to account for the succinct and emphatic "bad egg." People have been called "eggs" since Shakespeare at least ("What, you egg! Young fry of treachery!" from *Macbeth*). The strong impression always created by a bad egg is probably the reason why the term came into vogue so much earlier (1853) than the correlative "good egg" (1914).

egg. See BUTTER AND EGG MAN. GOOSE. LAY AN EGG.

Egyptian. See GYP.

eight ball. See BEHIND THE EIGHT BALL.

elbow. The harmless joke to the effect that the best stuff for polishing furniture is "elbow-grease" has been kicking about ever since 1672. Brewer calls it, more eloquently than accurately, "perspiration excited by hard manual labor."

An "elbow-crooker" or "bender," meaning one who goes through the process of bringing a glass or stein to his lips (and presumably emptying it), is also a phrase of some antiquity. The French equivalent is *lever* (or *hausser*) *le coude*. (See AKIMBO.)

elevator. See LIFT.

ell. "Give him an inch and he'll take an ell"—"Make him a slight concession and he'll take an indefinite amount"—comes honestly, it would seem, by its idea of indefiniteness. For the ell varies from 27 to 48 inches, depending on whether you mean the Flemish, the French, the Scotch, or the English ell; the reason being, no doubt, that the length of a man's *ulna* (cognate with *elbow*) was never standardized. The proverb is very old (16th century at least).

Empire. See HOLY ROMAN EMPIRE.

end. See BITTER END.

enemies. See DEFEND ME FROM MY FRIENDS.

enfants perdus. See FORLORN HOPE.

engine. See GIN.

English. See KING'S ENGLISH. REVERSE ENGLISH.

English leave. See FRENCH LEAVE.

entangling alliances. This rhythmical and resonant expression which has done much to hamper the development of an international consciousness in this country is usually blamed, unjustly, on George Washington. Thomas Jefferson used it in his first inaugural address, in 1801. What Washington said was that we should "steer clear of permanent alliances," and that we should not "entangle our peace and prosperity in the toils of European ambition."

entered into his soul. See IRON.

en tout cas. This used to mean (from the French "in any case") a contraption that could be either an umbrella or a sunshade. Now that the former is somewhat under a cloud and the latter entirely out, the term has been transferred to a tennis court of a brick-dust composition that absorbs a perfectly astonishing quantity of rain before becoming unplayable.

erase. See WORKS.

errand. See SLEEVELESS ERRAND.

estate. See FOURTH ESTATE.

etaoin shrdlu. See CLICHÉ.

euphuism. Don't confuse this with a euphemism. The latter means, we might say, calling a spade a "spatula for excavating the humus" (though the original *spade* of the proverbial expression may have been a mistake for something very like a bed-pan); i.e., finding a roundabout way of dodging profanity, four-letter words, and other dangerous allusions to the facts of life. Euphuistic style, on the other hand, is elaborate and affected, characterized, as Webster points out, by antithesis, alliteration, elegance, and abundance of similes. It does not mean, by derivation, "fine writing," but rather "well endowed by nature," Euphues being simply the name chosen by Lyly (c. 1579) for the hero of his book. Although euphuistic writing is generally condemned, Matthew Arnold did not seem to think so ill of it when he, in a famous passage, asserted that "the *euphues* tends towards sweetness and light." He was not, however, specifically referring to Lyly's work.

Here is a brief illustration, chosen at random from it: "For as the Bee that gathereth Honnye out of the weede, when shee espieth the fayre floure flyeth to the sweetest"—etc., etc.

even. See HONORS ARE EASY.

even Steven. Very little information is available about this emphatic term for "absolutely even." Thornton found it in America, in 1866, relative to an exchange of Confederate money for Federal money, "even Steven" (believe it or not). OED overlooks it altogether. But Stevenson, without making any display about it, lists a quotation from one of Swift's *Letters to Stella* which may easily be the source: "'Now we are even,' quoth Steven, when he gave his wife six blows to one." This, plus the lilting rhyme of it, may have started "even Steven" on its way to fame in the New World.

even tenor. See TENOR.

Evers. See TINKER TO EVERS TO CHANCE.

every man has his price. See PRICE.

everyone to their liking. See COW.

Excalibur. It is not necessary to struggle with *ex cal(ce) liber(are)*, "to free from the stone" (in allusion to one of the two different legends as to where King Arthur's sword came from), in order to find a source for Excalibur. An Irish hero had a sword named *Caledvwlch* or *Caladbolg*, implying "hard-belly" (i.e., voracious). Authorities are tolerably well satisfied that Excalibur was a corruption of this.

excelsior. See COLYUMIST.

exception that proves the rule. So many of the "tough-minded" (phrase in William James's *Varieties of Religious Experience*, 1903) have pronounced this silly that superhuman efforts have been made to explain the seeming paradox. In the original Latin a phrase was added which showed that this was meant: "To give a list of exceptions strengthens the application of the rule to the cases not excepted." Surely more was intended than just "When you name an exception you are admitting the existence of a rule." A logical explanation of this curious aphorism is that "proves" here means "tests" the rule, to see whether it will still hold water after an exception has been discovered.

expecting. See INFANTICIPATE.

extra river. See WATER.

eye. See MUD.

eyelids. See FED UP.

eyewash. Apparently British-Indian army slang dating from about 1884, this equivalent for our *buncombe*—"He came in with some eyewash or other"—derives, I believe, rather from the weakness of the liquid (somewhat as we say "weak as dishwater") than from any connection with *whitewash*, as Webster suggests. A bottle of eyewash would certainly make an unconvincing tipple for an old toper.

F

Fabian. Fabius Maximus the Cunctator (delayer) was the Roman general who "by delay, restored the state"; by wariness, he wore down the impetuous Hannibal. Yet, in 1598, a Fabian was a swashbuckler and roisterer, a nickname suggested by the licentious antics of the priests of Pan at the Lupercalian orgies. Then William Morris founded the Fabian Society, in 1884, the purpose being to educate people to socialism, "to reform the government, not overthrow it." And thus the expression "Fabian tactics" obtained a new lease on life, in its old significance.

face. See LOSE FACE.

face the music. Though Mencken labels this "an obvious product of pioneer life," it seems equally possible that it refers to that peculiar type of courage necessary to face the footlights and the orchestra in the pit. In *Follow the Fleet* (Irving Berlin, 1936), Fred Astaire sang, "Let's face the music and dance." Thornton's first specimen is dated 1850. It may be army slang, an allusion to the Rogue's March played when a culprit was being drummed out of the service.

fag. Meaning cigarette, this is apparently from fag end, the butt or unsmoked portion. While fag end, in this sense, is probably related to "fagged out" and thus to *flag* (to get tired), it is perhaps worth noting that tufts of pasture grass are known as fag ends—and that corn-silk is not the only tobacco substitute that has been smoked, with singular results, behind the barn or down by the railroad tracks.

A "fag," schoolboy slang for an older student's errand-runner and shoe-shiner, is more likely from the idea of "tiring work" contained in *flag* than from Latin *factotum*.

fairy. See ANGEL. FATA MORGANA.

fall. "Autumn" is not such a very marvelous name for the season preceding winter, because it doesn't really mean anything, etymologically speaking. But take our *fall*: simply "the fall of the leaves," as it used to be given, in full, in the very early days back in Britain. In 1599 it was correct to use the word in England, but OED's last British quotation for it is 1862, and it was evidently obsolescent long before that.

fall for. See PLUMP.

fame. In *Lycidas*, Milton called the desire for fame "that last infirmity of noble mind," evidently meaning that as a noble character grows older the one vice that he retains to the last is the love of glory. By what Swinburne calls "the most inexplicable coincidence in the whole range of literature," sixteen years before *Lycidas* there appeared a poem called *Sir John van Olden Barnevelt* in which reference was made to the desire for glory as "that last infirmity of noble minds." But we need not get unduly excited about it. Milton would have been the first to acknowledge that the idea was in the air at the time, for Massinger expressed it thus, in *Very Woman*, four years before *Lycidas*:

> Tho' the desire of fame be the last weakness
> Wise men put off.

familiarity breeds contempt. The usual meaning of this proverb, which goes back, Stevenson finds, to 1160, is: "Familiarity with danger makes one contemptuous of it, and therefore careless." Illustrations would be the practice of driving while slightly drunk, or of surreptitious smoking in a powder factory. The saying may also be taken to mean seeing too much of one's associates, or becoming unappreciative of benefits too generously showered on one. A quaint version of it is "Too much freedery breeds despisery" (Sierra Leone). Chaucer's "Overgreet hoomlinesse engendreth dispreisinge" was an ancestor. Then there was the optimistic Slender, before his marriage to Anne Page: "I hope, upon familiarity will grow more contempt."

fan. In the sense of "baseball fan," this is probably short for "fanatic." OED, early in its career, gave this derivation, listed also the spellings *fann* and *phan*, and labeled the whole business "obsolete." However, the Supplement implores us to "delete obs." on the ground that "fan" has come back into British usage via the U.S.A.

fan my brow. This exclamation of surprise and excitement, found only in Weseen and now probably extinct, is interesting chiefly because it was so promptly and amusingly altered to "sand my brow."

fanny. See BUM.

farce. The early miracle plays were padded out with interludes or "gags" (as OED elegantly calls them). These comic and spicy bits that were stuffed into the main piece came to be called "farces," from Latin *farcire*, to stuff (ancestor also of *frequent*).

Farthest North. See ULTIMA THULE.

fast and loose. See DUCKS AND DRAKES.

fast one. "Pull a fast one," meaning to put over a trick or swindle, or just a pun or a joke, is recent slang, perhaps in reference to a speedy pitch in baseball; but OED lists the verb "pull" as considerably older slang, in the sense of "engineer a deception."

The reason *fast* means both "stuck" and "rapid," is, authorities agree, that rapidity enabled one to stick close at the heels of the object pursued. A similar usage, OED reminds us, is in the phrase "run hard" as contrasted with "hard and fast."

fat. See CHEW THE RAG.

fata morgana. Morgan le fay (the fairy), sister of King Arthur, was traditionally assigned a residence in Calabria, the toe of Italy's boot. A sort of mirage sometimes seen in that neighborhood has been dubbed the *fata morgana* in her honor. *Fata*, Italian word for fairy, is related to English *fate*.

father of the man. See CHILD.

faux pas. See FOOT.

favor. See CURRY FAVOR.

fawney rig. See PHONEY.

faze. The popularity of this slang word (also spelled *feaze* and *feeze*) has continued since as early as 1843. Originally, it meant "put to flight." Why, deponent knoweth not.

fear the Greeks bringing gifts. See GREEK.

feast. See DUTCH.

feather in his cap. The custom of sticking a feather in your cap for every enemy you have killed (roughly approximate to the jovial old practice of carving a notch on your gun) has been found not only among the American Indians but in Hungary, Turkey, Abyssinia, and the Himalayas. This furnishes good evidence of early intercourse between tribes now widely separated. The phrase goes back to 1678, according to E.P. (See WHITE FEATHER.)

featherbedding. According to United Business Service, this slang expression originated on the Rock Island Railroad, when freight crews complained the bunks in the caboose were too hard, and were asked: "What do you want, featherbeds?" It means being forced to hire more men than are needed for a particular job. Mathews' first quotation (1943) points out that unions use this procedure to make "more jobs for more members who pay more dues."

fed up. Weekley gives the French equivalent of this as *J'en ai soupé*, "I've had enough of that for supper," and Kastner & Marks list it as originally military slang. In English, "fed-up to the eyelids" is found as far back as 1882. The idea is, of course, disgust aroused by too much —even of a good thing.

feed. See CHICKEN FEED.

feeder. See STOOGE.

feed the kitty. See KICK.

feel his oats. A horse who is "feeling his oats" is "full of oats" (see BEANS). It means not only lively and full of energy, but also self-important, inclined to show off a bit. Men (not to mention women and children) may also with perfect correctness be said to "feel their oats."

feet. See COLD FEET.

Fell. See DOCTOR FELL.

feller. See ALLIGATOR.

fence. As "receiver of stolen goods," this goes back to *Oliver Twist* (1838), possibly its earliest appearance in print. The basic conception seems to be that the ordinary fence gives at least a modicum of security. Stevenson quotes a little poem by Mary Frances Butts which sounds like a case in point, though she certainly did not intend it so: it starts out "Build a little fence of trust" and even contains an allusion to "the sheltering bars," which might be construed by the suspicious-minded as having something to do with a jail. (See DROP.)

To "prevaricate" is, by literal derivation, to "sit on the fence,"— as Trench says, "straddling with distorted legs." (See MUGWUMP.)

fiasco. See FROST.

fiat money. From the Latin word for "Let it be done," this is paper that says it's money, but doesn't back up its statement; i.e., there's no "will pay to the bearer on demand" clause. The Latin word was first used in this sense in about 1879.

The famous automobile takes its name from the initials of the *I*talian *A*utomobile *F*actory (of) *T*urin.

fico. See THUMB.

fig. See THUMB.

file. See INDIAN.

filibuster. The constituents of legislators who boast of their filibustering ability might be embarrassed if they should happen to hear that a filibuster is, by derivation, a pirate who wages "unauthorized and irregular warfare," usually in quest of plunder (Webster). In our austere Halls of Congress, as everyone knows, hot-air artists are allowed to talk to death bills that they don't like. This is called a filibuster— from Dutch *vrijbuiter*, by way, probably, of French *flibuster*. It is the same thing as *freebooter*—which was influenced in its development by *booty*, stolen goods. (See GAG-RULE.)

fillip me with a three-man beetle. From Shakespeare's *King Henry IV*, Part II, this picturesque exclamation approximates in a general way our "Strike me pink!" *Fillip*, which is apparently imitative and cognate with *flip*, is still used, chiefly as a noun and in a figurative sense, to mean a smart blow with the finger, i.e., an incentive to action. This kind of a "beetle," one so heavy as to require three men to operate it, was a rammer for tamping pavements, driving wedges, etc.—a pile-driver in embryo. The old simile, "deaf (or dumb) as a beetle," more than likely had its eye on this thing, not the insect.

finagler. A fumbler; one who delays till somebody else pays for the meal or the tickets. Webster says it is a variant of *fainaigue* and thus connected with *feign*—which, through Latin *fingere*, is related etymologically to *dough*! To fenagle (also spelled phenagle) at cards is to revoke or even, perish the thought, to cheat.

finger-man. In underworld argot, *finger* seems to have at least two distinct slants. One definition of a *finger* is a policeman or police informer; this is indicated in the term "finger-mob," a gang under police protection. Another is the more obvious sense of one who points out, as a victim for a kidnaping. As the finger-man is also a sort of middleman between the kidnapers and the "kid," a fact of some interest but probably no significance is that "middle" is old cant for "finger."

finnan haddie. More correctly, Findon haddock, probably from the river Findhorn + the village Findon. It means haddock that has been smoked over a fire of green wood. The haddock is traditionally said to be the fish from which Peter took the tribute money (though Vizetelly identifies it as a John Dory, a yellowish food-fish); what proves it, in both cases, is of course the two indentations Peter's fingers left beside the gills.

fippenny bit. See PICAYUNE.

fire. Shakespeare has a passage about a bad angel firing a good one "out," and folks who delight in proving that "obnoxious Americanisms" have been imported from England assume this to be the source of our colloquialism meaning "to discharge." It is, however, not clear that the line from *The Passionate Pilgrim* illustrates our use of *fire*, i.e., having no connection with "burning" a person out. It is rather, I think, the figure of expelling suddenly, as from a gun. The adverb "out" is almost never added when the verb is used in its strictly technical sense of separating a man from his job. OED finds this sense only from 1885 on. (See THAMES.)

fire-new. See BRAND NEW.

first chop. See CHOP-CHOP.

first hundred years are the hardest. Of fairly recent origin, this not very profound remark owes its existence, probably, to the familiar injunction expressed thus by Emerson: "Keep cool, 'tis all one a hundred years hence." The natural retort was, "But the first hundred years are the hardest."

first-string. See TWO STRINGS TO HIS BOW.

first water. See WATER.

fish. "A nice (or pretty) kettle of fish," an expression of disgust, is explained by dictionary people (who conceivably don't like picnics) as originating in somewhat messy fish-fries on the banks of rivers (date, about 1740). It has been, less circumstantially, related to kiddle-nets, baskets set in the sluice-ways of a dam. (See DRINK LIKE A FISH. GAFF. I.H.S. RED.)

fish-like smell. See ANCIENT AND FISH-LIKE SMELL.

fish story. See DRAW THE LONG BOW.

fit. See CONNIPTION FIT.

flabbergast. In 1772 this was already creeping into polite society, but dressed in quotation marks as befitted a slang word. And it still is slang. The dialect dictionaries list it in almost the above form, but admit uncertainty as to its ultimate origin. Perhaps from *flabby* or *flap* + *aghast* (cognate with *ghost*), the thought being, if this be the case, "weak in the knees after having seen a ghost."

flag. See CARRY THE BANNER. FAG.

flak. This desolate-sounding short-cut for a German jawcracker, *fliegerabwehrkanone*, means "bursting shells fired by anti-aircraft artillery." It finally got into Webster (*Addenda*) in 1950. (See ARCHIE.)

flaming youth. Well publicized in the twenties (in part by the advocates of repeal, who have doubtless noted with pleasure how completely the young people have stopped flaming since the end of Prohibition), this phrase nevertheless goes back to *Hamlet*:

> To flaming youth let virtue be as wax,
> And melt in her own fire.

Here, incidentally, is an odd contrast with the same author's use of "salad days" (q.v.), in which the implication is that the blood of youth is somewhat cooler than that of maturity.

flapper. This is a convenient word. People get tired of it, it hibernates for a while, then pops up with an entirely new meaning. Swift put "flappers" on the island of Laputa, to "flap" the absent-minded. Brewer knew the word in the sense of fly-swatter. In 1893, 1897, and 1909, we find evidence that flapper meant, in certain circles, a young girl trained to vice. Harry Leon Wilson used it in 1912 as a substitute for *chicken* (young girl), and Scott Fitzgerald popularized it. According to Mencken, the flapper kept her integrity longer in England than in this country; over there, he pointed out, it meant "innocent miss" while here "the idea of innocence was not in it." It is apparently derived from a provincial English noun, *flap*, an unsteady young woman. (See BAGGAGE.)

flash in the pan. Short-lived brilliance that shows no results. It goes back to the days when a misfire meant that the priming powder in the "pan" of a gun burned without igniting the main charge.

Flatsville. See WELL-STACKED.

flat tire. See DUD. SQUARE.

flay a stone. See FLINT.

flesh. See RED.

flicker. If "Let 'er flicker" ever had, as B. & L. thought, the significance of "Let the issue remain in doubt," like a candle burning uncertainly, it has long been an exact equivalent of "Let 'er *rip*" (q.v.). In French, *allons* would express it.

"The flickers" was an apt name for the movies in the early days. With the absolute perfection of synchronization, the jest loses its sting and, like the bee, passes out of circulation.

flint. Weseen cites, without giving a date, a slang phrase, "lick one's flint," as meaning "make careful preparation." As I have been unable to find it in any other reference book, it would appear to be a local survival of a pioneer byword. Why a wet flint should give a better spark than a dry one, I leave to you.

A *skin flint* is one who would "skin a flint" or "flay a stone" in the hope of scraping something marketable off it.

floored. See GRAVELED.

flop. See DUD.

flotsam and jetsam. Spelled also *flotsan*, *-sen*, and *-son*, the first of this famous pair is from French *flottaison*, derived from Latin *fluere*, to float. The second is also from the Latin (*jacere*, to throw) and was once identical with *jettison*, to throw overboard (in reference to cargo, in an emergency). As it has nothing to do with floating, properly the whole phrase should mean "what floats and what has been abandoned to the sea," whether it belongs to the *genus* Ivory Soap or not. Roughly, however, the combination means anything that has drifted to shore. And an instructive parallel can be drawn between *beachcomber* (q.v.) and the uncomplimentary "flotsam and jetsam of life."

flowing hope. See FORLORN HOPE.

fluke. The flukes, or wings, of an anchor are probably so called because they are flat (from a German word *flach*, flat). A much later word that seems to have been born on a billiard table is *fluke* in the sense of aiming at one thing and hitting another; i.e., when you make a score in a way that you had not intended. As sources, Dutch *vlug*, a flying stroke, dialect *flack*, a blow, and a dialect form meaning "guess" have been suggested; but OED finds no very convincing evidence for any of them. (See FLAK.)

flummoxed. Though the earliest American quotations indicate that this old slang word meaning "upset" or "wrecked" (i.e., a failure) is native to the mountaineers of Kentucky and Vermont, its first appearance in print, according to OED, was in *Pickwick Papers*: "what the Italians call reg'larly flummoxed." Of course, the ascription to the Italian was facetious, as the word probably originated in an English dialect form vaguely imitative, similar perhaps to *slump* or *hummock*. The possibility that it may be related to collegiate slang *flunk*, to fail, is strengthened by the fact that one of the early examples of *flummox* is described as Williams College slang (1851); moreover, Williams is not far from the Green Mountains of Vermont.

flunk. See FLUMMOXED.

flush. See FOURFLUSH.

fly. "A fly in the ointment" and "flies in amber" are two quite different things. The former is biblical and suggests clearly enough that a little defect (such as a fly that has been dead long enough to have developed a fragrance of his own) has spoiled something valuable. The latter, derived from the fact that, before hardening, lovely transparent amber often ensnares insects or twigs which are thus preserved for ever, is used of the enshrining of something unimportant in a beautiful setting. Pope made use of the idea in 1735.

"To fly off the handle," as Mencken says, is an obvious product of pioneer life, for it means to lose your temper with the same suddenness as you lose the head off your ax.

"To take a flyer" is a football figure, according to B. & L., suggesting a risky venture (such as, in the American game, a forward pass in your own territory).

fly a kite. Meaning to raise money on a fraudulent note or a "rubber check" (one that bounces back from the bank, because of insufficient funds), this Irish phrase may have been related in some way to "raise the wind," meaning borrow money. It is perhaps never heard now, the last OED quotation for "fly a kite" being one from Tennyson, 1875. "Kiting" is, however, listed in Crowell's *Dictionary of Business and Finance*, and its commonest form is explained, in brief, thus: you overdraw your account, but before the bank gets excited you write another check, cash it at the A. & P. or somewhere, and deposit enough cash to cover your first shortage; etc. The definition—"incurring a fresh obligation to discharge an old one"—suggests the soaring of a kite, higher and higher.

fly cop. See COP.

fly the flag. See CARRY THE BANNER.

fodder. See CANNON-FODDER.

fogy. A Scotch use of *foggy*, in the sense of bloated or moss-covered (compare "old mossback") may be the origin of this old slang word for an invalid soldier, or a person becoming stupid with age. On the other hand, the aura of tobacco usually surrounding such a man may have had a finger in the pie—as *fogus* (perhaps from *fogo*, stench) is old cant for tobacco. "Old fogram" was once a variant of *fogy*, and just as difficult to explain.

fold (up). Many must have thought that the use of this to mean collapse or go bankrupt was a picturesque product of the depression. While this is largely true, it is worth noting that in 1250 *fold* could mean fail or give way. In 1934 Webster said this was obsolete, but by *Addenda* time in 1950 he had changed his mind.

food for powder. See CANNON-FODDER.

foot. "Now you *have* put your foot in it," a figurative way of indicating that you have made a *faux pas* (literally, a false step), goes back beyond 1800. When the soup was scorched, the saying used to be, "The bishop hath put his foot in it." This may have derived from the reputation bishops had for burning heretics, but more likely from the excuse a cook might give: that she had run to the window to see the bishop go by, in the Procession of the Host, and that while she was performing this pious duty the soup had burned. In this connection it is interesting to note that "bishop" is port that has been scorched. (A Chinese student of mine once paraphrased the familiar passage from *A Christmas Carol* as "Bring me a bowl of smoking head-of-a diocese.")

Of course, the literal interpretation, that you have put your foot into something undesirable, may be the actual source.

footpad. The *pad* (Dutch) was the *path*, the road, the highway. Highwaymen were at one time dubbed "knights of the pad"; hence, probably, the less aristocratic robber who worked the road on foot became a *footpad.* OED says it is "obsolete except historical," but it is certainly familiar to Americans.

Deriving from the same Dutch word is *pad*, an ambling, good-natured horse. And B. & L. list two slang phrases now out of use: "pad the hoof," to tramp (which should be "hoof the pad," as they properly point out), and "to stand pad," to stand on the road—which may have some bearing on "to stand pat." Which latter means, in poker, that you are satisfied with the hand that has been dealt you; presumably, because "pat" means fixed or firm.

Just at the moment (1960) "pad" also means a beatnik's apartment.

foozle. B. & L.'s guess that this, in the sense of "work hurriedly and badly," is of Anglo-Indian origin is overruled by later authorities who point to German *fuseln*, meaning just that (its Dutch equivalent, *futseln*, was also mentioned by B. & L. as a possibility). (See BAMBOOZLE.)

for crying out loud. See CRYING OUT LOUD.

forelock. See TAKE TIME BY THE FORELOCK.

forget it. See SKIP IT.

forlorn hope. At one time this was the technical term for the leading squad of infantry in an advance (known in the American army as the "point"). At first it was not "forlorn hope" at all, but *verloren hoop*, Dutch for "lost squad," itself a sufficiently disheartening name, one would think. *Verloren* is of course related to *forlorn*, but *hoop* is a near-cousin of *heap* and not connected with "hope" in any way.

The French call this band of death-defiers (as the term soon came to mean) *enfants perdus*, lost children. OED reports that English sailors have still further disguised the original phrase by mispronouncing it "flowing hope."

for the nonce. See NONCE.

fortitude, intestinal. See PLUCK.

forty winks. See NAB.

fourflush. There are various kinds of flushes in poker. This kind, known also as a bobtail flush, means four of a kind in a five card hand, and is good for nothing except to bluff with; i.e., to pretend to be worth more than you really are. Properly, a flush means all the cards in your hand are of one suit, and in this sense the word can probably be traced to Latin *flux*, a copious flow.

fourpence (**hapenny**). See PICAYUNE.

fourth estate. Carlyle said that Burke was the man who dubbed the press the fourth estate, but patient searchers after truth have concluded that Carlyle meant Macaulay, as it appears in the latter's works, under date of 1828, and not in the former's. The fact that Carlyle referred to the "reporters' gallery" in almost the identical terms used by Macaulay strengthens this belief. The traditional three estates, in England, were the Lords Spiritual, the Lords Temporal, and the Commons. Other countries use different classifications. "Fourth estate" has also been used, in English, of other groups, such as the army, the mob, and Fox's Board of Commissioners (1789).

fracture. See FRITTER.

fragile. See FRAIL.

frail. This half-joking adjective for a girl of questionable character (or indeed character about which there was no question at all) has evolved into a cant noun for any girl of marriageable age. The word *frail* is derived from *fragile.*

Frankenstein. While recognizing that the dictionary maker should record existing usage rather than preach reform, I feel justified nevertheless in pointing out emphatically that Mr. Frankenstein, in Mary Shelley's story, created a monster—*unnamed.* "A Frankenstein" is therefore not a mechanical man without a soul, but a person who starts something he can't stop.

freebooter. See FILIBUSTER.

freedery. See FAMILIARITY BREEDS CONTEMPT.

free speech. See GAG.

freewheeling. Our uninhibited ancestors who rode bicycles actually shortened this to "freeling," back in about 1906. It was all the rage, from about 1899 until the invention of the coaster brake, which combined the coasting advantages of the free wheel (i.e., the pedals went around only when you pushed them) with the phenomenal advantage that when you pushed back against the pedal the bicycle stopped. It is curious that though freewheeling as applied to automobiles was not first tried in America there is no reference to it in the latest OED Supplement (1933), at the height, perhaps, of its brief reign as the popular fad in motordom.

French disease. See PUNIC FAITH.

French leave. The French are, if nothing else, polite. Why then should it be considered characteristically *French* behavior to leave a party without saying good night to the hostess? Significantly, the French call it taking English leave, and I must say it sounds more like the self-conscious, retiring Englishman than the gallant and voluble Frenchman. However, rightly or wrongly, it has come to mean to go AWOL (absent without leave); in short, to desert or abscond.

frequent. See FARCE.

fresh. See SKIP IT.

fresh from the mint. See SPICK AND SPAN.

friable, friction. See MEALY-MOUTHED.

friends. See DEFEND ME FROM MY FRIENDS.

fritter. Apple *fritters* are fried—from French *friture.* But "fritter away" is related to *fracture*, the idea being, as it were, to break yourself, or your energies, into such small pieces that you are quite wasted. The colloquialism dates back to about 1700.

frolic. This is from the Dutch *vroolijk* (German *fröhlich*, gay). The

British appear to have had a phrase, "on the frolic" (not recognized by Webster), corresponding to "making whoopee."

from Dan to Beersheba. See DAN TO BEERSHEBA.

frost. "A complete frost" is a dismal failure; originally, a theatrical production that received a *cold* reception; in more modern slang, one that was "not so hot." *Fiasco* is another word for it, but just why is not clear, as this is the Italian word for a bottle or flask. Perhaps the sense is transferred from the crash of a bottle when it hits bottom.

frozen music. See ARCHITECTURE.

full house. See DRESS.

full of beans. See BEANS.

full of oats. See BEANS.

full of prunes. See PRUNES.

full of red ants. See BEANS.

fumble for the check. See FINAGLER. MOOCHER.

funk. This is musty old collegiate slang (Oxford, 1743). OED and Webster agree that Flemish *fonck*, fear, offers the likeliest source. Its vigorous survival can, however, be ascribed in part to its similarity to *skunk* and to one of the famous four-letter words.

funkelnagelneu. See BRAND NEW.

funny bone. Whereas Mencken says the American variant of this is "crazy bone," Webster, not entering into international disputes, shows a preference for funny bone. Less conservative than OED, however, Webster admits the possibility of a pun on *humerus*, Latin name for the bone of the upper arm.

fuss-budget. Why this word for a leather bag (enlarged to cover a statement of financial requirements) should have been attached to the obvious *fuss*, to mean one who worries and fidgets about trifles, is a mystery—unless one accepts a present-day political theory that a budget is something one should never worry about. "Fuss-box" and "fuss-pot" are to be found in OED, in this sense, and "mumbudget" in Webster, in the opposite. This may account for "fuss-budget" as having been coined for contrast. Still there is no explanation for the derogatory use of *budget*, unless, perhaps, we call in the Anglo-Indian *budzat*, scoundrel, blackguard. As a fuss-budget is seldom fat, there seems to be little use in pointing out that *budget* is related to *belly* and *bulge*.

futilitarian. This old humorous coinage goes back to Southey (1827) and the early days of the Utilitarian movement, but was revived a few years ago as a slur on the writings of the "lost generation," the post-war decadents (World War I, that is). Obviously, we have no decadents in the wake of World War II (see BEATNIK).

The adjective *futile*, incidentally, comes from *futire*, to run off like water.

G

gab. "The gift of gab" means "speaking ability" or, unkindly, "talkativeness." *Gab* is a very old word, in Scotch and Gaelic, for *mouth*. It may be related to French *gaber*, to boast, and certainly to *gap*, *gape*, *gabble*, *gobble*, and even *gable* (literally, "beak").

gabble. See GIBBERISH.

gadget. This first seeped into world consciousness as a sailor's word for a what-you-may-call-it. It has proved embarrassingly useful and bids fair to supplant all other technical terms whatsoever. But the same people who got tired of the adjective "intriguing" are frowning on "gadget," so there is hope that such rich products of our civilization as "electrodynamometer" and "superheterodynoscope" may continue to bud and flourish.

OED furnishes the best clue to the ancestry of *gadget*. Admitting that its origin is obscure, the Oxford Supplement points to a French *gâchette*, diminutive of a word meaning hook or staple, and used by the French to mean various pieces of mechanism. *Gadget* is not found in print prior to 1886, but is believed to have been in common use before that.

gaff. "Give him the gaff" and "stand the gaff" both trace their ancestry to a Provençal word for a boat-hook. The first means to spur or goad, the second to endure goading by someone else. The spur of a game cock is also called its gaff.

"Blow the gaff" is old thieves' cant for "blab," tell secrets; "blow" corresponded in a way to our "hot air," and this "gaff," which meant a hoax or trick, derived from the older *gaff* through the notion, perhaps, of "hooking some poor fish," as a large fish-hook was sometimes referred to as a gaff.

gag. In the sense of a joke or comic scene, this goes back first to the use of gag to mean an extemporary "crack" or bit of clowning, an interpolation (see FARCE). While this sort of thing might conceivably be related to the *gag* that Webster describes as "a mouthful that makes one retch," it must be recognized that a bad joke is seldom complimented by being called a gag. A gag-man (one who writes, or rather adapts, jokes for a comedian's use) does not remain a gag-man long unless he is successful. Hence, for the "interpolation" idea we may have to go back to a 1747 quotation in OED, relative to a temporary prop used in mining operations.

"Gag-rule" is the stock retort whenever Vox Pop. is raised in opposition to filibustering. Coming from the word meaning something "interpolated" in the mouth to hinder speech, the expression means that to set a time limit on a legislator's speech, or to require that he discuss the subject, is an infringement of the right of free tripe.

gaga. No satisfactory explanation for this, as meaning mentally unbalanced, has been offered. Maybe from Gauguin. Perhaps it is an imitation of an idiot's laugh. It is interesting that "cuckoo," meaning the same, bears some similarity in sound. The former, appearing in 1905, however, long preceded the latter in that sense. The British, according to OED, pronounce the first syllable like "gag" rather than "gah" as is customary in America; here, too, the word is more likely to imply a temporary aberration, or, indeed, simply "haywire" (q.v.).

gallery god. Either because they are "seated on high," or because there are usually Venuses and Cupids painted on the adjoining ceiling, the denizens of the top gallery are often called gallery gods. A less polite term for the topmost seats in a theater is "nigger heaven."

galley west. See KNOCK GALLEY WEST.

galligaskins. Influenced, perhaps, by *Gallic* and *Gascon*, this word seems nevertheless to be a corruption of something quite different, Old French *garguescans*, from *grechesco*, Grecian. Apparently some seamen from Greece affected these ludicrously loose breeches. A further association may have been with *gallows*, especially as converted to plural "galluses," suspenders or braces (colloquial from 1730 to nearly 1900).

galloping ivories. See DIE IS CAST.

galluses. See GALLIGASKINS.

galoot. This belongs in the same category as "Tell it to the marines," for it was originally (1812) applied by sailors to the despised marines, and has loyally kept its sense of awkward or worthless fellow. B. & L. connect it plausibly with Italian *galeotto*, galley slave, but Webster and OED pronounce its origin obscure.

galore. This somewhat overworked Irishism (Brewer says it was popular with seafaring men) means simply, in Gaelic, "enough" (*gu leor*). It has certainly grown; to us, "girls galore," for instance, signifies "lots of girls," more than enough to go around. The fact is that *enough* can have either the positive connotation of "plenty" or the negative of "barely sufficient."

game-cock. See COCK OF THE WALK.

game isn't worth the candle. See CANDLE.

game leg. Though OED says the etymology is uncertain, this *game* is apparently from the same Celtic root as French *jambe* and is related to such English dialect forms as *gam* and *gammy*, meaning "crooked." (See GAMMON AND SPINACH.)

gammon and spinach. This phrase for "bosh," made familiar to American school children through "A frog he would a-wooing go," is illustrated only once in OED (*David Copperfield*, 1850). The *gammon* part is really a play on words. In the first place, it comes from Old French *gambe*, leg, and is used of ham or bacon; *gammon and spinach*, then, is just our tried and true combination of "ham and spinach." But *gammon*, either through relation to *game* in the sense of "trick" or in the sense of "crooked" (see GAME LEG), or to the game of backgammon, came to be slang for treacherous nonsense. Returning to our spinach (spelled "spinnage" by Dickens) we find Webster listing nine ancestors for it, all the way back to Persian *isfanaj*—then saying "of unknown origin." There's a conscience for you!

gantlet. By spelling the chief word of "run the gauntlet" this way, Webster ingeniously emphasizes the fact that *gauntlet* (glove) is not in the picture; he concedes the "aw" pronunciation, however. On the other hand, OED declares *gantlet* an obsolete form of *gauntlet*. Be that as it may, the origin has been agreed on: the word was originally *gantlope*, from Swedish *gata*, a way (cognate with *gate*), + *lopp*, leap (related to German *laufen*, to run). The conception is that of a "way" between two rows of soldiers down which the man being punished had to "leap," while his companions took cracks at him with rope-ends. The institution dates back to the Thirty Years' War.

An expression that does carry the sense of "glove" is "throw down the gauntlet," meaning to challenge to combat. The formation is a diminutive from the French word for glove, *gant*—though we usually think nowadays of a gauntlet as a particularly heavy glove.

garble. From an Arabic word for "sieve," this meant originally to sift or sort. Thus, when meddlers took a passage and "edited" it, separating concepts from their context and destroying continuity, the dispatch or article was said to have been "garbled," i.e., mutilated.

garter. The Order of the Garter originated with Edward III ("the Brave") in the 14th century. Two or three stories of this sort have been told: that he picked up, or wore after somebody else picked up, a garter that a countess or some other lady lost while dancing; and that he chided moralistic critics with "*Honi soit qui mal y pense.*" However, Stevenson finds no historical authority for this derivation, and tells us simply that Edward used his garter as the signal for starting the battle of Crécy.

Gashouse Gang. Meaning a scrappy outfit from the wrong side of the tracks, this name was first applied to the St. Louis Cardinals (according to Frankie Frisch, *Sat. Eve. Post*, July 18, 1959) in August, 1934, when they appeared in the New York Polo Grounds wearing dirty uniforms. It seems they had played in a thunderstorm the day before, and the New York laundries were closed for the weekend.

gate. "Crash the gate" is an obvious metaphor, but picturesque enough—meaning to attend a party or other spectacle without an invitation or a ticket. The "crash" is misleading, as the best gate-crashers either sneak or lie their way in. The term seems to have been invented in about 1923.

To give someone "the gate" is to show him the door, to usher him out, delicately or otherwise. Stevenson quotes a couplet from a colloquial version of *King Lear*, about how his daughters gave him the gate, but says the author is "unknown." Why not F.P.A.'s staunch and talented assistant, Christopher Ward? (See GANTLET. HELL GATE.)

gauntlet. See GANTLET.

gay Lothario. See LOTHARIO.

gazabo. OED guesses this is a variant of *gazebo*, a summer house or a projecting balcony with windows, but Webster, closer to the point of origin (Southwestern U.S.), relates it to Mexican Spanish *gazapo*, clever fellow. Mencken agrees.

The British *gazebo*, while probably a joking formation from the verb *gaze*, may be related to German *Gasse-bau*, a bow window.

gazette. This is either from a coin, worth less than a farthing, paid for the privilege of reading the primitive newspaper (in manuscript form); or from *gazzetta*, little magpie, because the paper didn't always tell the truth.

gee-string. Often spelled "G string," though this is misleading, because even the heaviest string of a violin would be quite inadequate, this word for an American Indian's (or strip-teaser's) loin-cloth is obscure in origin. Thornton lists it as an Americanism of 1878, and OED includes it, but Webster decidedly slights it. Inasmuch as no Indian word has been proposed, it may be that the *g* is the initial of some English word, like *guts* or *groin*, considered at the time as indecently explicit.

geezer. The red-nosed and frozen-fingered musicians who are playing Christmas carols, on some of our greeting cards, should not resent being called "geezers," for it is a dialect pronunciation of *guiser*, a mummer, especially a Christmas mummer and therefore a close relative of the carol singers or "waits" (derived, Brewer thought, from *hautboy*, oboe, but believed more conservatively to be a distant relative of the weary *waiting* done by a night watchman). We seldom think of a geezer as feminine, but OED says that it is commonly applied to elderly women. There is no connection with *geyser*, though some fun was had over their similarity in one of Will Rogers's pictures.

general. See CAVIAR TO THE GENERAL.

General Taylor never surrenders. See DIES BUT NEVER SURRENDERS.

Geneva courage. About the same as *Dutch courage* (q.v.). No slander on the good people of Geneva is here intended, though there may have been once a punning allusion to the Calvinists. The situation is this: *gin* is short for *geneva*, which in turn is a corruption of *genièvre*, from Latin *juniperus*, the juniper berries used for flavoring the stuff. ("Juniper juice" is occasionally heard as slang for hard liquor.) I once knew a girl named Genevra, who will probably not be complimented to hear that she is cognate with *gin*; the name is, however, also associated with Ginevra, character in *Orlando Furioso*, and with Queen Guinevere.

genius. It has been said that this is a misquotation: "Genius is an infinite capacity for taking pains." And it is, if you are trying to repeat Carlyle's *mot* about genius, that it "means transcendent capacity of taking trouble, first of all." Stevenson, however, gives a plausible ascription to social reformer Jane Ellice Hopkins, 1870, who may first have used the exact words of our "misquotation." So striking an epigram was bound to become a target for the wits: Samuel Butler the Younger called it, rather, the supreme capacity for "getting its possessor into trouble of all kinds"; Elbert Hubbard—"for evading hard work"; and Christopher Morley—"for catching trains" (in reference, of course, to the harassed commuter).

The difference between *talent* and *genius* was well put by Lowell: "Talent is that which is in a man's power; genius is that in whose power a man is."

gentleman. Somehow this word has kept its manliness and nobility, while *ladylike* has had to yield to *womanly* in beauty. I can even conceive of a situation in which I should consider the exclamation, "That girl's a *gentleman*!" the highest of compliments. It has a courageous and generous stature which *lady* has unfortunately lost and *woman* has not yet attained.

One of Macaulay's most delightful balanced sentences is built around this word: "There were gentlemen and seamen in the navy of Charles II. But the seamen were not gentlemen, and the gentlemen were not seamen."

gerrymander. (Pronunciation with a hard *g* is approved.) When Governor Gerry of Massachusetts exhibited a map on which he had shrewdly indicated how certain districts could be reapportioned greatly to his political advantage, a companion noted its resemblance to a salamander, and sketched in claws and a beak; whereupon it was dubbed a gerrymander.

Gesundheit. See GOD BLESS YOU.

get. "Get (or put) across" and "get over," implying success, both seem to understand an object, the footlights, across which the play or the address must carry conviction. "Get away" and "get by" may also be used in the sense of achievement, though usually, either through modesty or bitter experience, the speaker implies that he barely escaped being showered with ancient vegetables. On the other hand, to "get away with murder" is to do something not quite right, or at best recklessly unconventional, and receive no commensurate punishment. As in a number of other cases, OED calls upon reliable old Christy Mathewson for its first (1912) example of this.

To "get a thing down cold," meaning to master it, to learn it perfectly, seems to derive from the prize ring, the thought being similar to that in "knock him cold," i.e., unconscious.

get home until morning. See HOME.

get in my hair. See BEARD.

get in on the ground floor. See LOWDOWN.

get my goat. See GOAT.

get the big bird. See RAZZ.

get the drop on. See DROP.

get the hang. See LEARN THE ROPES.

get the mitten. See MITTEN.

get the sack. See SACK.

get your back up. See HUMP.

ghost. This word, to mean one who writes your speeches or articles for you, was in the dictionaries long before "ghost-writer" became familiar to most people. The origin is presumably the idea of a ghost as an *alter ego*, a spirit distinct from oneself.

"The ghost walks," to mean "pay-day," was good theatrical slang as far back as 1867. It originated perhaps in the custom ghosts have of appearing infrequently and unexpectedly. Or perhaps, after the effort of raising the money for the salaries, the treasurer of the company would be as pale as a ghost. Again, we have the *Hamlet* story, about how the ghost "won't walk again until the company gets paid!" (See FLABBERGAST.)

gibberish. (The British pronounce the *g* hard.) Not from the Arabian alchemist, Geber, as Dr. Johnson thought, or the spelling would be "gebirish." It is probably imitative in origin, like *jabber* and *gabble*.

gift. See GREEK.

gift horse. "Don't look a gift horse in the mouth" is based on the fact that the age of a horse can be determined by examining his teeth. The thought is: accept presents gracefully, without asking embarrassing questions. It is found in Latin as early as A.D. 400, and is literally reproduced in both French and German.

gift of gab. See GAB.

gigolo. See MACARONI.

Gilead. See BALM IN GILEAD.

gin. (See also GENEVA COURAGE.) The "gin" of "cotton-gin," a cotton-picking machine, is believed to be nothing more technical than an abbreviation of "engine" (cognate with *ingenious*). That "spinning-jenny" is a similar formation is possible, but it is more often associated with the tendency to apply ordinary Christian names to implements with which one works (such as automobile jack, or the old boot-jack). As the spinning machine took the place of a certain number of girl spinners, the name Jenny (a counterpart of Jack) was the most natural one to use.

Ginevra. See GENEVA COURAGE.

gingham. Early etymologists—the word has been familiar in this form since 1615—were inevitably tempted by its similarity to Guingamp, in Brittany. But it is now agreed that it came into English, via the French, from Malay *gingan*, meaning "striped." In other words, a gingham apron just has to have stripes.

giraffe. See NECK.

girl for sale. See WEAKEST GOES TO THE WALL.

give a continental. See CONTINENTAL.

give a hoot. See HOOT.

give and take. See HOBNOB.

give an inch. See ELL.

give a rap. See RAP.

give her the gun. See GUN.

give him the dope. See DOPE.

give him the gaff. See GAFF.

give him the gate. See GATE.

give him the razz (etc.). See RAZZ.

give him the works. See WORKS.

giver. See INDIAN.

glove. See HAND AND GLOVE.

G-men. One of our leading public enemies, Machine Gun Kelly, is believed to have surprised his captors by calling them this as they closed in on him. It is applied to the detectives of the Federal Government, the *G* standing of course for Government. One of the letters of Dillinger to his father, during that blood-stained pursuit, helped make America *G*-conscious when he wrote, "The G-heat is something terrible."

go. See TOUCH AND GO.

goal. See KNOCK GALLEY WEST.

goat. "That gets my goat," meaning "That bothers me intensely," must be connected, I suppose, with the scapegoat idea expressed in "You're the goat," but I don't quite see how. The scapegoat is, of course, in Hebrew tradition the innocent victim who has to endure the penalty for the sins of others (the origin of the fraternity "goat-room"). Curiously enough, the Jewish goat, instead of being sacrificed, was allowed to escape into the wilderness where I have no doubt he was happier than in captivity. If the goat were the symbol of anger rather than of lechery, "That gets my goat" would be easier to understand. Can it be that there is a confusion with *goad*, to arouse, irritate?

goat. See SIN EATERS. ZANY.

Gobelin. See GOBLIN.

goblin. The authorities express cautious opinions that this is from Greek *kobalos*, knave. Related, probably, to this Greek word was Gobelinus, found in 12th century France as a popular name for the spirit haunting a certain locality. Dr. Johnson made an astonishing conjecture that *elf* and *goblin* came from *Guelph* and *Ghibelline*, rival parties in medieval Italy. Gobelin tapestries were so named because a French family of that name founded the industry. (See HOBGOBLIN.)

god. See GALLERY GOD.

God bless the Duke of Argyle. This Scotch saying may have reference to a noble lord who erected posts especially designed for his herdsmen to scratch their backs on. Walsh says the posts were put up to indicate a trail when it was covered with deep snow. Evidently, however, the hostess was supposed to make a graceful reference to the Duke of Argyle to relieve the embarrassment if one of her guests should back up to a pillar and begin a wistful wiggle.

God bless you! A sneeze, in almost any language, is a bad omen. The bystander should exclaim *Gesundheit!* or *Salute!* (Good health!) or *Crisce sant!* (Grow saintly!) or a dozen other pious hopes—though, to be practical, it would probably do the sufferer more good if the bystander administered bicarbonate of soda. Even our sanitary gesture of covering the mouth for a sneeze, or (less plausibly) a yawn, had a superstitious origin: one was simply, antiquarians tell us, making the sign of the cross. Incidentally, the word *sneeze* was originally *fnese*, but somebody miscued on that queer old *s* that looked like an *f*.

God is on the side of the heaviest battalions. While Voltaire is often given the credit for this, he was not by any means the first to express it, as he acknowledged when he started out with *On dit*, "They say." The date of this was 1770, whereas both Mme. de Sévigny and Marshal de la Ferté appear to have made this remark, with specific reference to "battalions," well before 1700, while Rabutin conveyed the same idea even earlier, using "big squadrons." And at that they were all borrowing from Tacitus and Terence. While not, perhaps, trying to find its first appearance in English, OED lists as its first quotation an American example of 1868, which seems curious.

God takes soonest those he loveth best. See GOOD DIE YOUNG.

God tempers the wind to the shorn lamb. Laurence Sterne was a clergyman, though he did occasionally yield to the temptation to be smutty in a snickering and dishonest way. And he was able to put this French proverb (*Dieu mésure le froid à la brebis tondue*) into such convincingly biblical phraseology that many have spent weary hours trying to find it in their King James versions. The author did not claim to have originated it—he even put it into the mouth of Maria, who was French.

Gog and Magog. Prince Gog, of the land of Magog, is prophesied against with some severity in Ezekiel. By the time of the Revelation, he was two men, Gog and Magog, representing the nations whom Satan induced to revolt, upon the expiration of his thousand year prison term.

When Englishmen who knew their Bibles heard of the legendary Goemagot, alleged descendant of one of the murderous daughters of Diocletian, they speedily converted the giant king's name into "Gogmagog." And soon he was two men again, doing duty in captivity as porters at the royal palace. The effigies of the two giants used to be carried in the Lord Mayor's pageant (remote ancestor, perhaps, of the Macy Thanksgiving parade down Broadway). Destroyed in the great fire of 1666, these effigies were succeeded by fourteen foot wooden figures at the London Guildhall.

goggles. Brewer receives no support in his effort to relate this word with the verb *ogle* (from Dutch *oog*, eye). It may be that "goggle-eyed," in the sense of having a squint, is, like *joggle* and *jiggle*, imitative; i.e., they somehow convey the idea of vibrating jerkily. The further sense of staring with protruding eyes seems to come from the early goggles made with short projecting tubes, like tiny telescopes, for people whose eyes needed protecting or strengthening. Evidently these horrifying glasses were called goggles because they helped to relieve a squint.

golden balls. See BALLS.

golf. Though Webster backs up Jamieson's theory that this is from Middle Dutch *colf*, club, and thus related to Latin *globus*, ball, OED is not satisfied, because the Scotch game is earlier than any similar Dutch game. The British authority suggests, in view of the traditional Scotch pronunciation as "gouf" (*ou* as in *ouch*), that the source may be Scotch *gowf*, a blow with the hand.

A famous quotation about golf for which the origin is often requested is this little jewel by Sarah N. Cleghorn:

> The golf links lie so near the mill
> That almost every day
> The laboring children can look out
> And see the men at play.

go like Sam Hill. See SAM HILL.

goober. While this is doubtless descended, as our experts on Africa inform us, from Angolan *nguba*, this Southern U.S. word for peanut bears an interesting similarity—especially in view of the advertising campaign for peanuts as the "nickel lunch"—to *gouber*, an old English word for "a gouster, an afternoone's repast, a nunchion."

good as a mile. See MISS AS GOOD AS A MILE.

good die young. Defoe says "die early," Wordsworth, "die first." But both were following the classic writers Menander and Plautus. N. & Q. records a 1626 quotation, "God takes soonest those he loveth best." Another N. & Q. writer presents statistics as to the high percentage of good boys that die in their fifth year—presumably because they have been burning the midnight oil over their alphabets instead of making mud pies in the fresh air.

good intentions. See HELL IS PAVED WITH GOOD INTENTIONS.

goods and chattels. See CHATTELS.

good-woolled. See WILD AND WOOLLY.

goofy. See CUCKOO.

gool. See KNOCK GALLEY WEST.

goose. At cricket, they say "duck's egg"; over here, "goose-egg." But they mean the same: a score of zero. 1860 and 1886 are the respective dates in OED.

The British seem reluctant to pin "goose-step" on the Germans, no doubt because they themselves used the goose-step from 1800 on; not, however, as a ceremonial march step supposed to look dignified, but as a marking-time exercise in calisthenics. The stiff-legged, jerky step of the Prussian guard has seemed to the less regimental-minded Anglo-Saxon to be symbolic of despotism. But the gloomy Mencken once asserted that "People's natural gait is the goose-step."

Since 1600 the heavy iron used by a tailor has been called a "goose," more probably because its handle resembles the neck of a goose than because it is constantly getting a roasting. (See COOK YOUR GOOSE.)

Though Weseen notes a cowboy expression, "Pork chops will hang high" (predicting a hard winter), Webster considers that "The goose hangs high" should really be, "The goose *honks* high," showing that the weather is good and everything propitious. This theory has been confirmed for me by Mrs. Percival Wraight, of Northampton, Mass., whose grandfather assured her that "honks" was the original form of the expression.

go places and do things. Using this once in his *Saturday Review* page, Christopher Morley felt it necessary to assure us that it was "a harmless phrase." It suggests spending money and making a moderate amount of whoopee. Weseen discovers in it a figurative use: to be successful, to get ahead.

Gothamites. This was first applied to New Yorkers by Washington Irving, in about 1805. The inhabitants of Gotham, in England, had long been celebrated as fools (though one story has it that they got their reputation by playing the fool intentionally to avoid the expense of having to entertain the king). Irving's satirical application of the name to New York was an allusion to the Manhattanite's traditional air of "knowing it all." (See CUCKOO.)

go the whole hog. See HOG.

go to Halifax. See HALIFAX.

go to Jericho. See JERICHO.

go to pot. See POT.

go to the dogs. While the obvious connection with "a dog's life" or "die like a dog" may be the correct derivation, "to go to the dogs" is strikingly similar to the Dutch saying *Toe goe, toe de dogs*, "Money gone, credit gone." Appropriately enough, in South Florida the expression is whimsically applied to an evening at the greyhound races.

go to the wall. See WEAKEST GOES TO THE WALL.

gowans. Not all of us who have wondered what "pu'd the gowans fine" meant, in *Auld Lang Syne*, have had the ambition to look it up. It means "pulled the daisies."

grace of God. "There, but for the grace of God, goes . . ." who? Some say Bunyan, others Wesley. But the one who seems to have said it first was John Bradford, as he watched some criminals going to execution. He himself was burned at the stake in 1555.

grade. See MAKE.

graft. Starting about 1889 as a synonym for our "racket" (q.v.), it soon took on a political tinge. The suggestion that it may derive from an early word meaning dig or work hard is out of order; the idea of *work* is not in it. It is more likely that the connection is with the grafting of a parasitic branch on a legitimate business.

grain of salt. To take a thing *cum grano salis* (of which the familiar phrase is a translation) is to accept it with reservations, to taste it gingerly, to avoid swallowing it whole. Stevenson found that Pompey used to add "a grain of salt" to a suspected drink as an antidote for poison (Pliny). Other plausible suggestions are scarce. A modern equivalent that I have seen is to take a story "with a good big chaser" (a mild drink calculated to cool somewhat the fieriness of a preceding shot of liquor).

Gramercy Park. Evidently the name of this exclusive section of New York City does not mean "thanks a lot" (*grand merci*). The problem here is to combine two Dutch sources that at first seem far apart: Walsh says *der Kromme See*, while R. R. Wilson, in *New York Old and New*, gives the old name as *Crummassie-Vly*. Breaking these down we find that the first means "crooked sea" (the *Zee* of *Zuyder-Zee*) and might easily refer to the East River, which is not a river at all but a winding and narrow branch of the sea; and that the second, which Wilson interprets as "Winding Creek," was probably *Kromme See Vliet* (as in *Watervliet*, N. Y.), "crooked sea brook."

grand climacteric. See CLIMACTERIC.

granger. The National Grange, or "Patrons of Husbandry," dates from about 1867. The word used to be applied regularly to the group of railroads which drew their main support from the grain industry; it was also at one time a nickname for a "rube," a country bumpkin (from *Reuben*). A "grange" is simply, by definition, a granary.

grapevine route. During the Civil War, a rumor that came by "grapevine telegraph" was one that arrived mysteriously and was $99\frac{44}{100}$% false. Its somewhat less proper successor, of World War I days, was "latrine rumor." As Webster compares the grapevine telegraph to the use of drums in the primitive sending of messages, it seems possible that the origin lies in the miraculous speed (familiar to all *Tarzan* fans) with which grapevine specialists can swing their way through the impenetrable jungle.

grass roots. John Hamilton, of Topeka, Kan., is probably the one to whom goes the credit for applying to the resurgent Republican party (in January, 1935) this "little classic of the poetic imagination," as *The New York Times* calls it. The phrase, "to get down to grass roots," so happily similar to the "brass tacks" expression, goes far back into prairie farm history. It is unlikely that Republican politicians will stress the etymological fact that one who gets down to *roots* is a *radical*.

grass widow. With his tongue in his cheek, Brewer tells us of how a forty-niner would put his wife out to grass (i.e., to board with some family) while he went off prospecting. A little more convincing is the derivation from *veuve de grâce*, a widow by dispensation of the Pope (a divorcée). But OED says "certainly not" from *grâce*, as shown by the parallels from other languages, such as *Strohwitwe*, straw widow.

Webster also lists MLG, *graswedewe*, a woman who has had an illegitimate child, calling it obsolete, but obviously suggesting where the idea of grass and straw came from.

The meaning of the term is disputed. Thornton (1893) gives the results of a Michigan professor's research on the subject. Of 100 students questioned, 19 thought a grass widow a divorced woman; 37, either divorced or informally separated from her husband; 42, one who had been deserted by her husband, or had left him—usually the former.

grate. See CRATE.

graveled. It is probable that this old word for perplexed, "floored," gets its figurative meaning from the grounding of a ship, though the uncomfortable predicament of a horse whose hoofs have been damaged by sharp gravel may also be considered.

grease. OED cannot show the identical phrase, "grease the palm," before 1807, but "grease the hand," in the sense of "tip," boasts a 1526 date. The metaphor in "grease" seems to be that of lubricating the machinery so that things will run smoothly. The French twin is *graisser la patte.* A similar figurative use of *palm* is Shakespeare's "itching palm" (*Julius Cæsar*).

No matter how you look at it, the American nickname for the Mexican peon, "greaser," is uncomplimentary, alluding either to a greasy appearance in general, the oily complexion, or the greasy food. Perhaps all three.

grease. See ELBOW.

Great Cham. See GRUB STREET.

great guns. See BLOW.

Great Scott. Though we cannot prove that this exclamation was in common use before the day of General Winfield Scott (Old Fuss-and-Feathers), there is little reason to suppose that the man who first started to say "Great God!" and hastily changed it to "Great Scott!" did so in tribute to the general. It is doubtless nothing but a euphemism. The German *Gott* helped things along.

Greek. *Timeo Danaos et dona ferentes*—"I fear the Greeks when they bring gifts" (Virgil's *Æneid*). Just as this wily Trojan suspected the Wooden Horse, we use the phrase to mean "I smell a rat" or "There seems to be a nigger in the woodpile."

"When Greek meets Greek, then comes the tug-of-war" is from a 17th century play, celebrating Philip and Alexander's bitterly contested battle with their fellow-Greeks. There is no foundation for the belief that the original form of this was: "When Greek meets Greek, they start a restaurant."

Greek to me. See GRINGO.

green room. In old theaters there was a room painted a restful green where the performers waited between their scenes; this pastoral provision has largely disappeared, in more than one instance because the temperamental star demanded a more magnificent dressing room. "Green room gossip" has likewise been outmoded.

grind. See AX TO GRIND. HIPPED.

gringo. The romantic "Green grow the rashes, O" explanation is probably as fantastic as the "green coat" one. The Mexicans may conceivably have heard hardboiled doughboys singing Burns's tender ballad, but Spanish authorities insist that *gringo* is just *griego*, Greek, i.e., just gibberish (as in "It's all Greek to me"). *Griego* was applied to any foreign language; but *gringo* has come to mean almost exclusively North American or British.

Another possibility decidedly worth considering is the Ringgold theory. The name (now familiar as that of an army post in Texas, and of other places in the South and West) was borne by Major Samuel Ringgold, a conspicuously gallant officer under General Zachary Taylor in the Mexican war. He was mortally wounded in the battle of Palo Alto (1846), but he had already become a veritable bogeyman to Mexican marauders, particularly through his development of a flying artillery corps. Incidentally, his brother, Cadwallader Ringgold, was in 1824 an officer in Commodore Porter's West Indies fleet. And OED's earliest quotation for *gringo* is 1844. By trilling the *r* of Ringgold and omitting the final consonants, as a Mexican would tend to do, we get something quite like *gringo*. Further, it seems possible that the border peons would be more familiar with the dreaded name of Ringgold than with the Castilian slang for "foreigner."

gripe. See BURN.

grit. See SAND.

grog. Admiral Edward Vernon wore a cloak of grogram (French *grosgrain*: "coarse grain," taffeta) and was called, in consequence, "Old Grog." In 1740, he issued an order requiring that the British sea-dogs' drinking water be adulterated with rum—or was it the other way? In any event, the mixture was therefore dubbed "grog," according to well-authenticated stories. One of the evidences was a jingle quoted by OED on the subject of grog. Here are two lines of it:

> The sacred robe which Vernon wore
> Was drenched within the same.

groom. See BRIDEGROOM. HENCH.

ground floor. See LOWDOWN.

ground-hog day. "Ground-hog" is certainly American for the marmot or woodchuck, and the tradition that if the hibernating creature sees his shadow on February 2, Candlemas Day, he will go back to bed, in anticipation of more severe weather, seems to be of American origin too. Though Sir Thomas Browne associates February 2 with predictions about the weather, neither OED nor the Encyclopedia Britannica makes any specific reference to "ground-hog day." On the other hand, E.P. traces the following proverb back to 1612: "If Candlemas day be fair and bright, winter will have another flight: If on Candlemas day it be shower and rain, winter is gone, and will not come again."

groves. See ACADEMIC GROVES.

grub. This slang word for food was familiar to Dickens. It probably comes from Gothic *graban*, to dig, hence to work hard. Then, too, there was a convenient word to rhyme with it: *bub*, slang for beer (derived from "bubble" rather than from "bubby," old word for a woman's breast). "Grubby," meaning dirty, is more nearly related to the word for "larva" than to the slang sense of "food." "Grub-stake," however, has to do with food: the furnishing of supplies to a prospector on the agreement that eventual proceeds will be shared. The "stake" part of it is probably from the idea of the risk involved. Just why "at stake" means "in jeopardy" is a question, unless we can establish a connection with the highly perilous pastime of being burned at the stake.

Grub Street. A century before Johnson's Dictionary, this street was already known as the stamping-ground of hack-writers (this *hack* comes from *hackney*, an ordinary variety of horse). The Great Cham (literally, "lord") of Literature, smiling perhaps out of the corner of his mouth, described the street as being much inhabited by writers of "small histories, dictionaries, and temporary poems." It is now called Milton Street, apparently in tribute to the mighty John.

grueling. Historically, there appears to have been some connection with the administering of gruel as a punishment; perhaps an allusion to the Medici poisonings.

Grundy. In Morton's *Speed the Plough*, the mother of a girl who has been compromised seems to be more concerned about what a conventional and critical busybody named Mrs. Grundy will say than she is about her daughter's welfare. The play is long dead, but the phrase, "What will Mrs. Grundy say?" is immortal. Later "sources," such as the tale about Mrs. Felix Grundy, Washington society leader, are obviously applications to any Mrs. Grundy to whom the shoe can be fitted.

G-string. See GEE-STRING.

Guard dies but never surrenders. See DIES BUT NEVER SURRENDERS.

guinea pig. Like Holy Roman Empire (q.v.) this name is misleading, for the beast is not a pig and does not come from Guinea (in West Africa). Though it is native to Brazil, which is not far from *Guiana*, the connection seems to be rather with the slave ships that used to ply between Africa and South America. One of these "guinea-men" probably introduced the South American rodent to the Old World on a return trip after the slaves had been delivered. Inasmuch as the prolific little creature does not bear any resemblance to a pig, it is curious that the highly scientific Germans should have allowed something about "swine" to creep into their name for it: *Meerschweinchen*, meaning apparently "little pig from over the sea."

guiser. See GEEZER.

guitar. See KIT AND CABOODLE.

gull. Our colloquialism, "swallow it whole" or "hook, line, and sinker," is intimately connected, in all probability, with *gull*, to deceive (cognate with *gullet*, throat). Since 1550, *gulled* has meant "fooled," and by origin seems related to the concept of feeding somebody full of lies. The French use the good-natured penguin in this sense, and it may be that the sea-gull is also easily tricked, but this is not believed to be the source.

gullet. See BEAGLE.

gumbo. This comes directly from the African name for the mucilaginous pods of the okra plant, indigenous to the dark continent. The slaves brought the name and the plant to our Southern states. It is a thick soup, sticky enough to have lent its name to particularly tenacious mud or clay.

gump, gumption. Here are paradoxes. The American *gump*, immortalized in Andy of the comic strip, goes back to the early 19th century as a chinless nitwit. Yet to most Americans *gumption* means initiative, even "guts." And to a Scot its primary meaning is, rather, common sense. Can it be that the American misuse grew up as a euphemism for the once highly improper "guts"?

gun. "Give her the gun" is an aviation term for "open the throttle wide." There is no reason to suppose that any other figure is intended than the terrific noise made by a wide-open pursuit-plane motor. Incidentally, the word *throttle* is curiously parallel to *choke*, as applied to the operation (now automatic in most cars) of sending a richer mixture (i.e., more gasoline, proportionally) into the carburetor when the motor is cold. What you are doing is *choking* down on the air intake, just as closing the throttle on a steam engine cuts down the steam intake.

The derivation of the ancient word *gun* is interesting. It is probably connected with the stately Gunhilda, name familiar to many in the dear dead days when people had Swedish maids. Both *gunn-r* and *hild-r* mean "war." Even before gunpowder, artillery men gave their missile throwers pet names, of which Gunhilda was a favorite. This compares exactly with Big Bertha, of World War I. (See also BLOW.)

gunny sack. As the word has been traced to India we need not worry about a gypsy word for bag or an Italian word for petticoat. Sanskrit *goni* means sack, one usually made of fibers of Indian jute. In America, *gunny sack* came into common use in Civil War time.

guts. See GUMPTION. PLUCK.

guy. Meaning to kid or razz, this can be traced to Guy Fawkes, ambitious dynamiter. Yet its first use in print, as a slangy verb, seems to have been by Mark Twain, in 1872. "You guys," as an equivalent for "chaps" and not in specific reference to a dressed-up Guy (Fawkes), appears in 1896, and (I suppose) "youse guys"—that too-logical plural—at about the same time.

A "guy-wire" is simply a shortened form of "guide-wire," used for steadying things like poles and tents.

gymkhana. From racket-court to race-course to horse-show, this Anglo-Indian word has not been idle since 1872. Deriving from Persian *ged-khana*, ball house, it borrowed the *gym* of *gymnastics* (from the Greek for "train naked") and came to be applied to various kinds of horse races and finally to an athletic exhibition of a general nature.

gymnastics. See GYMKHANA.

gynecology. See BANSHEE.

gyp. If we are to follow OED we may have to conclude that British gypsies (spelled *gipsies* in England) are more honest than those over here. For Webster derives our slang word *gyp*, cheat, from gypsy, while the British authority lists *gyp*, meaning "treat roughly," as apparently from "gee-up." However, B. & L. (1897) give *gyp*, thief, as from *gipsy*. A "gyp artist" is, of course, a swindler.

The word *gypsy* itself is from *Egyptian*. Their migratory habits account for their being known also as Bohemians.

H

hackney, hack-writer. See GRUB STREET.

had. The expression "She can be had," in the sense of sexual possession, is just a modern version of the old idea implied in "To have and to hold." B. & L. record "can't be had" as meaning "can't be taken in."

haddock. See FINNAN HADDIE.

Hades. Former name of Pluto, god of the dead, in Greek mythology, this was transferred to the land over which he reigned. And when the Revised Version of the Bible came out in 1885, it substituted Hades for Hell in a number of places, not because of squeamishness, but because it better translated the original Greek.

haggle. See HECKLE.

hail fellow well met. This term is often used to describe a good mixer. Stevenson has a 1550 quotation, beating out OED by 31 years, and has an even earlier one foreshadowing the phrase. Swift popularized it.

The exclamation "Well met!" is sometimes used alone to mean "Glad I met you!"

hair. Really serious medical books at one time advised applying to the bite of a mad dog some of the hair of the animal. With equally scientific justification it has been contended that a drink of the same liquor that put you under the table the night before will cure your hangover. An N. & Q. wag says that from being a cure for dog bite it has become a cure for "dog's nose" (described by Dickens as compounded of warm porter, moist sugar, gin, and nutmeg). The expression, "a hair of the dog that bit you," goes back to Heywood (1546).

Jane Austen was one of the first to use in print the "horsey" term—"he never turned a hair." The thought is that the hair of a well-groomed horse will remain smooth and glossy as long as he keeps cool; when he begins to sweat it roughens up.

hair. See BEARD. HIDE AND HAIR. SHORT HAIRS.

halcyon days. The fourteen days at the time of the winter solstice were supposed to be especially calm so that the kingfisher (known in poetry, chiefly, as the halcyon) could lay its eggs on the surface of the sea. Thus, traditionally, a time of happiness and prosperity. The Greek name for the bird, meaning literally "brood on the sea," is akin to *auk*. Politician Roscoe Conkling was at least momentarily forgetful of his etymology when he spoke of a "halcyon and vociferous occasion" ("peaceful and shout-making").

half-licked cub. See CUB.

half-seas over. The literal possibilities are less fascinating than the suggestion that the Dutch expression, *op zee zober*, "over-sea beer," may have fathered the English phrase meaning drunk.

half-sell a duck. See CANARD.

Halifax. For several reasons, "Go to Halifax!" is an unusually appropriate form of polite profanity. In England, Halifax has for centuries been associated with hell because of the long since abolished law authorizing beheading for a minor theft. However, no stigma of this sort attaches to the Nova Scotia city, unless it be a stigma to have suffered one of the most terrific and literally hellish catastrophes of World War I—the explosion of 3,000 tons of TNT in 1917. In any case, it is clear that "Go to Halifax" is just another euphemism like "Oh heck!" and "For crying out loud."

hallmark. Since 1721 this has been used to mean the stamp of genuineness, because the Goldsmith's Company, at their Hall, had an official mark for the gold and silver articles they tested. Anything that bore the hallmark was all right.

ham. In the heyday of American minstrelsy, there was a song called "The Hamfat Man," about a low grade actor. This, plus the similarity to *amateur*, plus the tradition that all seedy actors have been *Hamlets* in better times, sufficiently accounts for the expression "ham actor."

hammer. See HEAD LIKE A HAMMER.

hand. "Give the little girl a great big hand," threadbare entreaty of the cheerleader (or master of ceremonies) at a night club, means "Applaud." OED amusingly misunderstood a reference of the Prince of Wales to *successive* occasions on which he had been given "a hand." He modestly remarked that others had been doing the work and he had been "getting the hands"; OED promptly made a note of "get the hands" as meaning "receive applause," whereas the singular, "get a hand," should be used of a single burst of applause.

hand and glove. "Hand in glove" was an 18th century attempt to rationalize the older phrase, to make it sound more as if it meant "intimate," "inseparable." Either form is correct. The expression was already hackneyed enough, in 1738, to be satirized in Swift's *Polite Conversation*.

handle. See FLY.

hands and feet. See CLOSER IS HE THAN BREATHING.

handsaw. See KNOW A HAWK FROM A HANDSAW.

hand-shaker. See TUFT-HUNTER. CURRY FAVOR.

hand you a line. See LINE.

hang. See LEARN THE ROPES.

hangdog look. Though this has been in use since 1677, it is not yet clear whether it means the inglorious appearance of a dog-executioner, or of one of the executees.

hanged, drawn, and quartered. See DRAWN.

hang out. This is not modern slang, in the sense of "reside," but it is still slang nevertheless. In 1811, the English underworld had it, and by the time of *Pickwick*, the medical students did. In response to Bob Sawyer's question, it will be remembered, Mr. Pickwick stated that "he was at present suspended at the George and Vulture." The phrase is said to come from the custom of hanging out a sign at your residence.

It seems likely that the American "hang out your shingle," in reference to the sign of a lawyer or doctor, goes back to the actual use of a shingle for that purpose in pioneer days.

hangover. While there is considerable evidence that the phenomena accompanying the morning after the night before are not unknown in England, OED fails to recognize the existence of *hangover* except in the sense of "remainder, survival." And that, I submit, is putting it too mildly. (See HAIR.)

happy as a dead hog. See SNUG.

hara kiri. Literally "belly cutting," this is a colloquial and vulgar term seldom used by the Japanese. It does *not* mean "happy dispatch," as the English have been encouraged to believe.

Mencken lists "hari kari" as a name for a drink. Another common misspelling for the good old Japanese custom is *harikiri*.

hard. See FAST ONE.

hard lines. This is now used chiefly as an exclamation equivalent to "Tough luck!" The 1824 quotation in OED indicates popularity among seamen, but the figurative use of *lines* to mean fortune or lot has been traced to the 16th Psalm: "The lines are fallen unto me in pleasant places." Smith's Bible Dictionary admits the possibility of deriving this "lines" from the Jewish measuring rod.

hard tack. This is descriptive of bread or crackers baked hard enough to endure the vicissitudes of weather and rats through a long voyage or army campaign. Apparently from *tackle* (once used colloquially to mean food), the expression borrowed also, on its way to fame, from the strength and endurance of the lowly carpet tack. (See BISCUIT.)

hare. See HOLD WITH THE HARE. MARCH HARE.

harlot. Not until the 15th century did this become definitely feminine. Chaucer uses it of a hired man; but almost without exception, throughout the Romanic languages, it is "a fighting word," ranging in shade of meaning from "glutton" to "hedge-priest." The Italian *arlotto*, to which *harlot* has been traced, is a rogue or vagabond.

harp. Slang for a native of Ireland, this is doubtless an allusion to this musical instrument as the national symbol of the Emerald Isle. Indirectly, perhaps, this nickname was fostered by the gambling propensities of the Irish, as the shilling had a harp on one side, and the call was "harp" instead of "tails."

Harry. Though it is mildly entertaining to try to connect "the Old Harry" with the verb *harry*, to torment, or the adjective *hairy*, there seems to be no other reason for nicknaming the devil thus than the jocular desire to appear on intimate terms with him; hence, the use of the very familiar names Harry, Dick (the dickens), and Nick. The commonness of these names is evidenced by the expression, "Tom, Dick, and Harry," meaning everybody; but I confess I never heard the devil addressed as "Old Tom." Attempts have been made to relate Dick and Nick to Scandinavian *nickers*, water spirits, but without marked success.

hashish. See ASSASSIN.

hat. See DROP.

hatchet. See BURY THE HATCHET.

hatter. See MAD.

haul over the coals. Though illustrations of this in print go back only to about 1800, the idea probably persisted from the medieval ordeal by fire, used in heresy "trials." Today it means, of course, to "bawl out," to reprimand.

haunch. See HENCH.

have an edge on. See EDGE.

have something on the ball. See BALL.

havoc. See CRY HAVOC. HEFT.

hawk. See KNOW A HAWK FROM A HANDSAW.

hawker. See HOCK.

hawk of a buzzard. See SILK PURSE OUT OF A SOW'S EAR.

haywire. The wide-awake new Webster explains that the origin of this slang term, in the sense of "confused, out of order," is in the twisted mass of wire taken from bales of hay. Weseen, even more plausibly, points out that when anything goes to pieces the farmer tries first to mend it with old haywire. It has also been mentioned that live stock can get hopelessly tangled up in the stuff.

A British movie-critic said recently over the air from London that his compatriots were already trying to make a noun of this American adjective.

head like a hammer. B. & L. delve into Yiddish slang to bring us a possible explanation, in the shape of *hammar*, an ass. But why bother, when the well-known density of iron conveys so completely the idea of stupidity?

head over heels. When you stop to think of it, this should be "heels over head." It may originally have been "over head and heels," a translation of *per caputque pedesque* (Catullus).

heart. In addition to being the seat of affection, the heart was sometimes thought of as the seat of intelligence and memory, though it is customary today to make a sharp contrast between the emotional appeal to the heart and the intellectual appeal to the mind. At any rate, to "learn by heart" is exactly equivalent to the verb *record* (Latin *cor*, heart or mind) and the French *se recorder*.

heat. See HUMIDITY.

heave. See HEFT.

heaviest battalions. See GOD IS ON THE SIDE OF THE HEAVIEST BATTALIONS.

heck. See HALIFAX.

heckle. Related to *haggle* and *hook*, this unkempt-sounding word was familiar to the Scotch as meaning to bother or *badger* (q.v.) long before it was adopted by Parliament to meet a long-felt want. By origin, it meant to pluck or pull to pieces, to "tease," as hemp or flax.

hectic. This much-overused word suggests, by derivation, the habitual, slow wasting away of animal tissue in consumption. Thus, though a bit hard to believe, it is related to *scheme*, through the Greek word meaning to have or to "hold out." Of course, it is the related meaning of "feverish" on which we have seized to express a hideously busy time; one wonders how people ever got along without it, before 1922 or so. Kipling experimented with it in 1904, but evidently society did not become hectic-conscious until the exciting days following World War I.

hector. This lower-case word for browbeat or bully has fallen a long way from the exalted Hector, bravest Trojan. The catastrophe happened pretty much all of a sudden, in the second half of the 16th century.

hedge. If you bet 100–10 on a horse, and 90–10 against him, you can't lose; if he wins you make $10, if he loses you break even. This "hedging" of a bet derives presumably from the erecting of a barrier to protect yourself. The figurative sense of backing down a little, taking in your sails, leaving a loop-hole, "trimming"—all figurative senses, in fact—arose about the same time (16th century) as the betting usage. If anything, the "trimming" sense was earlier, which is curious.

A "hedge-priest" was an ignorant vagabond whose home and whose parish was the hedge along the highway. (See HARLOT.)

"Hedge-hopping," in a plane, is flying low over obstacles.

heeby-jeebies. This expressive term includes not only the wide range of animals from striped elephants to kaleidoscopic snakes, but has been extended from the delirium tremens to plain "nerves," corresponding to the "jitters," the "willies," and the "jim-jams." OED says the term derives from an American Indian word for a witch doctor's dance.

heeled. To be well-heeled is, presumably, to have good heels on your shoes, to be the opposite of "run-down"; hence, to be well provided with money. Yet modern slang (probably ephemeral) has "heel" for a cad, a good-for-nothing sponger. The classic Achilles' heel—the only vulnerable spot—is altogether too literary a source for this word "heel." But perhaps *ward-heeler*, a yes-man who does a politician's dirty work, is the proud parent.

heels over head. See HEAD OVER HEELS.

heel-taps. From meaning the layers of a leather heel, this was transferred to describe the dregs at the bottom of a liquor glass, perhaps because of the dirty appearance, or from the notion of adding one more layer to the drinks already inside. There seems to me to be a connection between "Here's *mud* in your eye" (q.v.) and the practically habitual condition of people's heels in the days before rubbers, Fords, and paved roads.

A "heel-tap glass" was one with no standard, so that it could not be set down on the table until it was entirely empty. This is probably the origin of "tumbler" for a table glass.

heft. Formed from *heave*, by analogy, apparently, with *thieve* and *theft*, this can be either a noun meaning "weight" or a verb meaning to lift something for the purpose of judging its weight. Both are considered a bit rustic in this country, and are distinctly dialect forms in England. Webster lists thirty words which are directly akin to it, including these surprising ones: *cop*, *havoc*, *prince*, and *susceptible*.

"Hefty" is a natural slang formation conveying effectively the idea of weight and power.

Helena. See SAINT ELMO'S FIRE.

Hell Gate. Though an effort has been made to derive this from Dutch words (which I have not found) meaning "whirling gut," this narrow passage, with its conflicting currents, where more than 2,000 vessels were wrecked before some millions of dollars were spent in blasting, undoubtedly seemed like the gate of hell to those Dutch mariners of New York. And they had a word for hell, *hel*, and a word for hole or opening, *gat*.

hell is paved with good intentions. This is Dr. Johnson's phraseology, modeled on a remark of George Herbert's, in 1633, though the idea was very much in the air at about that time. The most sensible form describes the *road to hell* as being thus paved.

helper-engine. See COCK-HORSE.

hen. See OLD HEN.

hench. "Hench bone," which is listed by Weseen as slang for the hip bone or thigh, seems to go straight back to Scotch dialect, as "hench" is the way *haunch* is pronounced in Scotland.

"Henchman," never a very polite word for follower or hanger-on, comes from *hengst*, horse, and thus means the same as *groom*. (See BRIDEGROOM.)

here's mud in your eye. See MUD.

hero. The cynical epigram, "No man is a hero to his valet," was given this English form by Samuel Foote, in 1764, but it was floating around France before 1700. Stevenson and Bartlett give Mme. Cornuel most of the credit, but the Prince de Condé and La Bruyère were dallying with the idea at the same time, as Plutarch had, some centuries before. Carlyle and Goethe gave it a sturdy twist when they insisted that a valet who could not appreciate a hero had "a mean valet-soul." *Valet*, by the way, is a near-relative of *varlet* and *vassal*.

The drug *heroin* received its name from the tendency it has to inflate the ego of its tragic victim.

heroes. See THIN RED LINE OF 'EROES.

heroin. See HERO.

heronshaw. See KNOW A HAWK FROM A HANDSAW.

herring. See RED.

he who runs may read. See RUN.

Hickory. See OLD HICKORY.

hide. See HUDDLE.

hide and hair. Used more often in the negative, "neither hide nor hair," the phrase itself is not very old (1857) but the suggestion goes back farther than that. The source of the metaphor seems to be that it must be a very hungry animal (probably having an admixture of goat in his lineage) that will devour the hide and hair of his victim. A similar phrase, equally alliterative but less popular, is "neither hoof nor horn."

highball. Society knows this as a long drink, usually whisky, and water (or other mixer). Why the "ball," I don't know.

Railroad men use the term in two loosely related ways: one, the "go ahead" signal from the rear, often acknowledged by two toots of the whistle; the other, the "all clear" signal of the automatic block system. Christopher Morley found that the fireman of the Broadway Limited used "Highball" in this second sense until well out of Chicago, when he changed his shout to "Clear."

highfalutin. The fact that this can be spelled six different ways indicates the uncertainty as to its derivation. Dutch *verlooten* and Yiddish *hifelufelem* have been invoked, as well as English *high-flighting*, *-fluting*, *-flying*, and *-flown*. The best bet, I think, is that it is simply a sonorous and elaborate mispronunciation of one of the latter group; this seems the more plausible because its precise meaning is "high-flown."

high-hat. See PUT ON THE DOG.

highwayman. See FOOTPAD.

hill. See COLYUMIST.

hillbilly. This nickname for the backwoods mountaineers has been in print since 1904, but people became conscious of them in the 1930's through the magic of radio. The "billy" is simply derived from the name Billy, in the abstract sense of a "fellow"; somewhat as the panhandler or the gyp artist with cheap furs or tires to sell hails you as "Buddy" or "Mac."

hinge. See CARDINAL.

hip. See HUMP.

hipped. If this were spelled, as perhaps it should be, "hypped," there would be less likelihood of people's connecting it, in the sense of "sore" or depressed, with being smitten "hip and thigh" or being had "by the hip." Steele, who used it in the *Spectator* in 1712, obviously thought of it as stemming from *hypochondria*, the "blue" disease of morbidly imaginative people. The disease was supposed to have its headquarters in the abdomen, the *hypochondros*, i.e., "below the cartilage of the breast-bone"; *chondros* was, properly, a grain, and thus managed to become also the ancestor of *grind*. Apparently from the idea of "crazy," there has developed in America the variation, to be "hipped on" somebody or something, meaning "crazy about," "bitten with."

hippopotamus. See NIX.

his nibs. See NIBS.

hit bottom. See FROST.

hitch-hiker. See THUMB.

hit the dirt. To a railroader who sees a head-on collision inevitable, this can mean only one thing: "Jump!" In baseball it is the order to slide into a base, the purpose being twofold: that you may stop when you get to the bag, and that you may be more difficult to tag with the ball than if you come in standing up. Phonetically, the explosives of "hit the dirt" are beyond all doubt preferable, under the circumstances, to the liquids of "slide." It should be said, perhaps, that the average American is not aware of the close association, by derivation, between dirt and excrement. We even have the jocular phrase, "clean dirt." (See SLIDE, KELLY, SLIDE.)

hitting on all six. See BALL. CLICK.

hoax. See HOCUS POCUS.

hobgoblin. The *hob* of *hobgoblin* is, like Bob, short for Robert or Robin (compare Robin Goodfellow, another name for the supernatural "Puck"). A similar tendency to give human nicknames to one's every-day companions in the spirit or animal world may be seen in Tom Tit, Jack Ass, and Jenny Wren. (See CONSISTENCY IS A JEWEL. GOBLIN.)

hobnob. There is a wide gap between the "give it or take it" sense, as Shakespeare defined it, and the cozy *tête à tête* before the fire. The former is reached directly from the source, "hab, nab," "have, not-have," "take it or leave it." The second usage, which is more familiar, may be from the "give and take" of drinking together, though Brewer's unsupported conjecture of something hot on the *hob* or the *nob* (a little round table) is very appealing. "Hob and nob," as a verb, is found in Tennyson: "hob and nob with brother Death." This *hob* is apparently unrelated to *hobgoblin* and *play hob*.

hobo. One of the too few etymological suggestions made in Weseen's valuable dictionary of slang relates this with *hoe-boy*, a migratory farm laborer. While Webster and OED refuse to guess at its source, they both recognize the "wandering workman" in the early *hobo*, and point out that he is rapidly losing this amateur standing and becoming a professional tramp whose distaste for work is a matter of principle. Since 1891, these vagrant folk have accepted the name *hobo* and even worn it as a badge of distinction.

Hobson-Jobson. This has so often been given as an example of the substitution of familiar words, unrelated in meaning, for a foreign term, that the procedure is sometimes referred to as the "law of Hobson-Jobson"; and the best-known book on Anglo-Indian expressions was ingeniously entitled *Hobson-Jobson.* The names *Hodge* and *Jobson* were traditionally rustic English surnames, and it may be that "Hodge and Jobson" was first used to represent the reiterated exclamation of Mohammedans on parade, "*Ya Hasan, ya Husayn*" (Hasan and Husayn were grandsons of Mohammed), and later became "Hobson" by reduplication. Another example of this "law" is *forlorn hope* (q.v.).

Hobson's choice. OED and Stevenson have both resigned themselves to acceptance of the Tobias Hobson story; he was a livery stable man (celebrated by Milton) who allowed no choice of horses—you took the horse due to go next. Yet it is a mysterious fact, pointed out by Weekley, that a merchant living in Japan used "Hodgson's choice" fourteen years before the carrier died and became legendary. Anyway, we know that the expression is not a slap at the kisses showered on Lieutenant Hobson after his *Merrimac* exploit.

hock. The slang sense of "prison" seems to have preceded that of "pawn," and perhaps suggested it, though no agreement has been reached. Webster finds some connection with a Dutch word for "nook," through *hawker*, a peddler, whereas others are much more interested in Dutch words of the "hook" family; for instance, *hok*, thief slang for credit or debt. Then there is an old card game, known as "hock" (perhaps from Latin *hoc*) in which there are certain privileged cards to which you can attribute any value you please—and that's the very backbone of the pawnshop industry. In short, nobody knows why "in hock" means "out of circulation."

hockey. At some time or other, this word has meant, in England, "harvest-home." In this sense, it is entirely unknown in America. The reason for its application to the rough-and-tumble game (ice or field) is obscure. Webster's guess is that it goes back to *hoquet*, shepherd's crook, from Middle Dutch *hoek*, hook.

hocus pocus. The existence of a 17th century magician named Ochus Bochus has not been proved. Nor has a connection been established with *hoc est corpus*, phrase used in the Mass. An early conjuror had a string of mock Latin with which he distracted his audience while he worked his tricks: *Hocus pocus, tontus talontus, vade, celeriter jubeo*. Yet here is a striking fact that must be accounted for before we abandon entirely the *hoc est corpus* theory: the "hocus pocus" formula familiar to our children today is "Hocus pocus dominocus," which looks strangely like a throw-back to a *hoc est corpus Domini*, "this is the body of the Lord."

A common word probably derived from *hocus pocus* is *hoax*, a trick; another is *hocus*, to drug someone's liquor. Perhaps, too, the hokey-pokey man (ice-cream vendor) comes honestly by the name, the thought being that one never quite knows what goes into cheap ice cream. Joaquin Miller used "hokee-pokee" of an American Indian dance.

hodgepodge. The stew from which the figurative meaning of "confused medley" comes is evidently the same as the French *hochepot* and Dutch *hutspot*. The spelling of the English variant, *hotchpotch*, may have been influenced by English dialect *hotch*, shake (see HOOTCHY-KOOTCHY). *Olla podrida*, the Spanish equivalent, has the least inviting name of all; it means "putrid pot," an exact translation of the French *pot pourri*.

hog. "Go the whole hog" means "go the limit." As is natural, both expressions have been used as euphemisms for the sex act; but in ordinary usage, as meaning "do something thoroughly," there is little likelihood of their being misunderstood. While Stevenson looks with favor on the theory that the Irish nickname, "hog," for a shilling may have been the source (i.e., "spend the whole shilling"), OED prefers the story about the pious but hungry Mohammedans, who had been ordered by their leader not to eat some unspecified part of a pig; having no way of determining which part was intended, they ate the whole business.

To "hog-tie" is to tie an animal by three legs. Hence, figuratively, to hamper or cripple a person or movement.

hog. See ROOT.

hoi polloi. Theoretically it enrolls you as a member of *hoi polloi* if you say "the hoi polloi," i.e., "the *the* common people." Every author quoted in the OED Supplement, however, including Dryden and Byron, uses the superfluous *the.*

hoist with his own petard. Hamlet looks forward to the sport of having the engineer blown up with his own explosive, as in mining an enemy fort. *Petard* derives from French *péter*, to break wind.

hoity toity. This reduplicated exclamation is from *hoyden* and, back of that, from *hoit*, "to romp riotously." Originating before 1700, it is what our grandmothers said when our mothers did something tomboyish. The note of patronizing reproof, plus the similarity with *haughty*, gave to the adjective form of the phrase the meaning of "high-hat," "stuck-up." Like *bugaboo* (q.v.), *hoity-toity* has been the innocent victim of a grave charge that it was originally a Scotch or Irish war-cry, perhaps in imitation of a trumpet.

hokey-pokey man. See HOCUS POCUS.

hokum. A happy combination of *hocus* and *bunkum*, this has been in print only since about 1920. Weseen quotes Percy W. White to the effect that it is an old gag, found by experience to be sure-fire. It is usually sentimental, melodramatic, not true to life—and we lap it up.

hold a candle. See CANDLE.

hold everything. A sort of descendant, and intensive form, of "hold your horses," this is rather a cheery and friendly admonition to wait a bit, or to "hold the fort."

hold with the hare and run (or hunt) with the hounds. In Heywood (1562) we find the proverb in this approximate form. But other early instances reverse the sense, though everything comes out much the same in the end—namely, that some people try to cheer for both sides. The above form strikes me as better; it would seem more natural for a man to hunt with the hounds while feeling an academic sympathy for the hare, than to run with the terrified hare, hoping all the time that the hounds would catch him and his little friend.

hole. See ACE IN THE HOLE.

hollow. "To beat all hollow" cannot be explained, apparently, on any other ground than that it means "to beat wholly" and therefore must be derived from "wholly." OED says its origin "has excited much conjecture," but fails to offer any for us to try our teeth on.

holy deadlock. This ingenious, if somewhat disillusioned, description of marriage was used in 1934 by A. P. Herbert as a title for a novel. As political slang for a complete tie-up because of conflicting views, *deadlock* dates back only to 1888, but a primitive form of lock without spring-catch was known by that name, before 1800. The idea of associating marriage with some sort of lock is of course as old as the word *wedlock*—which isn't a lock at all, but is from *lac*, a gift. Byron's contribution was, "And wedlock and a padlock mean the same."

Holy Roman Empire. H. G. Wells, in his *Outline of History*, gave perhaps the most effective description of this astonishing set-up, which was neither Holy, nor Roman, nor an Empire. (See GUINEA-PIG.) "For eleven centuries," he says, "Europe was like a busy factory owned by a somnambulist, who is sometimes quite unimportant and sometimes disastrously in the way. . . . The Roman Empire staggers, sprawls, is thrust off the stage, and reappears."

holystone. The likeliest way of accounting for the name of the soft sandstone used for scrubbing decks is that it is porous, "full of holes." Another guess is that it is connected with polishing up the ship in honor of Sunday. The dictionaries hesitate to commit themselves.

hombre. In the words of Mencken, "the common speech of the Southwest is heavy with debased Spanish." Though there is nothing particularly debased about this word for "man," it is generally used, Webster says, jocularly or contemptuously. "Tough hombre" is understood wherever American is spoken.

home. "We won't get home until morning" was the song the Pickwickians sang towards the end of the party at which Mr. Snodgrass imbibed too much "salmon." Stevenson has found the song in a slightly earlier play by John Buckstone.

Homeric laughter. This is the famous *asbestos* laugh (literally, "inextinguishable") of the gods, in the *Iliad* and the *Odyssey*. Strange, isn't it, that the material which to us means "unburnable" should mean in Greek "unextinguishable"? I suppose one might say that of course you can't extinguish anything that you can't set fire to first, but that unquestionably smells like a quibble.

honeyfogle. Thornton thinks this is the same word as *hornswoggle* (not to mention such minor variations as *honeyfackle* and *honeyfuggle*). In any case they all mean the same: to cheat by cajolery (the "line" of the confidence man). The smoothness and sweetness of honey sufficiently account for the first half, without bringing in the old identity, by rhyming slang, of *honey* with *money*. *Fogle* presents a problem, however. Dickens knew it as thieves' cant for pocket handkerchief (coming, possibly, from Italian *foglia*, a piece of cloth, though how the cockney pickpockets discovered there was a *g* in that Italian word is beyond me). Job Trotter (*Pickwick Papers*) was a honeyfogler if there ever was one, and he cried into his handkerchief a good bit. A clue?

honeymoon. This may have originated in the Scandinavian custom of drinking honeyed wine during that first month of married bliss, but evidence is lacking. The "honey" part may mean just "sweet," while the "moon" element, according to OED, refers not so much to the period of one month as to the supposed waning of love after the first flush of happiness.

honks. See GOOSE.

honky-tonk. Recent slang for a cheap song-and-dance joint, this is said by our leading British authority to be negro slang, and by our American to be, perhaps, from English dialect *honk*, to idle about. That is what is known, technically, as passing the *buck* (q.v.) The rhyming character of it indicates reduplication (cf. *hootchy-kootchy*).

honor. See ALL IS LOST SAVE HONOR.

honors are easy. Why our whist-playing ancestors chose to say "easy" when they meant "even" is not for me to explain. OED found that they did, in 1884, and Webster confirms this by listing "easy aces" and "easy honors" in that sense. But OED Supplement implies that since 1920 it has been correct—as well as sensible—to say "honors are even."

hoodlum. B. & L.'s guess that this California word is either Spanish or pidgin English is perhaps no worse than the story that a notorious thug's name was Muldoon, which, spelled backward, became "Noodlum"; and this by association with *hooligan* soon gave birth to *hoodlum*. The supposed derivation of *Hooligan* (q.v.) would seem to strengthen the possibility that another Hibernian surname may have figured in the development of the new word. However, Mathews (1951) says it is probably from Bavarian *hodalum*.

hoodoo. This and its twin, *voodoo*, appeared in print in 1880–1881. The negro slaves brought *vodu* from Africa, and George W. Cable, in *The Grandissimes*, popularized it as *voodoo*. Almost immediately, perhaps through hearing people refer to "the rites of voodoo," Americans corrupted it to *hoodoo*. And from the deadly seriousness that surrounded those rites there has emerged the somewhat frivolous and sporty use of *hoodoo* in the sense of bad-luck bringer or "jinx." For either, "black magic" makes an appropriate, if not too obvious, synonym.

hoodwink. As long ago as 1560, this meant "to blindfold," as in the game of "blindmanbuf" or "hoodman blind"—both very old names for our Blind Man's Buff. From "blindfold," the transition to "cheat, deceive" was easy. (See WOOL.)

hoofer. In the sense of a dancer, especially a clog or tap dancer, this has been in print only since 1928. But as one who travels on foot, it is probably earlier, being reminiscent of old slang, "pad the hoof." (See FOOTPAD.)

hoof nor horn. See HIDE AND HAIR.

hookey. There seems to be little or no connection between "play hookey" and the Victorian slang expression "hookey Walker" (or just "Walker!" as used in *The Christmas Carol*) indicating incredulity. The linking of "hook" with the idea of unceremonious departure or of being AWOL (absent without leave) is probably no harder to explain than "beat," in the term "Beat it." The latter may derive from "beat a retreat"—the former from "hooking a ride" (i.e., attaching oneself to a passing vehicle).

While "Hookey Walker" may well be a memorial to some eagle-nosed chap of that name who was addicted to telling stories nobody believed, the modern dictionaries are cautious about identifying him in any more definite way than this. Earlier writers, uninhibited, assert with confidence that he was one John Walker.

hook, line, and sinker. See GULL.

hook or crook. Implying "by fair means or foul," "by hook or by crook" has probably elicited more N. & Q. letters than any other single phrase. Most of the proposed sources, such as the lawyers Hook and Croke, and the two landmarks that were to be used by the pilots of a hostile fleet in the capture of Waterford harbor—are, as OED points out, chronologically out of the question. The same authority is also very cautious about lending its support to the only one that holds water: namely, that according to the ancient laws of the New Forest, peasants were entitled to carry away for firewood whatever dead branches they could break off "by hook or by crook."

hooligan. Again, OED hesitates to pin this unpleasant name too definitely on anybody in the immediate neighborhood. But everybody else, including Webster, seems to think that there was a rowdy Irish family of that name that lived in Southwark, London, in the 1890's. The fact that there was a music hall song, at about that time, celebrating the exploits of such a family neither proves nor disproves its existence. As for the conjecture of a "Hooley's gang," it is unlikely that this would so quickly have been corrupted into a repetitious "Hooligan gang," phrase found in police reports of 1898. (See HOODLUM.)

hoosegow. This disreputable-appearing word (rhyming with "snooze-how") is a direct descendant of one of the noblest Romans of them all: *judicatum*. It comes from the Mexican via the Spanish, *juzgado*, court. There is something reassuring in the revelation that "court" has come to mean "jail." (See CALABOOSE.)

hoosier. The origin of this nickname for a native of Indiana has been lost. B. & L. say that they remember hearing *hoosieroon* as early as 1834, and deduce from that form that the word may have been

Spanish. But Thornton and OED place "hoosier" quotations earlier than those giving "hoosieroon." The two leading guesses are the Husher theory (the bully who "hushed" his opponents) and the "Who's yere?" theory (based on the belief that when someone knocked at his door the Indianian would thus inquire who it was). Or it may be from Cumberland dialect, *hoozer*, anything unusually large (Mathews).

hoot. "I don't give a hoot"—or, more elaborately, "I don't give two hoots in Hades"—is just another euphemism for "I don't give a damn." B. & L. list a slang word, *hooter*, to mean "iota"; but it is hardly necessary for us to go beyond the fact that a hoot has always signified contempt.

hootch. Fortunately the origin of this word for home-distilled liquor (generally of very questionable quality) has apparently been established before it was lost in alcoholic obscurity. The Hutsnuwu, Tlingit Indians of Alaska, developed a potent poison which came to be called, after their name, "hoochinoo" and then "hootch." It was made, we are told, with yeast, flour, and either sugar or molasses.

hootchy-kootchy. "Origin unascertained," says OED. But Webster experiments with Eng. dialect, *hotch*, to shake, and *couch out* (like Quiller-Couch, pronounced "cootch," for purposes of this etymology), meaning to protrude. It seems agreed, anyway, that the Oriental-sounding name for this Turkish muscle dance (which almost got Beatrice Lillie into trouble, when she exclaimed over our carefully censored air-waves that she had "no stomach for that kind of thing") is not Oriental at all.

hope. See FORLORN.

Hopkins log. In preparing *Familiar Quotations*, a handsome and authoritative little volume, the library staff at Wesleyan University did Burton Stevenson a minor injustice: they quote his *misquotation*, on page 2069, ascribing the famous saying to Mark himself rather than to James A. Garfield, and appear to have overlooked the entry on page 530 where Stevenson brings in President Garfield, as he should have, though he rather spoils it by saying that "the tradition has never been verified" that Garfield made any such remark at any alumni dinner in 1872. Which is true, inasmuch as the historic banquet at Delmonico's took place on Dec. 28, 1871, as the Wesleyan book points out. Washington Gladden, author of the immortal "O Master, Let Me Walk with Thee," was there, and his version is the one adopted by Wesleyan: "A pine bench, with Mark Hopkins at one end of it and me at the other, is a good enough college for me." However, the learned librarians recognize the advantages in the variation which starts out, "Give me a log hut, with only a simple bench. . . ."—because it contains the *log* motif. Professor T. C. Smith, in his *Life and Letters of James Abram Garfield*, makes one thing abundantly clear, and that is that Garfield never visualized anybody sitting on a log with Mark Hopkins for four years.

horn. Careful research has convinced me that "come out at the little end of the horn" has no connection whatever with "the music goes round and round," in the words of the old song. For one thing, the music comes out at the big end. For another, the first phrase is Elizabethan. The thought is "to be swindled," and the picture seems to be that of a man being pushed through the Horn of Plenty from the wrong end.

hornpipe. See PIPE DOWN.

hornswoggle. See HONEYFOGLE.

horse. A dicing expression for an even score is "horse and horse" (or "hoss and hoss"). It may be related to "neck and neck." And a derivative may be "a horse apiece," meaning a score of 1–1.

To "horse around," as Weseen says, means to act foolish. We can derive it, perhaps, from "horse-play" (rough-and-tumble fun), if we remember that by the sophisticated college student of today boisterous fooling is frowned on—except in sacred precincts such as the gym and the fraternity "goat-room."

A "horse-laugh" is a scornful one approaching in volume the neigh of a lusty horse.

B. & L.'s explanation, a rather unusual one, of the much discussed "good luck" qualities of the *horseshoe* is that it was originally taken as a symbol of fertility because of its sketchy resemblance to the vulva. (See CART BEFORE THE HORSE. COCK-HORSE. DARK HORSE. GIFT HORSE. SWAP HORSES IN THE MIDDLE OF THE STREAM.)

horseback. See ANGEL.

horse-trader. See COZEN.

host. "Mine host," *hostility*, *hospitality*, and the *host* (consecrated bread) used in the Mass all come, apparently, from Latin *hostis*, enemy. The "enemy" softened to "stranger"; then the idea of "hospitality" crept in. Along a different track, *hostis* found its way to *hostia*, a sheep used as a victim for sacrifice, and thus arrived at *host*, the symbol of Christ's sacrifice. Webster says that the basic idea in both *hostia* and *host* is "food." The monstrance (akin to *demonstrate*) is the *transparent* vessel in which the sacred wafer is carried.

hot. Since about 1930, this adjective has acquired great popularity in two almost contradictory senses. The first is complimentary, meaning excitingly attractive, and seems to be contemporary with the vogue of "hot music," rowdy and thrilling. "Not so hot" is still a common description of something not altogether successful. The second is crook slang for stolen goods easily identifiable. For instance, the Lindbergh ransom bills were "hot money," especially after the gold notes had been called in. A transferred use is that in "hot oil," meaning oil illegally produced in defiance of state efforts to prevent over-production. (See DROP.)

hot air. See SHOOT THE BULL.

hot and bothered. See BUTTER WON'T MELT IN HER MOUTH.

hot and cold. See BLOW.

hot cha. The Cantonese word for tea is *cha* (the British still call it that occasionally). The British also have a dialect word *hotch*, meaning shake or joggle (perhaps related to *hootchy-kootchy*). All of which has, I think, no connection with the Broadway elaboration of "Ha!" as hurled down the extended nose of Mr. Durante. I propose the Spanish word for girl, *muchacha*, as a plausible source. The Spanish equivalent of "What a girl!" reiterated in tribute to some sexy Mexican dancer comes not very far from "hot cha" in either sound or meaning.

hotchpotch. See HODGEPODGE.

hot enough for you. See HUMIDITY.

hounds. See HOLD WITH THE HARE.

house. See BRING DOWN THE HOUSE. DRESS.

housewife. See HUSSY.

howdy-do. Meaning "noisy dispute" or "bad fix," the phrase "a great howdy-do" undoubtedly derives from "how do you do?" but it is hard to see why. Surely the arrival, at the scene of action, of a number of people polite enough to greet each other in this way would not indicate unusual tension. At the same time, anyone who has given a large party knows that a couple of dozen "howdy-dos," mixed with an equal number of cocktails, will make as much noise as a high-school fire drill.

hoyden. See HOITY TOITY.

huddle. This American football term—transferred, slangily, to mean a private conference—had not reached OED by 1933; "crowded together in hurried confusion" does not, of course, describe adequately the systematic and formidable appearance of eleven mighty men of valor crouching together to learn where next the lightning is to strike. In a very few years the system has, I believe, entirely replaced the old method of shouting the signals for all to hear, partly because the enemy generally caught on, and partly because your own side, in the heat of battle or the haze of semi-consciousness, occasionally didn't. However, OED's theory that *huddle* may be akin to *hide* fits in admirably with the purpose of the football huddle. The first dim hint for the huddle, by the way, may have come from the primitive circle of players formed about one of their number who had split his pants and had to put on a new pair.

hullaballoo. See HURLY-BURLY.

humble pie. The eccentric British *h* has had a hand in the evolution of "humble pie" from a homely but thoroughly edible dish made of the "umbles" (from Latin *lumbulus*, little loins), the heart, liver and entrails of the stag. The fact that the umble pie was served to the less important members of the household led to "eat humble pie" as a punning allusion to a humiliating drop in the social scale.

humbug. The origin of this word for a fraud is not known; it may be from Irish *uim bog*, soft copper (used in debasing the coinage).

humerus. See FUNNY BONE.

humidity. With the advent of air-conditioning, we are becoming increasingly aware of the importance of a high percentage of moisture in the air we breathe. It is not to be hoped, however, that this will keep people from saying, "It's not the heat, it's the humidity," which has always been, and probably always will be, the answer to "Is it hot enough for you?" Which reminds me of a characteristically British joke played by the *Newcastle Weekly*, and reminiscent of Mr. Pickwick's discovery of the "Bill Stumps" inscription: somebody wrote in, in all innocence, apparently, to ask the translation of this name of a tavern in Wales—"by the sign of Yssthahdt Hhoty Nuffohrue." The hoax evoked a number of learned suggestions.

humor. This has not always specifically referred to the laugh industry. By derivation it means something wet. According to ancient medical theory, there were four principal humors or bodily fluids: phlegm, blood, choler, and black bile (note the origins of *phlegmatic*, *choleric*, and *bilious*). Somewhat as endocrinologists talk of achieving a proper balance among the glands, early physicians strove to get the right mixture of the humors. Evidently from the frequent "imbalance," *humorous* came to mean "eccentric" (off-center), "moody," and finally "funny."

hump. Though OED lists "hump yourself" as from 1906, Partridge found it at Shrewsbury School in 1880, in the sense of "get going," hurry. Evidently it did not have the sexual connotation of plain *hump*. OED relates it to the aggressive arching of an angry cat's back, and thus to the phrase "get your back up." Though "hump yourself" does not mean "get angry," the explanation will do till we find a better one. The word *hump*, itself, is akin to *hip* and to *cymbal*, if that helps any.

The *hump* in a railroad yard is the artificial hill over which an engine slowly pushes a string of uncoupled freight cars which then roll down individually to the various sidetracks where trains for different sections of the country are being made up.

hundred years. See FIRST HUNDRED YEARS ARE THE HARDEST.

hunky-dory. "Hunky" has meant "O.K." for some time (Artemus Ward, 1861)—but why? A "hunks" (from Danish *hundsk*, stingy, doggish) is a miser; a "Hunker" a fogy; a "hunky" a Bohunk (i.e., Bohemian + Hungarian); and "on his hunkers" (haunches) means "desperate." On the other hand, "hunk" is said to be a word for "home" or "goal" in a game. As for *dory*, it might have some sort of rhyming association with *glory*; or the allusion may be to the famous seaworthiness of the fisherman's dory.

Looking now at the whole word (just as if this were a charade), I have the audacity to repeat a suggestion made in 1876 in N. & Q., that American or British sailors may have picked up the expression in Japan, because the principal street of Yokohama is Huncho-dori Street. Murray's Handbook of Japan (1913) still lists "Honcho-dori" as one of the important streets of that city. With even a small cargo of rice wine aboard, a seafaring man might find difficulty navigating some of the back streets. But on "Main Street" everything would be hunky-dory.

hunter. See LION HUNTER.

hunt with the hounds. See HOLD WITH THE HARE.

hurly-burly. Known from about 1540, and immortalized by the *Macbeth* witches, this word for "mob-scene" or noisy disturbance is apparently imitative of the howling of the wind, the *burly* being simply a reduplication of the original *hurly*. OED throws some doubt on Walsh's statement that it is cognate with *hullabaloo*, the Irish name for the *coronach*, the wailing at funerals. An interesting French parallel to this Irish word, which has come to mean just plain noise, is the *hurluberlu* found in Rabelais.

hussar. See CORSAIR.

hussy. Somehow the word "wife" keeps its tender beauty, for as often as one man encounters bitter disillusionment in marriage, another finds "the pearl of great price"—and a half-dozen more confidently expect to. But "housewife" is something else again. The housekeeping of the recent bride is seldom anything to write home about; and the over-meticulous housewife is capable of making everybody miserable. Thus, the word has, as Weekley makes clear, been long associated with unpleasant adjectives. And by 1800 it became so common to call a woman an impudent, idle, worthless *housewife*, that the noun had to be shortened to *hussy* to save time; or, more charitably, to preserve whatever notion of cleanliness and comfort there may have clung about the older word.

hustler. See RUSTLER.

hypochondria. See HIPPED.

hysteria. The old name for this was "mother-sick" or "fits of the mother"; but it did not imply, as you might think, that the victim was working herself up to the dread announcement, "I'm going home to mother's." Rather it was connected with the old belief (which arose because women were more subject to hysteria than men) that it was primarily a uterine disorder—a belief which was enshrined in the very word *hysteria*, derived from the Greek word for womb. The Germans used to call the complaint, similarly, *Mutterweh*, "mother woe," but have now borrowed the Greek root.

I

ice. See BAG. CUT.

I do not like thee, Dr. Fell. See DOCTOR FELL.

if there were no God, it would be necessary to invent Him. See SCRAP OF PAPER.

if the worse comes to the worst. See WORSE TO THE WORST.

if you don't like it, you can lump it. See LUMP.

I. H. S. To the unbounded admiration of Mrs. Winthrop, Silas Marner was able to read these letters that she had put on her lard-cakes, but he was as unable as she to interpret them. If he had expressed an opinion it would almost surely have been wrong, because the three commonest explanations, *Iesus Hominum Salvator*, *In Hac Salus*, and *In Hoc Signo*, are all erroneous. They mean, respectively, "Jesus, Saviour of Men," "In this (cross), salvation," and "In this sign (conquer)." The correct interpretation is that they were a Greek abbreviation of the name Jesus. This name, by a sort of play on words, was responsible for the adoption, by the early Christians, of the fish (Greek *ichthus*) as their secret symbol, though it was ordinarily thought of, in classical times, as signifying fertility. By a sort of acrostic, the Christians took ICHTHUS to mean the Greek equivalent of "Jesus Christ, Son of God, Savior."

ilk. "Of that ilk" is not equivalent to "of that kidney," meaning "that kind of person." *Ilk* is simply the word for "same." "McGregor of that ilk" is just "McGregor of McGregor," referring usually either to clan or place. The further extension of the phrase to mean "of that sort" is looked on with disfavor.

I'll bite. See BITE.

image. See SPIT AND IMAGE.

I'm from Missouri. See MISSOURI.

in camera. See COMRADE.

inch. See ELL.

incunabula. This belongs to the jargon of rare-book collectors. Meaning "swaddling clothes" first, then "cradle," it now refers to books printed before 1500. OED's first quotation for it, dated 1861, explains that it is "the name the Germans give" to those early books. They are sometimes called "cradle-books."

Indian. "Indian file" is another way of saying single file or, in the American infantry, "column of files," a file consisting of a front-rank man and the one directly behind him. Crowell says, plausibly, that the savages concealed their numbers and even, if they were lucky, the fact of their having passed along a certain trail, by stepping in the footprints of the man ahead, and detailing the last man to obliterate them behind him. He must have had long arms and a rubber backbone, to keep up with the procession.

As if poor Lo (a nickname derived amusingly from "Lo, the poor Indian!" in Pope's *Essay on Man*) had not suffered enough at our hands, someone devised the term "Indian giver" to indicate a person who expects to have his gift, or an equivalent, returned to him. In fact, Bartlett says in so many words that "when an Indian gives anything," he has that expectation. Granting the truth of the generalization, which is probably (like all generalizations—including, as is frequently said, this one) false, we can estimate the superiority of our civilization by the care with which we pay our social debts and give Christmas presents to those who do the same for us. In visiting a Chinese home, on the other hand, it is even risky for you to admire a precious possession, as the owner may insist on your accepting it as a present.

No one knows just why the Indians are given credit for the short period of mild and sunny weather called "Indian summer." In England the same phenomenon has been given the names of various saints. Several authorities refer to the haze or smoke on the horizon as being characteristic, but make no effort to account for it. As a native of northern Wisconsin, I venture to record the fact that early autumn, especially if it is hot and dry, is *par excellence* the forest-fire season.

Indian corn. See MAIZE.

inexactitude. See INNOCUOUS DESUETUDE.

infanticipate. As this may pass out of circulation before the more dignified lexicographers get around to it, it should perhaps be recorded as a portmanteau word coined by Walter Winchell, who by constant use wore out all the other ways of saying "expect a baby," and had to invent a shiny new one. A somewhat similar play on words is the French *entrer dans l'infanterie*, listed by B. & L. (1897).

infantry. The Infanta of Spain is no longer believed to have had anything to do with the origin of *infantry*. It comes to us through the French from the Italian word meaning boy, servant, and finally foot-soldier. This invidious distinction between cavalry and infantry resulted, Weekley says, from the proved veterans' being given horses while the young recruits had to walk.

infection. See CONTAGION.

infinite capacity. See GENIUS.

ingenious. See GIN.

inkling. Almost nothing is known about this word except that it does not come from *ink*. Its immediate parent was *inclen*, to hint, and there was an Anglo-Saxon *inca*, a scruple or doubt. An old use of *inkle* to mean "whisper" ("She inkled in her daughter's ear") suggests that the origin may have been partially imitative, by analogy with *trickle* and *sprinkle*. The liquids of *inkle* make it an easy word to whisper. There is also an *inkle* meaning a linen tape, about which we again have only the negative information that it is not connected with *inkling*.

in lavender. See LAVENDER.

in limbo. See LIMBO.

innocent. See INNOCUOUS DESUETUDE.

innocuous desuetude. Like "terminological inexactitude" (used by Winston Churchill in 1906, in reference to the accuracy of the word "slavery" as applied to Chinese labor in South Africa), this expression is famous as a sesquipedalian substitute (literally, "a foot and a half long") for a short and ugly word. It means about the same as the "junk-pile" when used to describe a law or a custom long disregarded. Grover Cleveland said that he thought these expensive looking words "would please the Western taxpayers." *Innocuous* (a favorite word of Scotch lawyers, according to OED) comes, like *innocent*, from Latin *nocere*, to hurt. "Terminological inexactitude" is easier to understand. In Parliament it is tantamount to "lie," just as in diplomacy "unfriendly act" used to mean war.

inside dope. See LOWDOWN.

insinuendo. See PORTMANTEAU WORD.

insult. See JUMP.

intentions. See HELL IS PAVED WITH GOOD INTENTIONS.

intestinal fortitude. See PLUCK.

in the air. See CASTLE IN SPAIN.

in the bag. See BAG.

in the buff. See BUFF.

in the cards. See CARD.

in the doldrums. See DOLDRUMS.

in the limelight. See SPOTLIGHT.

in the pink. See PINK.

in the spotlight. See SPOTLIGHT.

in the swim. See SWIM.

intrepid aviator. See CLICHÉ.

invent God. See SCRAP OF PAPER.

Irish bull. See SHOOT THE BULL.

iron. "The iron entered into his soul" perpetuates a mistake made in the Vulgate, the only Latin version of the Bible which the Roman Catholic church considers authentic. The Hebrew was, literally, "his soul entered into the iron," translated in the Revised Standard Version (1952) as "his neck was put in a collar of iron" (Psalm 105:18). The misquotation was given great currency through the 1539 Bible, but credit for its metaphorical use is assigned by E.P. to Sterne, 1768. In the form, "the iron entered into his soul," the mistranslation is still preserved in the Episcopal prayer book, edition of 1929, and in Msgr. Knox's Old Testament in English (1950).

"Too many irons in the fire" apparently derives from the heating of laundry irons and the danger either of damaging one by leaving it in too long, or of finding that those around the edges are not so hot. The latter seems to fit in better with the metaphorical sense of having too many activities, "biting off more than you can chew," and is the form preferred by E.P., as a Scotch proverb of the 17th century. Beaumont & Fletcher used "having two irons in the fire" as equivalent to "having two strings to one's bow," but this did not catch on in any big way.

iron. See PIG IRON.

is it hot enough for you? See HUMIDITY.

it. Though OED gives Elinor Glyn the credit (1927) of being the first to use, in print, "it" for "sex appeal," Stevenson has found it in Kipling's *Mrs. Bathurst*, in 1904: "'Tisn't beauty, so to speak, nor good talk necessarily. It's just It. Some women'll stay in a man's memory if they once walked down a street."

As used in games, to mean the one that has to do most of the work, "it" was known in 1888.

itching palm. See GREASE.

it's not the heat, it's the humidity. See HUMIDITY.

I.W.W. See WOBBLIES.

izzard. "From A to Izzard" was an English provincial way of saying "from Alpha to Omega," from beginning to end. The English pronunciation of *z*, "zed," is of course closely related. Dr. Johnson derived *izzard* from "*s* hard," Webster turns to the French *et zède*, and OED finds a 1597 dialect variation of "zed," "Ezod." All of them are descendants of Greek *zeta*.

J

jabber. See GIBBERISH.

jack. Starting in 1700 as a word for an English farthing, "jack" grew from a small or counterfeit coin (1897) to mean money in general. If this coin does not seem a sufficiently natural source for "He made a pile of jack," we might toy a bit with the idea of a jack as a labor-saving device—the boot-jack took the place of a boy, the automobile jack takes the place of a dozen men. And coupon-clipping is a substitute (though ultimately an unsatisfactory one) for an honest day's work. Another possible connection is with B. & L.'s 1897 expression, "He has made his Jack," meaning "attained his aim." They associate it with "Jack-in-office." (See GIN.)

jackanapes. Walsh was much impressed with "Jack o' naibs," one of the face cards in a Saracen card game (1379). Others have associated it with a 15th century shipment of monkeys from Italy; thus, "Jack from Naples." But OED has chronological evidence that the Naples explanation was more popular than scientific; the evidence seems to be that the common name *Jack* was applied very early to the *ape*, a word known in medieval England. But not until 1450, when a Duke of Suffolk, who wore a clog-and-chain on his coat of arms, became unpopular enough to win the nickname of "Jackanapes," did the expression gain literary recognition.

jackass. See HOBGOBLIN.

jacket. See DUST HIS JACKET. MONKEY.

Jack Robinson. See BEFORE YOU CAN SAY JACK ROBINSON.

Jackson, Andrew. See O.K., and OLD HICKORY.

Jackson. See STONEWALL JACKSON.

jakes. This ancient word for a latrine is surmised to be derived from the characteristic French name *Jacques*. If so, it is of a piece with

"French leave" and "Punic faith" in maliciously associating a hated foreign nation with something disreputable. Modern "john" for bathroom (possibly derived from *jakes*) is rapidly becoming respectable, and when it does will doubtless be dropped.

On the other hand, since 1924, "jake" has meant, to Americans, O.K., fine, dandy—possibly by connection with "jack," slang for money.

jamboree. B. & L. cite a gypsy word meaning a great noise or riot, as a possible ancestor, but conscientiously point out that the American sense is that of a joyful occasion, and that the origin may be negro, after all. As the words *jambone* and *jamboree* are both used in the game of euchre to describe various situations, it may be that there is a connection between them; but the origin of neither is known.

jape. Akin, perhaps, to *gab* (q.v.) and to French *japer*, to yelp, this has had a curious history. From its original sense of "trick," it relaxed somewhat into "joke," then returned to its first meaning, with the special significance of "seduce." When the 16th century labeled the word indecent, it was stored away, only to be revived in our day in its once obsolete sense of "joke" or "jest."

jayhawker. Sinclair Lewis wrote me that the preface to his play of that name contains the best information he had in regard to the origin of *jayhawker*. In it he mentions the tradition that one Doc Jennison, "a frolicsome immigrant from New York State," being known in Kansas as the Gay Yorker, was to blame for his men being nicknamed "Gay Yorkers"; and this was transformed, with the greatest of ease apparently, into "Jayhawkers." Which is a tough pill for an etymologist to swallow. In the first place, there is a linguistic chasm between hard *g* and soft *j*; in the second, the mid-western "or" would surrender to the Boston "aw" only after a terrific struggle. Mr. Lewis, however, adds a better clue, though admitting that there has never been a comprehensive definition or a satisfactory origin. He quotes a Kansas guerrilla, one Pat Devlin, as remarking that "in the old country, we had a bird called the jayhawk, which kind of worried its prey." Though I have found no such bird listed in books on ornithology, I feel sure that somewhere a particular kind of hawk has been given that nickname; the fact that the jay is a notorious thief would seem to support this theory. Thus we arrive at a definition of a jayhawk as a ferocious and dishonest bird that strikes with unpleasant suddenness, and loots, and kills.

jazz. Philologists have known for some time that little stock could be taken in the stories about how a negro musician named Jasper or Chas was accustomed to be brought into furious action with a "Come on, Jazz." Webster calls it a Creole word for "speed up," imported from the west coast of Africa. But Dr. Vizetelly finds interesting parallels in the Arabic: *jazib*, one who allures or attracts (which fits in with Hindustani *jazba*, meaning "violent desire," and with American slang use of *jazz* to mean sexual intercourse), and *jaza*, complaint or lamentation. Then there is *jaiza* (from an African language resembling Arabic), meaning the rumbling noise of distant drums. The natives of the north coast of Africa are closely related to the Arabs, and the latter were great slave traders. Webster's "Creole" word more than likely came from north-west Africa and had Arab ancestors.

Jehu. Ever since 1682, the simile, "drive like a Jehu," has been used of a coachman who drives furiously. His biblical prototype is to be found in II Kings 9:20. I have never seen it applied to a hell-bent motorist, though it is commonly believed that there are some. OED's last quotation was 1877. The name might appropriately have been given to the all-too-well-known hero of one of Leacock's *Nonsense Novels* who rushed out the door and "rode madly off in all directions."

jell. The picturesque American use of this has not, apparently, been brought to the attention of our more dignified authorities. Meaning to solidify into jelly, it was located by OED in one of the *Little Women* books (1874), but there is no example of its use to mean "succeed" (usually in the negative, as "It didn't jell," "It failed"). Weseen says it is theatrical, but it must ultimately be traced to the kitchen.

jemmy. See JIMMY.

Jenny. See GIN.

jenny wren. See HOBGOBLIN.

Jericho. The euphemism, "Go to Jericho!" used to be explained as a reference to King Henry VIII's love-nest, Blackmore Priory. This is all right in the sense of a remote place of retirement, but all wrong in the sense of condemning someone to the torture of the damned. At least, when Henry's courtiers remarked, "He's gone to Jericho," they implied that he was on pleasure bent. The biblical injunction to "tarry at Jericho until your beards be grown" (II Sam. 10:5) is usually given as the source. Note that the allusion is not to beardless boys but to servants of David who had been mistaken for spies and had half of their beards shaved off. The nearest quotation to "Go to Jericho!" that I have seen is the 1758 "He may go to Jericho for what I cares."

jerry-built. This adjective for "cheap, unsubstantial houses" (the sort that fall down when the builder removes the scaffolding unless he is careful to wallpaper the rooms first) has been connected with *Jericho*, "jerry" (gypsy for "excrement"), *jelly*, and Jerry Bros. of Liverpool. But Webster prefers to make it cognate with *jury* (from Fr. *jour*), as in *jury-mast*, "for the day," temporary.

Jesus, Saviour of Men. See I.H.S.

jetsam. See FLOTSAM AND JETSAM.

jettison. See FLOTSAM AND JETSAM.

jewel. See CONSISTENCY IS A JEWEL.

jew's harp. Though sometimes called, in radio circles, a "juice harp," and though Hyamson suggests that it may be a corruption of "jaw's harp," Bacon called it a *jeu trompe*, literally "play-trumpet," which Beaumont & Fletcher turned into "jew trump." And Webster says it is simply *Jew* plus *harp*. The implication is that the instrument is somewhat cheaper than a regular harp.

jib. See CUT.

jiggers. A phrase of my childhood, "Jiggers for the cop!" used when we were riding our bicycles on the sidewalk and a bluecoat appeared on the horizon, turns out to be particularly difficult to explain. It may be related to a gypsy word for "door," from which apparently the slang sense of "prison" developed. Thus the euphemistic exclamation, "I'll be jiggered!" may originally have meant, "I'll be arrested!" Or it may be a relative of the W. Indian *chigoe*, jigger, a parasite which gets into the blood through the foot, somewhat as the hookworm does. As a matter of fact, almost any fantastic sense of *jigger* should be easy to explain in the light of its use for some years to mean a what-you-may-call-it, a predecessor of *gadget*.

As a liquor container or measure, *jigger* goes all the way back to 1857.

Jim Crow. This name, as applied to street or railroad cars reserved exclusively for negroes, was that of a dusky dancer of about 1830, whose routine included a peculiar jump still known to schoolchildren as part of the "wheel about and turn about and jump Jim Crow" dance. The early song and dance won wide popularity as a minstrel number, and Jim Crow became the generic name for a negro. By 1861 it was in print as designating their special car, though it was not until 1875 (according to *Time*, Dec. 5, 1955) that the first Jim Crow transportation law was written in the United States. As late as 1887 such cars were still in use in New England (Boston to Salem). Beginning Jan. 10, 1956, the Jim Crow car in interstate traffic was legally abolished.

jimmy. The burglar's tool for prying open windows or doors derives its name from *James* in the same way, apparently, that Mr. Jingle's "green jemmy" (overcoat) did. As early as 1811 the crowbar-like instrument was known as a Jemmy Rook, while according to the 1897 slang dictionary *jimmy* could mean either such a bar or a concealed confederate.

jingoism. From a music-hall song of 1878, emphasizing an acute dislike of the Russians by the use of "By jingo." Excessive nationalism is called *chauvinism* by the French, and by us spread-eagleism or, at one time, *Hearstanity*. The origin of *jingo* itself is more difficult; perhaps it is from the god of the heathen Basque mercenary troops. If so, remarks Weekley, it is probably the only pure Basque word in use in English today. While agreeing with Webster that "By jingo!" may be just a formation of the "By Jove!" and "By Jabers!" type (in remote allusion presumably to Jesus), OED calls the Basque theory unsupported, adding that the "St. Gengulphus" suggestion was a joke.

jinx. OED quotes Christy Mathewson as using this slang term, in 1912, for a hoodoo of some sort, and also, without connecting the two, lists *jynx*, the wrynecked woodpecker, as meaning a charm or spell; but Webster overrules both OED and Mencken (who found the "etymology unintelligible") and logically links the two words. The explanation is that that particular bird was sometimes used to cast charms.

jitney. Webster invokes a French *jeton*, counter or token, to explain why "jitney" means a nickel, and hence an automobile furnishing cheap bus service. Mencken feels that it is an old American noun revived. OED says quotations indicate a Russian-Jewish origin, from the name of the smallest coin in Russia. A "jitney dance" is a *taxi* dance (q.v.) at a nickel a throw.

jitters, jittery. The authorities offer no etymology for this convenient term for dizzy, irritable, on edge. Let me suggest that you try to say "chatter" with your teeth chattering; you will, I think, find yourself saying "jitter."

jo. Our hearts have not, I think, failed to indicate for us in a general way what was meant by "John Anderson, my jo." But there is also an intellectual satisfaction in learning that *jo* is apparently the same word as *joy*.

Joan. See POPE JOAN.

Jobson. See HOBSON-JOBSON.

Job's turkey. See POOR AS JOB'S TURKEY.

Joe Miller. The history, with dates, of this synonym for a stale joke is as follows: an illiterate comedian of that name died in 1738; the next year, somebody got out a book of ancient wheezes, and without having said anything to Joe about it called it *Joe Miller's Jest Book*. Within fifty years "a Joe Miller" had become proverbial. The last quotation for it in OED is 1882.

joggle. See GOGGLE.

john. See JAKES.

John Bradford. See GRACE OF GOD.

John Bull. Issued under the title, *Law Is a Bottomless Pit*, the satire by Dr. Arbuthnot from which the Englishman took his immortal nickname was rechristened *The History of John Bull* when it was seen that the name had caught on. Others in the Arbuthnot essay, such as Lewis Baboon for the French, and Nicholas Frog for the Dutch, did not have the same luck. The first appearance in print of John Bull as a clearly generic name for an Englishman was in 1772, about fifty years later.

John Dory. See FINNAN HADDIE.

johnny cake. This might never have been corrupted from "journey cake" had the inhabitants of our Southland, light and dark, been as careful about their *r*'s as the present-day children of the Pacific Coast. In 1775, it is found as "journey cake," in 1793 as "johnny cake," and in 1868 the latter is condemned as "vulgar." The thought in "journey" was probably that this sort of cornbread was easy to prepare and convenient for the traveller to take with him. Thus, *johnny cake* may be akin to *jerry-built* (q.v.).

joint. This is not a new word for an opium den or low drinking place. It began to be applied to such places in about 1880. While its early association with Chinese might point to a Cantonese origin, the only source thus far suggested is the rather colorless one of a "gathering-place," where you *join* other people. Possibly the riskiness of the investment had dictated the desirability of building such structures as cheaply as possible, simply as additions *joined* to something more solid.

jolly. See YULE.

Jolly Roger. This is the third of Weekley's trio of unsolved mysteries. As both of the other two, Davy Jones and Mother Carey, have shown definite signs of emerging from obscurity, a little more pressure on Roger may bring results. Who the jovial pirate was who gave his name to the first skull-and-crossbones flag may, of course, never be known. By derivation, the name is supposed to mean "famous with the spear," which seems to give the proper warlike note.

Jonathan. See BROTHER JONATHAN.

Joneses. See KEEPING UP WITH THE JONESES.

joseph. As two of the great moments in Joseph's life (see Genesis) were associated with coats—that of many colors and the one he abandoned with the importunate Mrs. Potiphar—it is not surprising that 18th century tailors thought of "joseph" as a name for a coat, though why it should have been designed for women horseback riders remains to be seen. An amusing development (in memory of Joseph's younger brother) was the benjamin, soon shortened to "benny," a close-fitting man's coat, and now any overcoat.

josh. As the big dictionaries insist on no other source for this slang verb meaning "kid" or "banter," a form of local pride induces me to cast my vote for "Josh Billings" (Henry W. Shaw) as having at least helped it along. He was a native of Lanesboro, between Williamstown and Pittsfield. Being short for Joshua and, like "Rube" for Reuben, a stock name for a rustic, "Josh" made a good pseudonym for Shaw, whose misspelled philosophy made the cracker box and iron stove of the general store famous. Unfortunately it was 1860 before he began to be noticed, whereas Mathews found an example of *josh* in 1845, as meaning a friendly pulling of someone's leg. This first quotation's being American renders the more questionable B. & L.'s theory that English provincial *joskin*, bumpkin, might be the source. They mention also Joshua's making the sun stand still, and the stoutness of Josh Sedley and the Chinese Buddha (see JOSS).

joss. It is curious that when early visitors to China inquired about the superstitious burning of red paper before a voyage or in connection with a funeral, they were answered, apparently, with the Portuguese word for God, *Deos!* This, corrupted into *joss*, became the regular pidgin English word for anything related to their religion; such as *joss-house*, temple, and *joss-stick*, incense punk. The extent of Portuguese influence in the old days is shown also in the word *mandarin*, the Portuguese explorers' version of a Malay word meaning "minister of state."

journey cake. See JOHNNY CAKE.

journeyman. Originally, one who worked by the *day* (French *jour*); hence a qualified artisan between the classes of "apprentice" and "passed master." He is not his own master—which is the sense in which "journeyman clock," an early form of electric clock controlled by a master clock at a distance, is used. A famous quotation is that from *Hamlet* in which it is suggested that the mean creature called man must have been created not by Nature but by one of her journeymen.

joy stick. Usually abbreviated to *stick*, this is the vertical control lever of an airplane. It operates the elevators and ailerons. Not until World War I did the name come into prominence. And now it has been superseded by *yoke*.

jubilee. It is curious but not unexplainable why this word usually associated with negro spirituals should have been strictly Jewish in origin. Derived from the *yōbēl*, the ram's horn, the year of jubilee was decreed in the 25th chapter of Leviticus as a sort of sabbatical year, at the end of seven periods of seven years each; i.e., the 50th year, in celebration of the deliverance from Egypt, everybody was to have a rest, including the fields, which were to lie fallow, and the slaves, who were to be set free. Thus the word came to have particularly poignant significance among the negroes and to play an important role in their revival meetings. The British use of it (as silver, golden, or diamond jubilee) in reference to the number of years under one monarch, resulted from a confusion with Latin *jubilum*, a shout, from which *jubilation* comes.

judge. See SOBER AS A JUDGE.

jujube. See LOTUS-EATER.

jump. "Jump on," slang term for "rebuke severely," is of interest because it is a literal translation of the Latin *insultare*, to leap upon, from which *insult* comes. (See DESULTORY.)

"To jump over the broom" or "to marry over the broomstick" is to go through a mock ceremony or indeed to dispense with a ceremony altogether. The expression is found in both provincial England and southern U.S., the earliest quotation being 1774. Later dictionaries disregard Brewer's suggestion of *brom*, the bit of a bridle, but offer no substitute. Can there be a remote connection with the superstition of witches riding on their broomsticks to their unholy pleasures?

jumper. This word may be either masculine, feminine, or neuter. For men, a *jumper*, or *jumpers*, is a cover-all used, in the inclusive phrase of OED, by "sailors, truckmen, and Eskimos." For women, it was first a *jump* (probably from French *jupon*, upper petticoat, which had gone through a transformation since it meant "outer garment" in Arabic); then, a smock-like dress hanging from the shoulders and not tucked in at the waist. The child's jumpers are a miniature edition of the man's: a one-piece suit for romping about.

juniper juice. See GENEVA COURAGE.

jury-mast. See JERRY-BUILT.

K

kale. *Kale* (*seed*), meaning money, is probably from Ger. *Kohl*, cabbage, and connected with "the long green," slang for paper money. In British slang, *coal* or *cole* meant money; though Brewer explains it through rhyming slang for *gold*, its connection with *Kohl* seems equally likely. *Cole-slaw*, "kailyard school" (of literature about Scottish humble life), and *cauliflower* are all descendants of Lat. *caulis*, cabbage.

Kanonenfutter. See CANNON-FODDER.

keel-haul. This direct translation of the Dutch *kielhalen* describes a harsh but not necessarily fatal punishment used in the Dutch and British navies until well into the 19th century. The culprit was dragged under the boat, from one side to the other, or from bow to stern. If he succeeded in holding his breath, he nevertheless received a cruel scratching from the barnacles. It will be remembered that the erring seaman in *Mutiny on the Bounty* did not survive the ordeal.

keen. The sedate Webster gives "nifty" as a synonym for this in its latest slang sense; as in "It was a keen picture," meaning a splendid movie. In its earlier, and still understandable usage, "I was keen about it," meaning enthusiastic, it dates back, in OED, to 1714: "They were not so keen upon coming in themselves." Both senses sprout, I suppose, from the fact that a sharp ax is a desirable one.

keep. "Keep a stiff upper lip" seems to be of New England origin (about 1830). It means, "Don't let your lip quiver, as if about to cry," i.e., "Don't be a baby." The story is told of a singer who, making her debut on the radio, was advised by a friend experienced in radio technique to "keep a stiff upper lip." Unfortunately the novice was so flustered that she took the advice literally, and the result was that her first audition was a failure.

"Keep your pecker up," an equivalent for "keep a stiff upper lip," is related to "woodpecker" in that the mouth or head is referred to in each case. While "pecker" is also used, as Read points out, of the male organ, the "mouth or beak" definition fits much better here, as the contrasting expression, to be "down in the mouth," indicates.

Variants of "keep your shirt on" are: "keep your hair on" and "keep your back hair up." The idea is, obviously, "don't get excited." In the case of the first, there is perhaps some connection with the old British phrase, "They got his rag out" (or "his shirt"), meaning "They enraged him." This is probably the origin of *rag* as meaning to tease. When a fellow's shirt tails are waving in the breeze he is usually bothered about something. As for keeping one's hair on, it seems more likely that this is an exaggerated allusion to what one's hair is alleged to do in situations of extreme danger, rather than to an easily dislodged wig.

keeping up with the Joneses. For this, we are apparently indebted to I. Bacheller, comic strip artist, who in about 1911 inaugurated a cartoon series dealing with the perennial problem of how to show as good a front as our neighbors.

keep the wall. See WEAKEST GOES TO THE WALL.

Kelly. See SLIDE, KELLY, SLIDE.

kettle of fish. See FISH.

key of the street. When Lowten told Job that he was afraid Job had the key of the street (*Pickwick Papers*), he was not using an equivalent of the French *la clef des champs*. The former means to be locked out overnight; the latter, to be free to roam, through the fields, anywhere. As the *Pickwick Papers* quotation was the only one in OED, it is evident that the phrase did not have wide currency in literary circles.

kibitzer. In 1923, Mencken recorded *kibbets* as crook slang for a ring of receivers of stolen goods—gentlemen who are more than likely to be suspicious and critical. This is doubtless related to the Yiddish word which has come to mean "one who gives unwanted advice at a card game." Webster traces this word to the German *kibitz*, an imitation of a pewit's cry.

kibosh. A Mr. Loewe, who ought to know, wrote to N. & Q. that this is a Yiddish word formed from four consonants, representing eighteen-pence. When, at a small auction, an eager bidder jumped his offer to eighteen-pence, he was said to have "put the kibosh" on his fellow-bidders. B. & L. may have confused it with *bosh* in explaining it as "nonsense, rubbish." In 1836 it appeared as "kye-bosk," in 1856 Dickens used it, but it had not by 1891 become sufficiently naturalized to divest itself of quotation marks.

kick. The modern-sounding "kick up a row" goes back to before 1800. It is commonly agreed that the figurative use derives from scuffing up a cloud of dust with the feet.

"Kick in," used commonly at poker as a synonym for "feed the kitty" (put some of your chips in the pool in the center of the table), seems to have so little reason for being related to the legs that one is tempted to theorize about the old slang use of *kick* to mean a trousers-pocket.

kick one's heels. See DANCE ATTENDANCE ON.

kickshaws. That this Shakesperean word for tidbits of food is akin to *quality* is capable of proof: it is simply French *quelque chose*, something, which in turn is derived from Latin *qualis causa*, "of what kind." A "singular" form, *kickshaw*, is incorrect, because *kickshaws* is itself singular.

kick the bucket. This fine old slang term for "die" retains a surprising degree of popularity. In provincial English, the block of wood from which slaughtered pigs were hung by the heels was called a "bucket." There are possibilities here.

kid. Somehow the word for young goat has from very early times made an appealing slang name for a child. Even "kiddy," which to many sensitive ears is as painful as "all righty" and "okey-doke," goes back into the previous century.

To "kid" someone was considered new slang in 1897, by B. & L., but OED found an 1811 use in the sense of amusing or diverting a victim while the accomplice robs him. The 1879 example was, however, the first with a modern appearance about it. It was surprising to find the exclamation "No kid!" meaning "Seriously now," in 1897; it seems there to have been thought of as a noun, whereas ours is, I believe, just an abbreviation of the gerund, *kidding*. The thought behind it all is probably the alleged ease with which one can deceive a child. (See CHAFF. RIDE.)

kiddle-net. See FISH.

kidney. "Of the same kidney," meaning of the same disposition or sort, was slang in the 1700's (see BAMBOOZLE). The kidneys were thought of as the seat of the affections, and hence the determining factor, largely, in one's temperament. (See ILK.)

Kilkenny cats. "To fight like Kilkenny cats" dates back, according to some accounts, to a pleasant little custom among Hessian soldiers, stationed in Ireland, of tying two cats together by the tail and hanging them over a clothesline. On the approach of an officer, one of the men once sliced off both the tails, the cats fled, and the officer was told that the cats had eaten each other, leaving nothing but the tails. However, conservative authorities prefer the derivation from the furious boundary struggles which continued for years between Kilkenny and Irishtown.

kilter. Webster offers no solution for "out of kilter," out of order. Most of the words that resemble *kilter* imply, when put into the phrase "out of kilter," almost the opposite meaning; for instance, OED lists *kelter*, rubbish, and *kilter*, a "bust" (a useless hand, at cards); or *kilthei* (Gothic for "womb"), from which we get "children"—and much as we like children we dare not assert that the presence of children guarantees perfect order. Slightly better possibilities are: a dialect form, *kilt*, to tuck up, to make neat; a Dutch *keelter*, stomach (by association perhaps with the frequent use of "out of order" in reference to one's digestion); the German word for money, *Geld* (pronounced "gelt"), the theory being that if you are out of money things will shortly be "out of kilter."

king. See DIVINE RIGHT OF KINGS.

kingdom come. This old way (1785) of referring either to life after death or the triumphant second coming of Christ goes back, no doubt, to the negro revival meeting and the Lord's Prayer.

kingfisher. See HALCYON DAYS.

king's cords. See CORDUROY.

king's English. Perhaps the leading use to which this phrase is now put is in wise-cracks leading up to "Of course I know he's English."

The expression became common shortly before Shakespeare. There's no great mystery about how it developed; the idea is "the kind the king would approve"; hence, the best.

Kingsley, Charles. See MUSCULAR CHRISTIANITY.

kissed her cow. See COW.

kit and caboodle. Whereas the second element sometimes appears as "bilin'" (probably "boiling") or as "boodle" (from which "caboodle" apparently derives), the "kit" part remains invariable. It is more likely that it is the same word as in *tool-kit* than that it is connected with the old name (derived ultimately from Latin *cithara*, and cognate with *guitar*) for a little fiddle, a "kit." As for this "boodle," it may be the same as the slang word for loot or tainted money or, indeed, money in general, the most plausible source being Dutch *boedel*, property or household stuff. If this is the proper derivation of *caboodle*, the notion conveyed by the entire phrase would, in fact, be something like "the whole outfit."

kit-cat. Since Kit (Christopher) Catt—or Kat or Catling—was the proprietor of a pastry shop where the Kit-Cat Club met, back in Addison and Steele days, kit-cat has been a technical term for a 36 × 28 inch portrait, as that was the size that fitted best the panels of the club-room, where the portrait of each member was supposed to be hung. It shows less than half the length of the sitter, but includes the hands.

An early name for the pencil-and-pad game of tit-tat-to was kit-cat-cannio, for no discernible reason. Kit-cat was also sometimes heard as a variant of tip-cat, an old game still seen on school-grounds: a piece of wood shaped like a double cone is tapped up into the air and knocked as far into the offing as possible, after which the batter proceeds somewhat as in baseball. This is probably the origin of the name "one o' (old) cat," for a simplified form of baseball played when there aren't enough boys to play sides.

kitchen police. The fateful letters *k.p.* have spoiled many a doughboy's anticipated holiday. OED lists the verb "police," in the sense of keeping a camp neat and orderly, as in good American usage in 1893, but by some strange oversight finds no illustration of *kitchen police* in print before 1930. Yet it is my impression that we had it during World War I. Anybody doubt it?

One army post is said to have issued these instructions on how to "police" the grounds: If it's small enough, pick it up; if not, paint it; but if it moves, salute it!

kite. See FLY A KITE.

kitten. See CHIT.

kitty. See KICK.

kittycorner. This is a playful variation on *catercorner* (which OED is inclined to think should be pronounced with a long *a*, but which Standard says is usually pronounced "catta"). Webster connects the *cater* with French *quatre*, four, but does not explain why "four-cornered" should mean "diagonally across from." Another variant is *catty-corner.* (See CATAWAMPUS.)

kleptomaniac. See LIFT.

knave. See BOWER.

knickerbocker. Washington Irving probably coined the name from Dutch words suggesting "baker of clay marbles" or, as one writer says, "of fancy cakes"; then Cruikshank drew pictures of burghers in voluminous breeches, to illustrate the Knickerbocker "History of New York." Eventually the name knickerbockers came to be used of men's baggy golf trousers and (ordinarily as "knickers") of women's silk bloomers. "Plus fours" were golf knickers made four inches longer than they used to be, for no known reason except to furnish more employment in the woollen mills.

knock. The origin of the superstitious "knocking on wood," with the hope of averting for a while longer a calamity thus far escaped, is not known, unless it be a verse in the sixth chapter of Galatians, "God forbid that I should glory save in the cross of our Lord Jesus Christ." The argument is that you can be forgiven for a boast if you will immediately turn your thoughts to the wooden cross of Christ.

To "knock under," in the sense of "give in," seems to come from an old practice of rapping on the under side of the table when beaten in an argument, though Webster connects it with drinking oneself under the table. "Knuckle under" is, it is thought, a derivative.

In some localities, "knocked up" is a harmless expression for "tired"; in others it is taken to mean "pregnant," and should be used with some care. B. & L. list "knocking shop" as a synonym for brothel.

knock-down. If your slangy friend asks you, at a dance, to give him a knock-down, don't take him too literally. All he wants is to be introduced to some divine creature. Why, I don't know. I mean, why the phrase, unless the thought is the very gallant one of being overpowered and, in short, floored, with joy at the introduction.

knock galley west. This equivalent for "knock into a cocked hat" is said by EDD to be an alteration of "collywest," or "collyweston," related to "collywobbles," and conveying, for no apparent reason, the notion of things going wrong.

The "cocked hat" business may have originated in the fact that that type of hat can be crushed and carried under the arm without the serious damage one would expect.

Other parallels are: "to knock for a gool" (i.e., *goal*, in some sport —cf. "gooled 'em," theatrical slang for "won the favor of the audience"); "to knock for a loop" (apparently referring to the loop a body is supposed to describe if a sufficiently powerful blow is applied on the end of the chin); "to knock all of a heap" (self-explanatory); "to knock *cuckoo*" (q.v.); "to knock cold" (i.e., unconscious); and "to knock the spots off" (origin obscure, but see DANDER).

knockout. See CORKER.

know a hawk from a handsaw. Unless *hawk* is a builder's tool and not a bird, *handsaw* should probably be *heronshaw*, a heron. Learned etymologists have battled about the derivation of *heronshaw*, but with that we are less concerned than with getting the two articles into the same general field. A bird cannot be compared to a saw any more than a spark to an elephant. For effectiveness in a phrase of this sort, the two must be dissimilar, but not too much so. One might say, for instance, "You can't tell a spark-coil from a speedometer," or "a radiator from a road-map," both of which have the important feature of alliteration that is seen also in the *Hamlet* quotation under discussion. In addition to bringing *handsaw* into the bird kingdom, the *heronshaw* reading suggests pursuer and pursued, as if one were to say, "You don't know the difference between a hound and a hare." That the phrase about the hawk and the handsaw is not entirely dead is suggested by its having been used informally in 1886, in *Harper's Magazine*.

But the fact is that a hawk *is* a builder's tool and has been since 1700 at least! The chances are good that Shakespeare knew one kind of hawk to be the mortar-board which a plasterer holds in his left hand and on which he piles his "mud." A Deep South secretary of a plastering firm told me it was called a "hoke," while a descendant of Governor Bradford of Massachusetts assured me it was a "hock"! Referee Webster, however, runs a picture of it under *hawk*.

know beans about it. See BEANS.

knuckle-duster. One definition of this, in Webster, is "a stone artifact of uncertain purpose." Be that as it may, and what it may, we are interested in it as another name for the brass knuckles which gangsters use in their more playful moments. It is a descendant of the cestus, or mailed fist, with which gladiators used to kill each other in the *arena* (literally, sand). The name *brass knuckles* has been in use since 1860. It is not clear what "dusting" had to do with this device for damaging one's opponent the most and oneself the least.

knuckle under. See KNOCK.

kobold. This German name for the familiar spirit of a house (like Robin Goodfellow), or a brownie, or a gnome, has a curious relation to the mineral, *cobalt*, used largely in alloys. German miners considered this ore not only useless but a nuisance, because of the arsenic and sulfur in it which were bad not only for the silver that it touched, but for the miners as well. Thus it was in no wise a compliment to the spirit that his name was given to the metal. The word *kobold* probably means "houseruler," and is related to *cove* and *wield*; and to *koben*, pigsty. One wonders whether *caboose* and *cahoots* (q.v.) may not be akin to this *koben*. Then too we have the *cobalt* bomb, perish forbid (q.v.).

Kodak. See COMRADE.

kowtow. This has been spelled several ways, but our leading authorities now favor this form, which to me is significant in that it seems to represent best the Cantonese pronunciation of the phrase meaning "knock your head" (i.e., touch your forehead to the floor in submission). Probably those adventurers who opened up China got their first taste of kowtowing in Canton. Yet Webster recommends pronouncing it to rhyme with "know how," which is neither Cantonese nor Mandarin. But why not rhyme each syllable with *bow* [bau], as that is what it means?

k.p. See KITCHEN POLICE.

Kriss Kringle. That this is not to be found in OED does not, in itself, prove that there is no Santa Claus. It is a jolly Dutch name for the spirit of Christmas, and yet it goes back to fundamentals, for it is descended from *Christ-kindlein*, the little Christ child. Incidentally, the only *kriss* in OED was "a Malay dagger" (var. of *creese*).

kudos. Popularized, in our day, by TIME, which was seeking a space-saving synonym for *praise* (saved one letter, anyway), this was frequently used by Victorian writers, to most of whom a Greek word looked little more outlandish than a French one. It is well understood today as a colloquialism for glory or fame. Note that it is not a plural form.

kumquat. See DOLLARS TO DOUGHNUTS.

L

labyrinth. The classical word for an intricate maze originated not far from Egypt, in all probability. Webster is much more positive than other authorities that the word goes back to *labrys*, a double ax used frequently as a religious symbol. As the various labyrinths seem never to have been primarily religious in significance, one wonders why this double ax makes any better source than the Egyptian king, Labyris, mentioned by Brewer.

lace. In the sense of mingling a dash of spirits with some other beverage, such as coffee, this is by no means recent slang, as it goes back to 1687; though formerly it was capable of application to so harmless a "lacer" as a sugar lump.

lack of money. See MONEY.

lady. See GENTLEMAN.

Lady Bountiful. Farquhar created this beneficent character for his *Beaux's Stratagem* (1707). It was not until a century later that the name appeared in print in the generic sense common today.

lag. The slang use of this verb to mean arrest or transport is not explained by the big dictionaries. B. & L. relate it to the old sea-lawyer's word *lagan* (*ligan* is preferred) meaning goods attached to a buoy and sunk under the sea. With an agile imagination, one can see the figurative connection with the situation of a man who is seized by the law and sunk in a penal colony. Far-fetched, though. Hotten lists *lag* as meaning also to urinate; in this sense it may possibly be connected with Cornwall *lag*, to make wet and soiled, and may have helped to give currency to the modern *leak*, though the latter is, of course, easily explainable without recourse to *lag*.

lager beer. *Lager* is a German word that is akin to *lie* and *lair*, and is properly a bed or resting place. The beverage is therefore beer that has been for some time "bedded-down" in a warehouse, for aging. Not all German beer is *lager*.

lair. See LAGER BEER.

lallapaloosa (and variants). This highly complimentary term is, Mencken thinks, a French expression, *allez fusil*, which became in County Mayo "allay-foozee," a sturdy fellow. The French term, meaning "Forward the muskets," was stamped on Irish consciousness at Killala, where the French troops landed in 1798. The all-day sucker, or *lollypop*, is possibly a distant relative.

lamb. See GOD TEMPERS THE WIND TO THE SHORN LAMB.

lame duck. To a Britisher this means a defaulter, a bankrupt, one who has been financially crippled on the Stock Exchange. In America, the word should now, theoretically, fold its wings and expire, by act of Congress; for the Constitution has been amended—no longer does a congressman who has failed of reelection have any further chance to "represent" his disaffected constituents. However, a lame duck may still, as in the past, be given a diplomatic appointment. Notice an important difference between a congressman who has been voted out of office and a President who, by Constitutional amendment, is not permitted to serve a third term.

lamp. See SMELL.

landing. See DEAD STICK LANDING.

landlubber. See LUBBER.

land office business. OED quotes an 1853 reference to the rushing business actually done in a land office, registering applicants for territory just opened to settlers; and an 1882 example of the figurative use of *land office business* in something other than land—in this case, it was ore crushing. The phrase is clearly one that could have been included by Mencken with many other "obvious products of pioneer life," such as "fly off the handle" and "log-rolling."

land of Nod. As meaning the country to which we go when we fall asleep, this would never have attained its widespread popularity had there been no more to it than just the nodding of a drowsy head. There is surely a pun intended on the "land of wandering" to which Cain was exiled (Genesis 4:16). The similarity between "land of Nod" and "land of Oz" has helped to further the success of a noteworthy series of books for children.

language. See LIMEHOUSE.

larboard. See STARBOARD.

lariat. The Mexican cowboys had two Spanish names for the highly specialized ropes they used in their business: *el lazo* and *la reata.* The former became our *lasso*, the latter begat twins—*riata*, and *lariat*, but *riata* has never been completely naturalized. *Reatar*, Spanish verb meaning to bind again, is from the Latin, *re-aptare.*

lascar. No seafarer from the Far East ever thinks of a lascar as a soldier. Yet this word for a native East Indian sailor comes from an Arabic word for army or army-camp. Notice that when there is any sort of an accident on a P. & O. liner someone invariably blames it on the lascar crew.

lasso. See LARIAT.

last. See BALLAST. STICK TO YOUR LAST.

last ditch. See DITCH.

last infirmity of noble mind. See FAME.

lather. This is just the Anglo-Saxon word for washing-soda, hence akin to *lye.* For centuries it has been used with reference to the flecks of foam on a vigorously perspiring horse, and it is from this, apparently, that the notion of a beating or whipping got into the word *lathering*; i.e., the horse is beaten with the whip until he is "all of a muck of sweat" (Goldsmith). Here, too, we may find the origin of "work oneself into a lather" as a synonym for "get hot and bothered," angry or worried.

Perhaps, also, there is a hint here for the as yet unexplained bit of baseball slang, "Cream it!" meaning hit the ball hard.

latrine rumor. See GRAPEVINE ROUTE.

laughter. See HOMERIC LAUGHTER.

lavender. "Laid away in lavender" means "put away in moth balls," the point being that the aromatic mint, sprinkled between the freshly laundered sheets in a linen closet, was supposed to keep moths away. That the method was not 100% effective is indicated by the 1677 quotation that "The seeds of lavender, kept a little warm and moist, will turn into moths." Though used in connection with linen closets and perfumed baths, it should not be related to Spanish *lavandera*, washerwoman. Webster guesses that it is from *lividus*, a bluish or blue-red color. (See LIVID.) In slang figurative application, the phrase may mean "in hock" or "in prison."

law. See POSSESSION.

law and order. See LYNCH LAW.

lay an egg. No self-respecting hen would admit that to lay an egg was to achieve a conspicuous failure. Yet that is what theatrical people mean by it. The reason, deponent sayeth not.

lay away in lavender. See LAVENDER.

lay them in the aisles. See AISLE.

lazy as Ludlam's dog. See POOR AS JOB'S TURKEY.

lead a double life. See TWO-TIMER.

lead with your chin. The dictionaries are as yet officially unconscious of this lively variant for "stick out your chin," i.e., expose yourself to a knockout blow. In boxing, you may lead with your right, or lead with your left; but if you lead with an unprotected chin, it won't take a Joe Louis to flatten you. (See STOOGE.)

leak. See LAG.

leap. See GANTLET.

learn by heart. See HEART.

learn the ropes. In use since the middle of the last century to mean "get the hang of it," i.e., learn how to do something, this is explained by Brewer as an allusion to the reins by which a horse is directed. In the absence of a better theory, it is my guess that it derives rather from the maze of ropes on a sailing vessel. Any landlubber who has tried to be helpful on a yacht knows that ropes (i.e., "sheets") are not learned in a day. To return to "get the hang of," this has, I believe, no connection with ropes, but refers to the balance of an ax, and the best way to hold it.

leather and prunella. See PRUNELLA.

leatherhead. See LOGGERHEADS.

leatherneck. There have been some amusing guesses as to why this should be the standard nickname for a marine. Some have thought "roughneck" might furnish a clue; others have investigated the leather-producing qualities of a tropical sunburn. It is now generally agreed, however, that it was a term of ridicule applied by the sailors of the gay nineties, whose Adam's apples were not muzzled, to the marines, whose uniforms included high leather stocks. The "blouse" of the American soldier of World War I had a tight-fitting collar, a somewhat similar relic of the chamber of horrors.

leave no stone unturned. During the lean years of depression, many of us knew the brutal goading of this challenge. In origin, it had to do, not with finding a job, but with buried treasure. The slippery old Delphic oracle, that knew all the answers and was as famous for loopholes as a Swiss cheese, gave this infallible recipe, according to Euripides, for finding a hoard that had been cached by a fleeing general.

lecture. See CAUDLE LECTURE. CURTAIN LECTURE.

leery. If a *leer* may be a look of "fear, defiance, and cunning mixed up," as an OED quotation suggests, then the slang expression, "I'm a little leery about it," meaning doubtful or suspicious, may derive from *leer* rather than from provincial *lere*, to learn. *Leery* is not a new word, being found in the sense of "on one's guard" in 1796.

left hand, left wing. See DEXTEROUS.

leg. Stevenson (1934) was not "pulling your leg" (intentionally cheating or kidding you) when he dated this phrase as nearly four centuries old. He evidently mistook the unusual name Churchward, author of *Blackbirding in the South Pacific* (1888) for the equally unusual one, Churchyard, Elizabethan author quoted *elsewhere* by OED—but not under "pull one's leg"! Where Stevenson got that exact date (1563) is just one of those things. A strange feature of it is that OED includes in the 1888 quotation (its earliest) the entirely non-Elizabethan expression, "that chap Mike," which Stevenson replaced with a row of dots. In the *Addenda* to the 1944 edition, Stevenson corrected his mistake.

"Shake a leg" has penetrated the British consciousness as meaning "to dance," but this American synonym for "hurry" is not yet recognized by OED. (See GAME LEG.)

leg of mutton school. See MUTTON.

leopard. "Can a leopard change his spots?" is found in Jeremiah 13:23, alongside the one about an Ethiopian's changing his skin. The animal was supposed to be a cross between a lion (*leo*) and a pard, a panther similar to the ounce, a Tibetan wild-cat said by Webster to be "one of the most beautiful" of felines. This ounce, about which I read a poem in *St. Nicholas* a great many years ago, and which I long believed to be a fabulous creature like the unicorn, is akin to *lynx*; the French source of *ounce* was *lonce*, the *l* being later mistaken for the definite article.

let. The tennis expression, sometimes given (logically but not correctly) as "net," is the same as in the phrase "without let or hindrance." It means that the ball has been "hindered" on its progress toward the proper court by touching the top of the net. The word is also used, in top-flight tennis circles, when a disputed point is to be played over; thus, "Play it *let*." Brewer thinks the historic spelling *lett* should have been preserved to mark the distinction from ordinary *let*.

To "let a person down," in modern slang, is to fail him, to leave him in the lurch. There is a hint in OED that the figure here might be that of breaking through thin ice. An earlier use, generally with *easily*, *softly*, or *gently*, means almost the opposite: to be lenient with a person, or at least to cushion his fall. A third variation which seems to have borrowed from both of the others is "I let him down" in the sense of "I did not keep the challenge high enough; I let him compromise with his conscience."

B. & L. list a slang term, "let in," meaning defrauded. The picture is that of a swindling merchant "seeing you coming" (i.e., as a likely prospect) and letting you into his shop, or in on some crooked deal. Under the same word, B. & L. give "attack" as a meaning of "let in." I feel sure that "lit in" was what they had in mind (the past tense of "light in").

let 'er flicker. See FLICKER.

let 'er rip. See RIP.

let the cat out of the bag. See PIG IN A POKE.

let them eat cake. While very little can be said for Marie Antoinette's tact and discretion in dealing with the Paris proletariat, it has been asserted that the famous retort to their plea for bread was of an earlier date. Other defenders think that she had reference to the *crust* (brioche) of the bread as opposed to the soft or crumby part. There is certainly reason to believe that she was capable of saying it, not in giddy indifference, perhaps, but as one of her cute little jokes.

Leviathan. The Hebrew word (literally, according to Crowell, "that which gathers itself together in folds") denoted, in various connections, either the crocodile, the whale, or a dragon. Since about 1800 it has been often applied to ships of great size. In Hobbes's book (1651) it meant the commonwealth.

lewd. Through the years this has had seven different meanings, of which only the last has survived. They are as follows: lay (as in *lay-man*), unlettered, low, bungling, vile, lawless, and licentious. In the famous "lewd fellows of the baser sort" (Acts 17:5) the idea is rather that of lawlessness than of indecency.

Lewis Baboon. See JOHN BULL.

Lewis, Sinclair. See BABBITT. JAYHAWKER.

lick. See CUB.

lickety split. B. & L. connect this, and *lickety-cut*, with "putting in big licks," but later dictionaries class both formations as "fanciful." The rapid-fire, explosive *k*'s and *t*'s of *lickety-cut* should make it a slightly better vehicle for the sense of headlong speed than *split*, with its *l*; conversely, *lickety-brindle's* failure to gain equal popularity may be ascribed in part to the liquid *n* and *l*. Why the word *lick* should be associated with speed and effort ("I haven't done a lick of work") is not clear; perhaps from the rapidity with which we can move our tongues, and the intense earnestness of a cleanly cat or dog washing up.

lick your flint. See FLINT.

lie. See LAGER BEER.

lieutenant. See LOCUM-TENENS.

life. See SEAMY SIDE OF LIFE.

life is just a bowl of cherries. See CHERRY.

life of Riley. There seems to be strangely little enthusiasm about relating this metaphor, which means a life of joyous loafing, to James Whitcomb Riley and his poems about barefoot boys and drowsy summer days. Stevenson, admitting the origin as uncertain, remarks that a song called "Is that Mr. Riley?" was popular in the nineties.

lift. Meaning steal, this is one of those weasel-words (like *liquidate* for "kill") which remain slang because they are not honest. It has been known in this sense since 1526. Pointing out that it is used especially of cattle-stealing, Webster admits that it may be from Latin *clepere*, to steal, and hence akin to *kleptomania*, a mania for lifting things. But people who call stealing "lifting" do so because it sounds less like a prison offense. The French equivalent, also slang, is *soulever*.

The British word for elevator is becoming familiar in this country, partly because it is one of those short synonyms that headline writers dream about.

light. See SWEETNESS AND LIGHT.

light into. See LET.

lily-livered. "Livers white as milk," says Shakespeare. Somehow the liver, the largest gland in man, received credit, along with other important organs of the body such as the heart and bowels, as being the seat of love. However, there was also attached to the liver the notion of passionate violence. Thus a person with a pale liver was a coward.

limber. The artillery term, "limber up" (to attach the gun section to the ammunition-carrying truck) seems to be no relative whatever to the term meaning to exercise your muscles until they are flexible. The former is perhaps from a French *limonière*, meaning the shafts and chassis of a wagon. The latter seems to be akin to *limp*.

limbo. Technically it is incorrect to use this in any case but the ablative ("in the limbo"); the nominative case is *limbus*. Our present sense of being confined somewhere, forgotten, derives from its application to the borders of hell, where dwell Dante's "praiseless and blameless dead," the Old Testament saints, and the newborn babes who did not take the precaution of getting themselves baptized before slipping back into the Unknown.

lime. See BIRD-LIME.

limehouse. Burke's *Lime-house Nights* are sufficiently well known in America to have given the name a strong flavor of fog, sinister figures, and sudden death. In England, however, since a 1909 speech there by Lloyd George, it has conveyed much the same meaning as "billingsgate" (originally a fish market noted for bad language). Limehouse is a district in the East End of London; and the politician "spoke their language" of violent abuse.

limelight. See SPOTLIGHT.

limerick. Lear's *Book of Nonsense* (1846) did much to popularize this form of verse. But the first instance in print is said by Stevenson to be in a *History of Sixteen Wonderful Old Women*, in 1820. The way the town of Limerick, Ireland, got mixed up in it was that after each ridiculous stanza a chorus would be sung about "coming up to Limerick."

limey. It is probably well known that this nickname for a British sailor is an abbreviation of *lime-juicer*. To prevent scurvy, the drinking of lime-juice is compulsory in John Bull's navy. The name has been generously stretched so that it covers any Englishman.

limit. See HOG.

limp. See LIMBER.

line. It would never do for a sub-deb to be natural. She must have her "line." She may be gushing, or super-sophisticated, or appealingly naive. His "line" is also the memorized speech the salesman rattles off with his foot in the door. "He handed me a line" would mean about the same as "took me for a ride" (see RIDE) in its less deadly form. (See HARD LINES. PATTER.)

lion hunter. In the sense of a person whose hobby is entertaining celebrities, this undoubtedly owes its widespread popularity to *Pickwick Papers* (1837) though it was found by OED in a work by one R. C. Sands, in 1829. Dickens was ingenious enough to give his celebrity chaser the name of "Mrs. Leo Hunter" without patronizingly explaining that Leo was Latin for lion; this flattered thousands of his readers into thinking that they really did remember their Latin marvelously, and accounted largely for the overnight rise of the expression to fame. Carlyle adopted it in 1840.

lion in his den. See BEARD.

lion rampant. See RAMP.

lion's share. Æsop's lion announced that he was entitled to one fourth of any kill the pack made, because of his prerogative; another fourth, because of his superior courage; a third fourth for his dam and cubs; and as for the last fourth, "let who will dispute it with me." Though not personally acquainted with any lions, I gather that this fellow's intention was to have it all. Yet the ordinary definition of "the lion's share" is "the best or largest part." This would indicate that "Who Will" did successfully dispute the fourth quarter with him often enough to establish a precedent.

lip. See KEEP.

liquidate. See LIFT. WORKS.

lisp. By derivation (from Old High German) this means also stammer. The poet who "lisp'd in numbers" was Pope. Whether or not free verse is poetry, it is certainly not "numbers," the rather unromantic name for poetry that has a specified number of feet.

little army. See CONTEMPTIBLE LITTLE ARMY.

little bird told me. See BIRD.

little end of the horn. See HORN.

Little Nell. See NELL.

little Willy. See WILLIES.

lively as a chipmunk. See CHIP.

liver. See LILY-LIVERED.

livid. Who among us has not been thrilled, at one time or other, by a scene in which somebody, "his face livid with horror," did something heroic or dastardly? But who among us knew then what we know now, that *livid* means "black and blue"? It comes from the Latin word for a bluish-leaden color, and is related to an Old Slavic word for plum, and to our *lavender*. As a matter of fact, *livid* can mean "ashy pale"; and "livid white" is a perfectly good expression.

Lo. See INDIAN.

loaf-eater. See BEEF-EATER.

loafer. As the word was known to New Yorkers before the Mexican War, it is more likely that it has Dutch or German ancestors than that it comes from Mexican *gallofero*, a vagabond. B. & L. say the Dutch word *loever* meant "one who idly strolls about." Lowell thought German *laufen*, to run, was indicated, but that is a little too energetic a word. However, *landläufer*, a German term used by Scott, in *The Antiquary*, in the sense of "loafer," implies a connection somewhere.

lob. See LUBBER.

loco. The weed which drives horses and cattle crazy takes its name from Spanish *loco*, insane.

Though the *loco-focos* of the 1840's were considered by many to be crazy radicals, no connection has been established with the above *loco*, which did not become Americanized till forty years later. They were a branch of the Democratic party who made so much disturbance at a Tammany Hall meeting that it was adjourned and the gas turned off; whereupon they lit candles with their *loco-focos* (early form of lucifer matches), and completed their organization. The name seems first to have been attached to a self-igniting cigar (an idea which was applied, without notable success, to the cigarette in the seventies). The wild flare of the primitive matches (from French *mèche*) may, in the opinion of B. & L., have suggested the "barbarous combination" of *loco* and *fuego*, crazy fire. But Webster chooses to refer *loco* to the idea of "self-moving" mistakenly supposed to be in *locomotive*, and to substitute Italian *fuoco* for its Spanish equivalent.

locum-tenens. This Latin term for which French *lieutenant* is an exact translation is familiar in England but practically unknown here. It means one who is taking the place of another, especially of a clergyman or doctor.

log. See BUMP. HOPKINS LOG.

loggerheads. This seems to have been used as a synonym for *leatherheads* or *blockheads* for many years. But just how it worked itself into the phrase "at loggerheads," meaning engaged in a violent quarrel, is not clear. Fielding has something about hindering "these two loggerheads from falling foul of one another," which may have had something to do with the development of the squabbling idea. Then, too, there was a long-handled instrument with a sort of soldering iron on the end, for heating in the fire; it was then plunged into a bucket of liquid to warm it, much as the barber boils water by putting a miniature "loggerhead" (electric, and under a different name) into a glassful. Two ancient loggerheads, with red-hot tips, would make admirable weapons. But if you don't like the above theories, experiment with the fact that a loggerhead is also a very large snapping turtle.

log-rolling. This has two literal meanings and one figurative. Getting logs into place for a cabin was arduous work for one or two men, but all sorts of fun for a crowd, while the rum held out. Thus, on the principle of the ancient proverb, "I'll scratch your back if you'll scratch mine" ("Claw me, claw thee"), our pioneer ancestors found life just one log-rolling after another. By 1838 the striking similarity to the game of politics had been noticed, and the age of deals ("You throw your support to my man, and later I'll throw mine to yours") was ushered in. Nor has literary log-rolling, in the field of book-reviewing, been unheard of.

The other literal sense has been increasingly taken care of by the word *birling*, a competitive sport in which two lumberjacks, with spiked shoes, get on the same floating log and try to spin each other into the water. This was called *log-rolling* at one time, though OED's description of it as "propelling a log on which one is seated" is amusingly wide of the mark. The derivation of *birl* is obscure; while it may bear some relation to *burl*, a knot on a log, it is probably, like *whirl*, imitative.

logy. While the very inertness of a log makes it a possible source for *logy* in the sense of dull, slow, awkward, the dictionaries point also to Dutch *log*, meaning just about that. Thornton spells the word *loggy* prior to 1888.

lollard. This was a contemptuous name for the followers of Wyclif. Authorities agree that it can be traced to Dutch *lollaerd*, a mutterer, one who mumbles over his prayers and hymns. Webster says it is akin to our word *lull*.

Lombard Street to a China orange. See DOLLARS TO DOUGHNUTS.

long bow. See DRAW.

long count. See DOWN FOR THE COUNT.

long green. See KALE.

look. See HANGDOG LOOK.

look a gift horse in the mouth. See GIFT HORSE.

loop. See KNOCK GALLEY WEST.

loot. Indian Nationalists have doubtless pointed out with glee that when John Bull wanted a hot and fast word for booty or plunder he went to India for it. From Hindustani *lut*, plunder, it appeared in 1788 as a native word (in italics) and in 1839 it seemed right at home in England, though still recognized as Anglo-Indian.

Lord's Prayer. See PATTER.

lose face. In our present primitive civilization, it is still necessary for nations to go to war, or to continue a ridiculous war, in order to gratify a curious invention of the late cave-men, National Pride. One of the best illustrations in all history of the alleged importance of "saving face" was when Mussolini seized the Lion of Judah by the tail and dared not let go. Both were desperately uncomfortable, but nothing could be done until a face-saving formula could be found. The Chinese, who invented the phrase, "lose face," and taught it to the Europeans in about 1870, have traditionally been willing to accept defeat philosophically if the other side would make the tiniest flicker of a compromise.

Lothario. A "gay Lothario" goes back to an unscrupulous rake of that name in Rowe's play, *The Fair Penitent.* He is not by any means held up as a model of conduct, for the fair penitent, Calista, after being seduced by him, stabs herself. A contemporary, Davenant, introduced a Lothario of somewhat similar habits.

lotus-eater. Though Webster chooses this spelling, Tennyson and most of the other poets have stuck to the Greek, *lotos.* Inasmuch as eating the fruit induced a form of insanity, wherein the victim idled and dreamed all day—or perhaps you don't agree on the insanity diagnosis—one wonders wistfully if there might not be a remote connection between Spanish *loco* and Greek *lotos.* The one-time popularity of *jujubes*, lozenges flavored (or alleged to be flavored) with that fruit, may have been helped along in certain quarters by the belief that the jujube was the original *lotos.* They were supposed to be soothing to an irritated throat.

love. As late as Smollett's translation of *Gil Blas*, "no love lost between us" could mean "a perfect love," all of it being mutually absorbed. About that time (mid-18th century) people began making wise-cracks about the absurdly contradictory meanings of the same phrase, and soon the above sense was dead and buried. We explain it now as a case of reciprocated antagonism where neither party wastes any of his valuable love on the other. Middleton uses a phrase that is sufficiently hard to figure out: "no hate lost between us."

In tennis and some other games, *love* has meant "nothing" since 1742 at least. An ingenious conjecture that it might come from French *l'œuf*, egg—hence, zero—is not supported by the dictionaries. The credit is usually given to such a phrase as "play for money or play for love," i.e., for nothing.

"Love-apples" were tomatoes between 1550 and 1825, though the name was at one time applied to the eggplant. French and German equivalents were *pommes d'amour* and *Liebesapfeln.*

love of money. See MONEY.

love their lords. See WOMEN WHO LOVE THEIR LORDS.

lowdown. In undergoing transformation from an adjective to a noun, this slang word somehow lost its disreputable meaning of "no good," and came to be a highly desirable thing, the "inside dope," the basic facts. The figure may be related to "get in on the ground floor."

lower the boom. See BOOM.

lubber. Milton's "lubber fiend" (*L'Allegro*) and the familiar "land-lubber" are said to be related to a French verb *lober*, to deceive, influenced by English *lob*, a hanging mass of fat flesh. That may be the correct situation, but it looks to me as if the influencer had been more important than the source. Norwegian *lubba*, a short, stout person, may be related. In cricket and tennis, a *lob* is, by derivation, an arched ball which moves heavily and slowly.

An old nautical expression, "bass the lubber," was explained in the *Olio* (a magazine of 1828) as meaning to put a clumsy seaman ashore on the island of Bass.

Lucifer. Too bad that the devil had to ruin such a fine upstanding name—meaning "light-bearing," and first applied to the morning star. Yet, because of his diabolical pride, he was driven out of heaven. And "proud as Lucifer" has been an English proverb since 1394. In 1831, the new phosphorus matches were nicknamed Lucifers, and the expression was revived by the British in World War I ("While you've a lucifer to light your fag . . .").

luff. See STARBOARD.

luggage. See BAGGAGE.

lugger. Made famous as the title of a novel by A. S. M. Hutchinson, "once aboard the lugger" has been traced to one of those double-title melodramas of the eighties, *Jack and Jack's Brother, or The Gipsy Farmer*. In it (according to N. & Q.) the villain says: "I want you to assist me in forcing her on board my lugger; once there, I'll frighten her into marriage." The writers of *Floradora* (1899) made use of the compact phrase into which this thrilling scene had, by common consent, been condensed. A lugger, by the way, is a small vessel equipped with one or more four-sided sails known as lug-sails.

luggs. See SILK PURSE OUT OF A SOW'S EAR.

lull. See LOLLARD.

lumber room. American readers of *A Christmas Carol* have doubtless wondered why Scrooge kept a room full of planks as part of his suite. The explanation is that lumber is a British term for useless articles; it derives from the Lombard pawnbrokers.

lummox. In the sense of a fat, awkward bungler, this is not clearly of American origin, though it has been found here since 1825. It is probably related to *lump*, and to provincial English *lummock*, to move heavily or clumsily.

lump. "If you don't like it, you can lump it" is the more primitive version of "take it and like it" (the allusion being to something unpleasant). The ordinary *lump* may have had influence here, in the sense of gulping down something hard to swallow; also, words like *glum* and *dumps* reek with gloom; and there is actually an old English verb *lump* that means to look sulky.

luncheon. Originally *nuncheon*, from *none-chenche*, "noon-drinking" (from Anglo-Saxon *scencan*, to pour). Drinking during the heat of the day was, we may deduce, more important than eating, as the early *bever* for noon-meal was derived from *bibere*, to drink.

Nuncheon collided with *lunshin*, dialect for "a hunk of bread," to give *luncheon*. The American use of *lunch* for a snack, or informal meal, at any time of day or night is not usual in England.

lushy. This slang word for intoxicated has been replaced by half a hundred others; there are more synonyms for this than for almost any other situation humanity gets itself into, apparently because of the extreme prejudice existing against saying bluntly, "I was drunk last night." But *lush*, in the sense of liquor or drunkard, was common all through the previous century. B.& L., as usual, advance a gypsy word as source, but others simply point to the adjective *lush*, succulent or full of juice, as a possibility. A drunkard in the exuberant stage is not entirely dissimilar to a tree bursting with luxuriant foliage.

lye. See LATHER.

lynch law. The doubtful honor of having one's name associated with this curious device for preserving law and order has been given to: a warden of Galway who condemned his son to death; two Virginians, James and Charles Lynch; and a creek in South Carolina. Now Sir William Craigie pops up, quite positively, with a third Virginian, Captain William, who in 1786 organized a body of citizens to rid the countryside of undesirables; their humane method, according to the captain, was to set the man on his horse, tie one end of a rope to a tree limb and the other around his neck; sometimes, Captain Lynch admitted, "there was an accident and the horse walked away" (NANA, June 8, 1935).

The expressive word "rolphing" (suggestive of "wolfing") might have supplanted "lynching," had not the governor of California died when he did.

lynx. See LEOPARD.

lynx-eyed. As the modern lynx is not noted for keen eyesight (though its name, related to Latin *lux*, must originally have had reference either to light color or good eyes), the expression may be a corruption of "Lynceus-eyed." Lynceus could see objects nine miles away—in point of fact, he could see right through the earth, according to the most reliable mythologies.

M

McCoy. "The real McCoy" appears to be a ringing tribute to some honest and dependable Irishman of that name, but no candidate for the honor has, I believe, come forward, unless it be pugilist "Kid" McCoy (Partridge). Of course it may be ephemeral, but if it should persist, in the sense of something genuine and wholly admirable, people will be asking why we didn't locate Mr. McCoy before it was too late —as happened in the case of *hoodlum*, for instance. On the other hand, "the real McGoo" is flagrantly an imitation of the other, and is not a name at all but an attempt to insert the idea of sticky and slightly soiled sentiment into movie slang for "sex appeal."

macaroni. The mistaken belief that Italian manners, and hence Italian food, were incomparably the finest in the world, led a group of gigolo-type Englishmen to form the Macaroni Club in 1764. Thus a perfectly edible and sometimes excellent dish (akin, as it happens, to the worthy *macaroon*) became the badge of the dude or fop. English authors, from Shakespeare down, seem to have found the "Italianized coxcomb" a bit hard to bear. A surprisingly accurate translation of *gigolo*, by the way, is "jigger."

Macassar. See ANTIMACASSAR.

machine politics. The use of *machine* in this sense seems to have arisen in the early nineteenth century, as Hawthorne, Aaron Burr, and the Duke of Wellington are variously credited with the parentage of the phrase. Walsh suggests a possible connection with the political activities of the volunteer fire companies, who doubtless learned the value of teamwork on the levers of the pumping machines.

mad. "Mad as a hatter" has yet to be convincingly explained. There have been references to various eccentric or vigorous hatters (including the father of the poet Collins); to Australian miners (called "hatters") who work alone and get a bit queer; and to infuriated adders. In view of the complexities that surround the pronunciation of *h* in England, and of the fact that "nattered" is provincial for "ill-tempered," I find it possible to believe that this was once "mad as a 'atter," i.e., an adder. Thackeray and Lewis Carroll did most to popularize the expression.

"Mad as a March hare" is easier; it derives from the characteristic wildness of the hare during March, the breeding season. Chaucer used it and Heywood (1562) explained it.

Mae West. See ANNIE OAKLEY.

mafficking. The *Pall Mall Gazette* appears to have coined this curious-looking verb in 1900. It served its purpose—to describe the sort of riotous celebrating in the streets that greeted the relief of Mafeking after Col. Baden-Powell (later to be the founder of the Boy Scout movement) had defended it capably, but somehow a little too light-heartedly, against the Boers for six long months—and was not even resurrected, I believe, to embellish newspaper accounts of Armistice Day demonstrations. Its chief value lies in the hint it gives as to the correct pronunciation of Mafeking.

Magog. See GOG AND MAGOG.

mail. See BLACKMAIL.

maize. Comes from a West Indian dialect, through the Spanish. It was used by many early colonists instead of the cumbrous "Indian corn," but was abandoned when the latter was shortened to *corn*, which in England still means grain in general. Apparently the American usage arose because Indian corn was the only corn worth mentioning at the time.

makari. Perhaps the most important single word in chapter VI of volume III of the Cambridge History of English Literature is *makari*. Yet it is not explained there, it is not listed in the index, and it is not to be found, in just that form, in either Webster or OED. I finally found *makar* in EDD and, with some difficulty, in other dictionaries, as being a variant of "maker," archaic Scotch way of denoting a "poet." Thus one learns, to his relief, that Dunbar and some others were not African headhunters but just "makers of verse."

make. Until recently, "on the make" meant "out for money." A Barrie play (*What Every Woman Knows*) has "a Scotsman on the make" in this sense. During the depression, it came to mean "out for love," perhaps because it was easier to make love than money in those historic days. Anyway, *make* became the fashionable slang word for "pick up" or "flirt with"; as in "That fellow tried to make me." Inevitably it developed, under less polite circumstances, into a synonym for "seduce."

Somewhat similar in meaning is the modern "make a pass at." "He made a pass at me" usually conveys that the honest and virtuous girl telling the story resisted successfully the boy's attempts to kiss or pet her. The expression came into society from the prize ring, where it still can mean "to take a poke at," especially if the poke does not connect. Or possibly from the noble game of crap-shooting.

OED discovered "make the grade" in 1930, in the sense of "reaching a proper standard." This implies derivation from the *grade* of "Grade A milk"; but I think it just as likely to be a railroad figure—that of a heavy train laboring up a long hill.

make no bones. See BONES.

make three bites of a cherry. See CHERRY.

make whoopee. See WHOOPEE.

mandarin. See JOSS.

mandolin. See BANJO.

maneuver. See MANURE.

mangle. The ironing machine to which Mr. Mantalini ultimately descended did not take its name from the verb meaning to mutilate. It comes rather from Greek *manganon*, to cheat (ancestor of *monger*, peddler), the point seeming to be that to smooth out wrinkles is an artificial way of imparting beauty (similarly, a college "smoothy" will not let considerations of honesty interfere with his gracious plausibility). Or else it comes indirectly from the same Greek word via *mangonel*, a catapult operated by pulleys and counterweights, for the early mangles were weighted with stones, having evolved from a heavy wooden club or "battledore" (q.v.). Why *mangonel* should have come from a word meaning "cheat" is not clear, unless the enemy at first thought that catapults, like poison gas and tanks and nuclear rockets, were not altogether fair. A colloquial question that Queen Victoria most likely knew about was: "Has your aunt (or mother) sold her mangle?" It was considered vaguely insulting, being roughly equivalent to "So's your old man," a silly come-back of the middle twenties in this country.

manhandle. While this may have been influenced by *mangle*, to mutilate, it seems clear that the source of our word meaning "to knock a person about roughly" is the same word under the harmless definition of "perform by manpower." The difference in connotation evidently resulted from the substitution of an animate object for an inanimate.

man of straw. That such men are ideal for burning in effigy probably accounts for the term's meaning a puppet or a worthless person. Perhaps its development to mean also a perjured witness or one who offers fraudulent bail was aided by the custom such miserable men had of wearing straws in their shoes. We most commonly use the expression to mean a fictitious opponent which some argumentative person creates and then demolishes, much to his own satisfaction; the metaphor is most useful when our own position has been misrepresented.

manure. Originally a polite word related to *manu opera*, *main-œuvre*, "manual labor," this was degraded into a euphemism by those who did not like the word *dung*—and, as always happens, it has taken on the characteristic odor of the word for which it was substituted. The fact that *manure* and *maneuver* are doublets should make life a trifle easier for those apostles of frankness from the garden clubs who maintain that fertilizer is a dinner-table topic. (See DIAPER.)

marble. See ALLEY.

March hare. See MAD.

Maria. See BLACK MARIA.

marines. "Tell it to the marines" doubtless arose from the belief among seamen that the comparatively inexperienced soldiers aboard ship would believe any wild story about the sea that an inventive sailor could devise. The expression means, of course, "I don't believe you—tell your tale to some greenhorn who will." (See GALOOT. LEATHERNECK.)

market. See DRUG ON THE MARKET.

Mark Hopkins. See HOPKINS LOG.

maroon. From French *marron*, meaning two entirely different things, we have a color (ranging from reddish-blue to reddish-yellow) and a verb meaning to abandon in an isolated place. The color was originally *chestnut*, the translation of the first French word. The second, from Spanish *cimarron*, wild (from *cimarra*, bushes), meant a fugitive slave, one who had escaped into the "bush."

marquee. The French word *marquise* (figurative word for an additional protection spread over the tent of an officer—the idea being, perhaps, that of a member of the nobility extending her protection over her gallant friend in the field-tent) was misunderstood as a plural, and, like "heathen Chinee," became a singular "marquee." It now means, in circus parlance, the main entrance to the big top, or a projecting canopy of some sort.

marriage. See MORGANATIC MARRIAGE.

marrow-bone stage. See SHANK'S MARE.

marry over the broomstick. See JUMP.

martinet. In spite of the efforts of some really scholarly men to find a better source for this than Col. Martinet, Louis XIV's drill master, on the grounds that Wycherley used the word in its uncomplimentary sense about forty years before the disciplinarian died, and that the term was not known in France in that sense (a goose-stepping stickler for the rules)—yet the fact seems to be that he made so profound an impression with his reorganization of the French infantry that almost overnight his name came to be known, and feared, and then ridiculed, in England.

mascot. The immediate origin of this, as an English word, was the appearance of an opera, *La Mascotte*, in 1880. Webster and OED trace the word to Provençal *masco*, sorceress. Connection with *masqué*, born with a caul and hence "lucky," has not been established.

masher. B. & L.'s gypsy origin for this, in the sense of a male flirt, is a word that means "allure." OED's first quotation for the slang term is 1882, though B. & L. traced it back to 1860. While suggesting no more definite a source than does OED, Webster points out the similarity with slang "have a crush on." The notion seems to be that one's heart can be softened by pressure!

Mason-Dixon. See DIXIELAND.

massive retaliation. See BRINKMANSHIP.

match. See LOCO.

maundy Thursday. This phrase commemorates either Christ's "new commandment," *mandatum novum*, or the "maunds," baskets, in which food was distributed to the poor on the day before Good Friday. Webster prefers the former, the reference to "Love one another!" "Maundy silver" was the name given at one time to certain small coins struck off for use as alms at that period of the year.

maverick. Samuel A. Maverick, Texas cattleman, having his ranch on an island, didn't bother to brand his calves. Thus, any unbranded calf came to be called a maverick. A descendant of Samuel, member of Congress in 1936, organized a block of "mavericks," insurgents or independents who do not acknowledge any party leadership. (See MUGWUMP.) However, the word was understood in this political sense as early as 1886. Mencken was mistaken in characterizing *maverick* as "an entirely new invention."

mazuma. Everybody admits that this is from a Yiddish word for money. The only hitch in it is that it is supposed to have risen to fame in Kansas. One might expect Hebrew words to influence the speech of New York City. But why Kansas?

mealy-mouthed. Meaning soft-spoken to the point of insincerity, this adjective, listed by Weseen as American slang, goes back to 1572 in England as well. Webster's explanation is that meal is soft, dry, and friable (which does not mean "capable of being fried," but "easily crumbled," being a distant relative of *friction*, from *fricare*, to rub).

mean valet-soul. See HERO.

measly. It struck me as something of an original discovery that this word for insignificant or worthless might somehow be connected with the disease of measles. I rushed to the dictionaries and learned that no one had ever, apparently, thought otherwise. The point seems to be that there is something singularly unheroic and even miserable about a child with the measles.

Meerschweinchen. See GUINEA PIG.

melt. See BUTTER WON'T MELT IN HER MOUTH.

melting pot. Israel Zangwill gets the credit for this, in the sense of a country (the United States, specifically) that welcomes all sorts of people and gradually breaks down their racial and national prejudices. His 1910 play of that title, which was a study of problems of immigration, gave the expression immediate prominence.

merry. See EAT, DRINK, AND BE MERRY.

Mesopotamia. While the story attributed to Garrick—that an illiterate old saint confided to George Whitefield, after one of his affecting sermons, that she "found great support in that blessed word *Mesopotamia*"—is too good to be true, there is evidence that the revivalist could intone commonplaces or even incomprehensibilities in a way to wring the heart strings. If ever he "put the fodder too high for the calves to reach," as Walter Hard says John Bascom did when he preached in a little Vermont church, he surrounded it with a fragrance that itself nourished and satisfied. It was a little like the Negro preacher who announced: "Dis mawnin I is gwine to describe de indescribable, explain de unexplainable, and unscrew de inscrutable."

middle-aisle. See AISLE.

middleman. See FINGER-MAN.

middle of the stream. See SWAP HORSES IN THE MIDDLE OF THE STREAM.

midriff. Listed as prizefighters' slang by Weseen, this word for diaphragm has been good English since Anglo-Saxon times, *middhrif* being the word for bowels or womb.

mild. See DRAW.

mile. See MISS AS GOOD AS A MILE.

mill about. Apparently from the circular motion of mill stones or mill wheels comes this mid-19th century invention to describe a rotating and usually panicky herd of cattle or other animals. The first use of it in print seems to be Kipling's, in 1874, in reference to India. The word has been extended to include the turbulent actions of any rioting mob.

Miller. See JOE MILLER.

millions for defense. Bombaugh, in 1905, and the more recent Stevenson have, I think, caught the mighty Webster in a mistake. Both Bombaugh and Stevenson state, with seemingly unassailable documentary backing, that General Pinckney did not say "Millions for defense, but not a cent for tribute!" when a French diplomat tried to touch Uncle Sam for a quarter of a million. It was Robert Goodloe Harper, at a public meeting, June 18, 1798. What Pinckney says he said is: "No, no; not a penny." (See the 1950 Webster, under *tribute.* Too bad he didn't read the 1936 *Phrase Origins* more carefully.)

Milton Street. See GRUB STREET.

Milwaukee. See CREAM CITY.

mince matters. Found also (in *Othello* and elsewhere) as "mince the matter," this is almost always in the negative. "He didn't mince matters" means "He spoke out frankly"; i.e., it was not hash that his hearers had to swallow, but tough beefsteak. *Mince* is related to Latin *minutia.*

mind your p's and q's. Meaning "be careful," this may have arisen because of the similarity—especially to a type-setter who has to read the letters upside down—between *p* and *q.* Or perhaps the phrase meant this, to a tavern keeper figuring up the monthly beer bill: "Be careful not to mix up the *pints* and *quarts.*"

minion. The trite phrase, "minions of the law," has led many to associate this with brutal force. Yet it is the same word as French *mignon,* small, which may derive from a Celtic word of that meaning or a German word for "love"; properly, a minion is a pampered darling, hence an obsequious follower. Perhaps there has been somewhere a mix-up between minions and *myrmidons* (q.v.).

mint. See MONEY.

minute drops. Of course this might mean "tiny drops" (with the accent on the *nute*), but in *Il Pensoroso* it is used as in: minute gun, minute steak, minute man, minute hand; i.e., the accent is on the first syllable and the reference is to the period of time. The guns and the drops follow each other at intervals of a minute; the steak takes only a minute to cook; the minute man is prepared to fight on a minute's notice; the minute hand of a clock tells, of course, the minutes.

mislead. See MIZZLE.

miss as good as a mile. Troubled by the belief that in its present form the old proverb just doesn't make sense, Walsh falls back on those sturdy old soldiers of Charlemagne, Amis and Amile, who were exactly alike, even to martyrdom. However, the 1614 form, "An inch in a miss is as good as an ell," shows better what the original intention was. Sir Walter Scott appears to have been the first to use the alliterative *mile* in place of *ell.* It may be characteristic that the British OED explains the phrase pessimistically, as "a failure is a failure," whereas the American Webster allows also its converse: that an escape, be it ever so narrow, is still an escape. That this, which is certainly the more common interpretation in this country, is historically the one to be preferred is, I think, borne out by OED's admission that only rarely has the proverb appeared thus: "A miss is as *bad* as a mile."

The expression "near-miss" seems to me a misnomer. It appears to mean "nearly a miss," which is pretty bad. Actually, "near-hit" would better describe the suspense and then the relief when the bomb *just* missed its target, namely you.

Missouri. Starting in a derogatory connection, "He's from Missouri, you'll have to show him," i.e., he's dumb and hard to teach, the phrase was quickly adopted by Missourians as a badge of distinction, signifying, rather, a native shrewdness capable of seeing through the veneer on a gold brick. *The Literary Digest*, for Jan. 28, 1922, gives data indicating that the "show me" phrase originated farther west, perhaps in Colorado, in the 1870's, but that it did not become nationally known until about the turn of the century, when Congressman W. D. Vandiver used it in the course of a joking speech explaining that the reason he was the only man without evening clothes was that the toastmaster had stolen Mr. Vandiver's. It is curious that OED found no example of "I'm from Missouri" before 1912, for in 1911 the *New York Herald* started an inquiry into the origin of the colloquialism. (See SHIBBOLETH.)

mitten. "To get the mitten," i.e., to be jilted, may be from a French-Canadian custom involving the presentation of a pair of *mitaines*, or from the Latin *mittere*, to send (about one's business), or from the jocular notion that when one's hand is asked for, one can part only with the mitten. Webster wisely refrains from offering an explanation.

mizzle. This and its synonym *drizzle* got off to a fairly good start, but the latter has outdistanced the former, even though *mizzle* had the slight advantage of an influential relative, *mist*. Even Thomas Hood's famous wise-crack about how George IV first reigned and then mizzled did not succeed in immortalizing this word for a mist-like rain. British sometimes use it as a verb to mean to drift in to an assemblage uninvited; i.e., not to crash the gate, but, as it were, to percolate through. About the only "mizzle" that is known in America is the purely fictitious verb that any number of children have postulated as the present tense of *misled* (properly, of course, the past tense of *mislead*), ours being the world's greatest breeding-ground of people who learn to read before they learn to pronounce.

The source, perhaps, of the "drift in" sense just mentioned is the other meaning of *mizzle*, to decamp or vanish, derived probably from Shelta *misli*, to go. (Shelta is an argot, chiefly Celtic, formerly used by tinkers and gypsies.)

mob. Latin words used most commonly for *mob* by classic writers, and usually thus translated, were *multitudo*, *populus*, *mobilium*, and *mobile vulgus*. The last-named was adopted bodily into English, and, in the 17th century, abbreviated to *mob*, which represents in all probability, the way people then pronounced the first syllable of this *mobile*. Inasmuch as *mobile vulgus* means "movable crowd," the expression "fickle mob" is redundant ("overflowing"), i.e., pleonastic ("more than enough"); that is to say, it kills one bird with two stones.

mob scene. See HURLY-BURLY.

mogul. The Great Mogul (corruption of *Mongol*) was the Emperor of Delhi. We apply the word not only to a type of locomotive, but to the "big shots" (derived probably from "big guns") of business, society, or the sporting world. At one time the best playing cards were known as mogul cards because they had the Emperor's picture on them. In this day of testimonials, one wonders if the descendants of His Imperial Highness remembered to collect their rightful percentage of the sales.

moll. This supposedly modern term for a gunman's girl friend has been crook cant for a couple of centuries and has somehow never graduated into respectable speech. Moll, a familiar diminutive of Mary, by the law of averages became notorious as the name likely to be borne by feminine thieves: Mary Carlson, Moll Cutpurse, Moll Flanders, Molly Mog. Then there was "Moll Blood," old Scotch slang for the gallows, and "mob," old slang for a prostitute—both of which may have contributed to the rich background of "the gangster's moll."

money. This, and its cousin, *mint*, are descendants of Juno *Moneta*, the admonisher (from *monere*, to warn). The mint, where money was coined, was attached to her temple.

An old misquotation hit the front page during the 1936 investigation of the Morgan war activities. When Thomas Lamont remarked that "money was the root of all evil," J. P. Morgan corrected him, pointing out that it should have been, "The love of money is the root of all evil" (1 Tim. 6:10). Shocker Shaw, with the old twinkle in his eye, has proclaimed that "the lack of money is the root of all evil." (See FIAT MONEY.)

monger. See MANGLE.

moniker. Your "moniker" is your name in the vernacular of the road. B. & L. guess that "monarch" is the source, the idea being "Every Man a King," but "monarch" is a pedantic word for a tramp. The same objection applies to "monocle." Partridge agrees with Jack Black (1926) that it may be a corruption of *monogram*. If it could be shown that "moniker" is very old, an interesting connection might be established with *Moneke*, the name of the ape's son in one of the beast epics (1498), the word from which Skeat derives "monkey," connecting Moneke with Italian *mona*, ape. However, the hook-up of Moneke with *monkey* may be made through *Simon*, for which Moneke may have been a pet name; and Simon is associated with *simian*, from the Latin for "flat-nosed."

monitor. From a teacher in a nursery school, to a grim "cracker box set on a raft," to a senior adviser in a preparatory school—all of these senses are easily traced to Latin *monere*, to advise or warn. Captain Ericsson's barge with its heavily armored gun-turret was especially designed to be "a severe monitor" or admonisher to the Southern forces in our Civil War. In a boys' school, the students who are chosen as the leaders in their class are usually so highly respected that I do not remember to have heard it mentioned in one's austere presence that a monitor is a large and rapacious lizard.

monkey. The "monkey jacket," abbreviated white dinner coat developed in the navy as full-dress equipment, can be found at college proms but not in the big dictionaries, except in the sense of a *tailless* jacket (from which it gets its name) used by the sailors in their work since about 1800.

"Monkey wrench" is a good example, like *crane*, of a thing named after a living creature because of a fancied resemblance. The sliding jaw of the wrench must have reminded someone of the monkey's chewing apparatus.

Only since the Civil War have the verb "to monkey" and the noun "buzz saw" been in print. But the two ideas have long been happily married, though no official cognizance of the union has been taken by the leading authorities. The instinctive urge of the monkey to "fool around," plus the menace of an unprotected circular saw led inevitably to "monkey with the buzz saw" in the figurative application of gay experimentation in the face of screaming danger. (See MONIKER.)

monkey-shines. See SHINNY.

monkey trial. See BIBLE BELT.

monkey wrench. See PIG IRON.

monstrance. See HOST.

months without an "r." See OYSTER.

moocher. When it is realized that this old slang word for petty thief or "sponger" might also be pronounced, and spelled, "mowcher," one can appreciate better the distress of the "volatile" little woman who protested to Dickens against his all too faithful portrayal of her oddities in *David Copperfield*. It will be remembered that the author changed his plans so that she finally emerged somewhat of a heroine.

This word for one who pretends poverty or "fumbles for the check" (i.e., is purposely slow in offering to pay the dinner check) is probably from Old French *muchier*, to hide or skulk. The comic strip character, Minnie the Moocher, offers a direct contrast to Tillie the Toiler. (See FINAGLER.)

moolah. See PAYOLA.

moon. "Once in a blue moon" meant, originally, "never"—it being considered as ridiculous to think the moon blue as to believe it was made of green cheese—but the "never" (like that of the *Pinafore's* captain) has softened into "hardly ever." In a 1934 song-hit (Rodgers & Hart), a rather ingenious use of the expression "blue moon" was made. It told of how a blue moon turned to gold when love came. That idea, transferred from Tin Pan Alley (where the popular songs are hammered out) to the football field, might have been rated a "triple threat" (a man who can run, pass, and kick with about equal skill)—for we have (1) the sentimental value of the moon, (2) the gloom value of "blue," and (3) the miracle connotation of "once in a blue moon."

The crack about green cheese goes back to the early 16th century in both French and English. One writer turned it into "cream cheese."

Meaning illicit whisky, *moonshine* is earlier than *boot-leg* liquor (q.v.). Even before 1800, it was English slang for smuggled spirits, presumably because, paradoxically, business was best when there was no moon. Scott, in 1809, used the word *moonlight* in the same sense.

That the light of the moon is supposed to make one "loony" (Latin *luna*, moon, source of *lunacy*) is reflected in the uncomplimentary phrase, "transcendental moonshine," applied by both De Quincey and Sterling to certain remarks of Coleridge, and said also to have been used by Carlyle in reference to something of Emerson's.

As OED seems at a loss to explain the use of "Moonlights" in reference to a Commencement oratorical contest at Williams College, I plead special knowledge, and reveal that the contests were, for nearly a century, held (as often as possible) outdoors under a June moon. (See HONEYMOON.) Mathews (1951) devoted four quotations to it, but neglected to mention that the "tradition" was quietly allowed to expire *twenty-one years ago* (1939) after "inclement weather" had twice driven the contest indoors, and reduced the attendance in 1938 to forty persons.

moot question. Originally a question proposed for debate in an assembly (from *mot* or *maethel*, Anglo-Saxon for meeting), this is now a decidedly trite term for a question actively under discussion. (See BLACKMAIL.)

mop up. This bit of military slang, which even the new Webster implies originated in World War I trenches, goes back to the Boer War. It means to clear out the last trace of enemy from territory just taken over, and it derives from the household mop that you hunt for when Junior spills his milk.

morganatic marriage. This term for the marriage of a royal personage with a commoner is derived from Old German *morgangeba*, morning gift. After the first night of their life together, the husband would make the wife a substantial present, often secured beforehand by contract, which was understood to wipe out all her future claims to his title or estate. An instance often cited is that of Archduke Ferdinand of Austria, whose wife died with him in the assassination that set off World War I; another is that of King Carol and Mme. Lupescu. It must be admitted, however, that the former union was a good deal more than morganatic, the latter a good deal less.

Morgan le fay. See FATA MORGANA.

morituri salutamus. In this form, the phrase made a rhythmic title for a poem of Longfellow's. The gladiators, passing in review before the emperor, probably gave it as "Morituri te salutamus," "We who are about to die salute thee," or the first person may have been replaced by the third person, *salutant*, as being more respectful.

morning after the night before. See HANGOVER.

morning shows the day. See CHILD IS FATHER OF THE MAN.

mosey. See VAMOOSE.

mossback. See FOGY.

most admired disorder. See ADMIRE.

moth balls. See LAVENDER.

Mother Carey's chickens. In 1934, Weekley was still of the opinion that, despite ingenious guesses, the origin of Mother Carey "remains as obscure as that of Davy Jones or the Jolly Roger." However, Webster and OED think that she is none other than the Virgin Mary, by way of *mater cara* or *madre cara*, "mother dear," protector of sailors. In any event, her chickens or geese belong to the petrel family, and when she plucks their feathers and lets them drift down on the water it looks like a snowstorm. In fact, it is.

Petrel is probably the diminutive of *Peter*, who walked on the water. When they fly close to the water, they give the appearance of running along its surface.

motorcade. *Cavalcade* is a French word derived from Italian *cavalcare*, to go on horseback. *Motorcade* is therefore a barbarous combination of English and French, with no etymological decency about it at all. But our new network of Interstate highways will make motorcades less difficult and dangerous, so I suppose we have to have a word for them.

mourners' bench. See AMEN CORNER.

mousse. See BOZO.

mouth. See BUTTER WON'T MELT IN HER MOUTH. GIFT HORSE. KEEP. SILVER SPOON IN HIS MOUTH.

mozo. See BOZO.

Mrs. Grundy. See GRUNDY.

muchacha. See HOT CHA.

muckey-muck. The title of "high muckey-muck" (spelled by Webster "muck-a-muck") appears to have been a childish invention without much excuse for living. One guess is that it is a fanciful enlargement on "high mogul." Certainly the *m*'s are easy enough to account for, when we have this and Great Mufti and Mumbo Jumbo from which to choose.

mud. "Here's mud in your eye," an invitation to drink, can plausibly be related to "Bottoms up!" for the sediment in the bottom of the glass would feel very little better than mud if splashed into the eye as a result of too enthusiastic inversion. In an entirely different connection, OED says that "mud" is a colloquial word for "dregs." (See HEEL-TAPS. KNOW A HAWK FROM A HANDSAW.)

muff. To "muff" a ball, or a chance, is to bungle it, to handle it badly. This useful piece of cricket and baseball slang probably arose from the pleasing spectacle (imaginary) of a man fielding a hard grounder with both hands in a muff. The word itself is from the Latin *muffula*, a fur-lined glove. However, dull blunderers have been called "muffs" since 1774 at least, when such a character in a play was given the name Sir Henry Muff. But "muff" as crook slang for girl or woman may be from association with the old-fashioned hand-warmer, or even complimentary (along lines of softness and warmth)—unless indeed it be a wretched pun on "a miss."

mufti. Many have puzzled over the problem: why should this Anglo-Indian word for priest or judge have come to mean civilian clothes? One guess is that it was in joking reference to the costume in which the Great Mufti was usually represented on the stage: dressing gown, smoking cap, and slippers. (See MUCKEY-MUCK.)

mug. It is not considered a compliment to have your face referred to as a mug, perhaps because the faces that were carved on 18th century beer mugs were not particularly noted for beauty of feature. Learned linguists have dredged in many places for some other source for this slang word, but today's dictionaries cautiously call our attention to just such drinking vessels as Varden's "Toby" in *Barnaby Rudge*, and drop the matter there.

mugwump. From American Indian *mugquomp*, which meant "big chief," this is sometimes still used ironically in that sense. But since Harold Willis Dodds, president of Princeton from 1933 to 1957, gave the uproarious definition that a mugwump was a man with his mug on one side of the fence and his wump on the other, its meaning has been fixed for ever as a "bolter," one who, in the words of B. & L., "professes to study the interests of his country before those of his party." The word is said to have been thus used first in Indianapolis in 1872.

Mumbo Jumbo. Dickens once wrote to Forster his surprise that "Carlyle, who knows everything, don't know what Mumbo Jumbo is," and went on to point out that it was not an idol or a fetish, but a disguised man representing the combined determination of the men of the tribe to keep the women strictly in their place. After one has tasted OED's dejection as to the possibility of finding its source ("origin unknown . . . no light from the languages of the Niger . . . Kongo *nzambi* geographically unlikely"), it is a relief to turn to the new Webster and find an authoritative *mama dyambo*, Mandingo dialect for "ancestor with a pompon" (wearing a tuft on the front of his hat). In confirmation of Webster's finding (though not explicitly so) the Encyclopedia Britannica mentions the Mandingo tribe as the originator of the useful bugaboo.

mumbudget. See FUSS-BUDGET.

murder. See GET.

muscular Christianity. Disraeli did as much as anybody to popularize this quite appropriate nickname for Charles Kingsley's broad-church movement. Nigel, in Disraeli's *Endymion*, was a fair sample, as was Mr. Crisparkle, in *Edwin Drood*. But as for the Reverend Charles Kingsley himself, he found the term "painful if not offensive." Brewer describes muscular Christianity as "healthy or strong-minded religion, which braces a man to fight the battle of life bravely and manfully."

music. See ARCHITECTURE. FACE THE MUSIC.

music of the spheres. The idea goes clear back to Job—"the morning stars sang together." Pythagorus taught that the moving planets were separated by intervals corresponding to the strings of a violin, and that, as the heavenly bodies revolved, harmonious notes were given off. Chaucer, Caxton, and Shakespeare were among those who gave expression to this theory, but it was not until 1798 that the exact form, "the music of the spheres," appeared in print, according to OED. One school of thought contends that this highly publicized music is the glorious click of billiard balls, but the proponents of this speculation are evidently prejudiced.

mustang. These were wild, or half-wild, horses descended from stock left in Mexico by the Spanish conquerors. The word derives from two Spanish words, *mestengo* and *mostrenco*, both of which meant "having no master." The later *mesteño* was understood to refer specifically to a graziers' association which was formed to avoid arguments as to the ownership of the vivacious animals: they all belonged to the association until they were impartially assigned to the various members.

mutton. The figure utilized in "leg of mutton school" is similar to that in "pot-boiler"; i.e., a group of writers or artists who earn their daily bread by flattering their patrons.

"Mutt" (as in "Mutt and Jeff") is evidently an abbreviation of *mutton-head*, familiar as early as 1804 in the sense of "blockhead."

myrmidon. Though the fact of ants in the ancestry is so remote that neither Webster nor OED recognizes it, Crowell is right in calling attention to it. Ovid accounts for the similarity between Greek *myrmax*, ant, and *Myrmidon*, one of the savage and brutal followers of Achilles, by asserting that they were descended from a tribe of ants. Today as applied, contemptuously, to the police, the reference is not so much to cruelty as to an unthinking or even unscrupulous obedience.

N

nab. There is nothing new about this slang word for seize—1686 is OED's first date. There was a contemporary *nap*, of Teutonic origin, that meant about the same. The word for a short sleep and that for the fuzz on wool or felt are also from the Teutonic, but their connection in meaning is not clear. Surely there can be no relation between "tearing off a nap" (catching forty winks) and plucking the nap off a carpet!

nabs. See NIBS.

nain jaune. See POPE JOAN.

naked truth. In the fable, Falsehood stole Truth's garment while Truth was in swimming; Truth, unwilling to put on Falsehood's clothes, went naked. *Nuda veritas* appears in Horace, and its translation is found in English from 1585 onward. While the naked truth is a very good thing indeed, it has been said with some wisdom, in regard particularly to the Santa Claus legend, that "Truth is not always most true when it is naked."

namby pamby. Poor Ambrose Philips wrote some wishy-washy verses for children, about 1700, and was satirized by Henry Carey in the same book in which first appeared the well-known barber-shop ballad, "Sally in Our Alley." "The Wasp of Twickenham," Alexander Pope, who was an acquaintance of Carey's, was charmed with the new nickname, Namby Pamby, for Philips.

nap. See NAB.

nasty. According to OED, this always means something foul, in England, and something still fouler, in America. Yet "he slings a nasty foot," meaning that he dances neatly (cf. *wicked*), is not only 20th-century slang that would be understood in both countries, but is found in B. & L. (British, 1897), and in Thornton as an Americanism of 1834! Webster has also, it seems, overlooked this.

nation of shopkeepers. Though this is usually ascribed to Adam Smith, in whose *Wealth of Nations* (1776) a similar phrase appeared, Stevenson has found "a shopkeeping nation" in a book by Josiah Tucker, 1766. Napoleon applied it, contemptuously, to his enemies across the channel, though he did not, as we know now, originate it; but it is characteristic of the English that they could not see anything particularly uncomplimentary about being called that, any more than they could at first see objections to "business as usual" as a national motto in the dark autumn of 1914.

nattered. See MAD.

nature-faker. See CROCODILE TEARS.

navvy. The man who plots the course of a trans-Pacific plane through the skies might raise his eyebrows (you can't surprise those fellows much) if you told him a navigator was a ditch digger. Yet that is how the British *navvy*, day-laborer, got his name. In derision at first, perhaps, the canal digger was described as a "director of ships." But do not be misled; Bowditch's *Navigator* concerns itself not at all with shovels.

nearer than hands and feet. See CLOSER IS HE THAN BREATHING.

near-miss. See MISS AS GOOD AS A MILE.

neck. Until 1927, about the only meanings this had as a verb were: to kill by striking or straining the neck (Webster); and to tie an unruly cow to a tractable one (Weseen). Since neither of these seemed to fit with any plausibility into accounts of parked-car or dance-floor activities, the lexicographers investigated a bit, and concluded that to neck a girl was to put your arm around her neck. So far, so good. Let me suggest only that it is a complete, and a silly, equivalent of *pet.* A natural outgrowth of it was the name *giraffe* as applied to one who enjoyed necking.

neck and crop. See COME A CROPPER.

neck and neck. See HORSE.

neck-verse. See BENEFIT OF CLERGY.

necromancy. See BLACK ART.

neither fish, nor flesh, nor good red herring. See RED.

neither hide nor hair. See HIDE AND HAIR.

neither rhyme nor reason. See RHYME NOR REASON.

Nell. I have not found the source of our melodramatic, shotgun wedding catchword, "do right by our Nell." It may be an echo from *Nellie, the Beautiful Cloak Model*, an early play by Owen Davis, contemporary American. That it goes back to Charles II's dying thought on behalf of his mistress, Nell Gwynne, "Don't let poor Nelly starve," is certainly a better possibility than Little Nell of *Old Curiosity Shop*. It is not believed that *nelly*, the sooty albatross, has anything to do with it.

nerts. See NUTS.

net. See LET.

never surrenders. See DIES BUT NEVER SURRENDERS.

never turned a hair. See HAIR.

new. See BRAND NEW.

news. Some one got a thrill when he noticed that this word contains the initials of the points of the compass, North, East, West, South. But science almost always frowns on the discoveries of P. B. Trovato (see BEFORE YOU CAN SAY JACK ROBINSON). A clue to the source of *news* lies in the statement (Acts 17:21) that the favorite sport of the Athenians was telling or hearing "some new thing." The plural of that, as in the case of French *nouvelles*, was *news*. Yet the word is commonly construed as singular. A famous anecdote about this was ascribed by Dr. Fernald to Horace Greeley, and a similar one told of Herbert Bayard Swope. Unable to get in touch with Mr. Greeley (then dead 64 years), I wrote Mr. Swope and received the following cordial reply from his secretary:

> Your letter of January 30th reached the office in Mr. Swope's absence. I talked with him over long distance telephone and he asked me to say that the phrase about which you inquire has been attributed to him, in certain correspondence he had with one of his young reporters at the time when the young man was out of town on an assignment. Mr. Swope called him and asked if there was any news. The young man replied, "No." Mr. Swope then said, "Ain't there even a single new?" Mr. Swope added, further, that he doubts that this was the first time the phrase was put in use.

nibs. "His nibs," as a jocular substitute for something like "his Majesty" or "his highness," was also given as "his nabs," here and there, all through the 19th century. Both were probably related to *nob*, a swell, which may have come from *notable* or simply from *knob*, head. *Notable*, by the way, used to have a meaning almost entirely unknown to Americans, that of "thrifty" or "capable" (see *Silas Marner*, Chapter XIV). The first syllable rhymed with *hot*.

nice. From Latin *nescius*, ignorant, this word derived its earliest English sense, "silly." From this it slipped easily into wanton or lascivious, which is interesting in the light of Webster's last definition as "pleasing" and "properly modest." This bad sense was largely obsolete by the time of Shakespeare, though Swift has "A nice man is a man of nasty ideas"—and by that he could not have meant the "nice fellow" that some people apply today to a man with an odoriferous collection of smoking-room anecdotes. Almost universal usage has rendered it no longer incorrect to use *nice* in other senses than that of particular or fastidious. However, as far back as 1881, observers were deploring the overuse of *nice* in indiscriminate praise. Hardy amusingly showed how far this could go, in speaking of "a nice unparticular man."

nice kettle of fish. See FISH.

Nicholas Frog. See JOHN BULL.

Nick. See HARRY.

nickel. See NIX.

nicker. See NIX.

nickname. Reversing the process seen in *an adder* (q.v.), this developed from *an eke-name*, an also-name. It is curious that Dr. Johnson, sturdiest of Englishmen, should have gone to the French *nom de nique* when there was a good Anglo-Saxon source available.

nick of time. Brewer finds some connection with being "pricked" as present at Cambridge University chapel service if you arrive "in the nick of time," while Hyamson refers to notches on a tally-stick. But more conservative authorities think of this figurative nick as merely marking a precise point of time.

nifty. Bret Harte thought this was short for *magnificat* (see OED's 1868 quotation), but the more conscientious dictionaries express doubt as to its origin. It is slang for "fine and dandy."

nigger heaven. See GALLERY GOD.

nigger in the woodpile. As the Negro was legendarily more often associated with missing chickens than with a suspiciously dwindling woodpile, it may be that the color in the case was derived simply from the "obscure factor," as Webster puts it, which has entered a situation. An entry in N. & Q. indicates that at one time the phrase was confused with the old skeleton proverb, the expression appearing as "There is a black man in her closet." (See also GREEK.) Another N. & Q. fan is under the impression that Abraham Lincoln started the whole thing, presumably by means of his Emancipation Proclamation.

nincompoop. When anger or disgust stimulates a creative artist to hitherto unreached heights of inventiveness and he explodes with such a word as this, it is seldom any use asking him where he got it. Scholars will wander about for centuries, if it really takes hold, and propose all sorts of ingenious solutions—when all that can be said with certainty about it is that to the originator it seemed like a good idea at the time, as the man said to the judge in explanation of his drunken dive through a plate glass window. A few guarded comments may however be made: *ninny*, a simpleton, is earlier (perhaps derived from *innocent*); the French use *Nicholas* for a fool, as we say "dumb Benny"; Johnson's brilliant *non compos mentis* guess (followed by Skeat) does not, says OED, agree with the earliest forms; and, finally, some of those early forms sound enough like "non-com" to suggest to the unwary a derivation of *nincompoop* from the hated *noncommissioned* officer.

nine. This mystic number was formerly used, in both singular and plural, to represent perfection. "Dressed to the nines" was usually a very complimentary way of expressing our "all dolled up." Later dictionaries do not take much stock in Skeat's idea that "to the eyes" might have borrowed an *n* just as "for the nonce" did. (See NONCE.)

nine days' wonder. In Skeat's book of *Proverbs* we find "A wonder last but nyne night never in towne" (1374), which, though sufficiently obscure, seems to have some bearing on our phrase "nine days' wonder," meaning something pretty marvelous, though not by any means one of the Seven Wonders of the World. Nine, as well as seven, has always been a mystic number, and that is probably the best reason why these two numbers appear in these expressions relative to wonders. One suggestion is that, just as kittens are blind for a number of days after birth, people's eyes may be blinded with astonishment for a while, until suddenly they discover what it is all about. The difficulty here is that we ordinarily speak of opening our eyes wide *when we are astonished.* An amusing offspring of the old pre-Chaucerian expression was the 1917–1918 nickname for the lieutenants trained for only three months: ninety day wonders.

nine points of the law. See POSSESSION.

ninny. See NINCOMPOOP.

nip and tuck. The earliest form of this equivalent of "neck and neck" is "rip and tuck" (American, 1832). This would tend to discredit, but not eliminate, B. & L.'s Cornwall wrestlers' expression, "nip and go tuck" (*nip*, for *nab*, and *tuck* for *chuck*, throw). Both *tack* and *chuck* are to be found in OED quotations. As the phrase most often appears in reference to contests of speed (which is not perhaps the word for a wrestling match) it may be that the *rip* of "let 'er rip" (q.v.) was originally intended. Then Mark Twain's "tuck," meaning pep or vigor, might serve satisfactorily as a running mate.

nip it in the bud. See SMELL.

Nira. See SOCCER.

nix, nicker. The Scandinavian root suggests demon, water-nymph, or hippopotamus (river-horse). Experiences at the old-fashioned opera to the contrary, we must not assume this to be a fair picture of the well-shaped Teutonic water-nymph. Though "Old Nick" has not been successfully traced to this, the word *nickel* has; it seems the Germans profanely called the metal *kupfernickel*, copper-demon, when it promised copper but failed to yield it. (See KOBOLD.)

Slang "nix" and "nixie," emphatic substitutes for "No," are from the German *nichts*, nothing.

nob. See NIBS.

nobbler. See WOBBLIES.

no better than she should be. Understatement is supposed to be characteristically American. But the British way of saying, "She is no better than she should be" to mean "She is immoral" is certainly mild. Its kindly originator probably intended to say, as pretentiously as possible, as little as possible. It is found in the Motteux translation of *Don Quixote*, in Beaumont & Fletcher, and in Fielding.

noble mind. See FAME.

Nod. See LAND OF NOD.

noiseless tenor. See TENOR.

no kid. See KID.

no love lost. See LOVE.

no man is a hero to his valet. See HERO.

nonce. "For the nonce," meaning "for the particular purpose" or "for the time being," is nothing more nor less than "for the once." The early form, "for then anes," indicates that the *n* got there as the sign of the dative case of the definite article. Then it was shifted to the following word, just as "an uncle" became "nuncle."

A nonce-word is a temporary one. Lexicographers are wary of using the term, as the word in question may happen to catch on, and the dictionary have to "eat crow" (see CROW). Perhaps *mafficking* (q.v.) is as good an illustration of a nonce-word as any.

no room to swing a cat. See ROOM TO SWING A CAT.

nose. See PAY THROUGH THE NOSE. THUMB THE NOSE.

notable. See NIBS.

not a cent for tribute. See MILLIONS FOR DEFENSE.

not a red (**cent**). See RED.

notch on his gun. See FEATHER IN HIS CAP.

no thoroughfare. See TABOO.

not so hot. See FROST. HOT.

not worth a nickel. See PICAYUNE.

not worth a rap. See RAP.

numbers. See LISP.

nuts. "It's the nuts," indicating high approval, is obsolescent. "I'm nuts over you" is following it into well-deserved oblivion. But "Nuts to you," with its variants "nerts" and "nurts," is just naughty enough in sexual connotation to be occasionally still heard among the so-called best people. "Nurts" is supposed to represent the sidewalks-of-New-York pronunciation.

When Maj.-Gen. Anthony C. McAuliffe, commander of surrounded American troops at Bastogne in 1944, sent his famous one-word answer to the German demand for surrender, he explained to the enemy messenger that it meant the same as "Go to hell"—and then to his own astonishment heard himself wish him "Good luck!"

"Nut" has long been used as a synonym for head, and "off his nut" for crazy.

O

oak. See SPORT YOUR OAK.

oats. See FEEL HIS OATS.

Ochus Bochus. See HOCUS POCUS.

odious, odorous. See COMPARISONS ARE ODOROUS.

odor of sanctity. As a figurative way of saying "a reputation for holiness," this derives from the curiously unscientific tradition that at death, or even at disinterment, the body of a saint would exhale a fragrance that would make the career of a "resurrection-man" a positive joy—provided he chose nothing but saints to work on.

off his nut. See NUTS.

off the handle. See FLY.

off the old block. See CHIP.

off your chump. See CHUMP.

of that ilk. See ILK.

of the same kidney. See KIDNEY.

oil on troubled waters. Since medieval days, oil has been used this way, at first with superstitious awe. In fact, Pliny and Plutarch knew about it. Only as recently as 1934 was it found that too much of it was also a menace, when some members of the crew of the sinking *Usworth* suffocated in the oil slick spread by the *Ascania*. The phrase has been in literary use in England since 1774.

ointment. See FLY.

O.K. Though Woodrow Wilson justified his use of "okeh" by tracing it to Choctaw, "It is so and in no other way," there is no evidence that President Andrew Jackson, who first popularized O.K., knew any Choctaw. In fact, he was sufficiently illiterate to have made possible the story that he thought those the initials for "Orl Korrect," a slander which has never been successfully refuted. It is conceivable, however, that the original initials used by him as his endorsement on documents were "O.R.," "Ordered Recorded." Edwards, whose work is more interesting than accurate, says that Jacob Astor, "who was a fine judge of solvency, if not of spelling," was the original "orl korrect" man.

One might here tell the story of the office boy who showed up at work with a big "O.K." badge on, and explained that it meant "All Confused." Being gently reminded that that wasn't the way to spell it, he said, "But you don't know how confused I am!"

okey-doke. See KID.

okra. See GUMBO.

old codger. See CODGER.

Old Contemptibles. See CONTEMPTIBLE LITTLE ARMY.

old fogy. See FOGY.

Old Harry. See HARRY.

old hen. The assertion that a woman is more sensitive about her age than a man need hardly be proved. But it is revealing that while some of the most affectionate pet names men have for each other make use of "old" (such as "old man" and "you old bum") a woman is insulted if you call her "old" anything—"old hen," for instance. That was the mistake that the slightly deaf cashier made at the bank, though it wasn't really anybody's fault. The Ladies Aid Society had made some money on a cake-sale, and the treasurer brought it down to the bank to deposit it. As she handed it to the cashier, she remarked, "Here's some Aid money." Thinking she had said "egg money," he replied pleasantly, "The old hens did pretty well, didn't they?"

Meredith applied the term to a disagreeable woman in 1880, but there is no reason to believe that he was the first.

Old Hickory. Here we have an admirable illustration of how conservative authorities, seeking a derivation, reject a story-origin in favor of something quite sensible and prosaic. The legend is that General

Andrew Jackson was sleeping under a tent of hickory bark when a drunken citizen, kicking over the improvised tent, hailed him as "Old Hickory." But the scholar's answer is simply that the old boy was physically as tough as hickory.

Old Nick. See HARRY.

olive branch. Seriously, this symbolizes peace (from the leaf that the dove brought back, indicating to Noah that the flood waters were abating), and facetiously it means children (from a reference in the Psalms to "children like olive plants, round about thy table"). It is clear that there is no connection between the two, for peace can hardly be said to be one among the many blessings that accompany the arrival of children.

olla podrida. See HODGEPODGE.

on a bat. See BAT.

one o' cat. See KIT-CAT.

one jump ahead of the sheriff. See BUM.

on his (tin) ear. See TIN EAR.

on ice. See BAG.

on the ball. See BALL.

on the bum. See BUM.

on the cards. See CARD.

on the carpet. See CARPET.

on the cuff. See CUFF.

on the frolic. See FROLIC.

on the make. See MAKE.

on the qui vive. See QUI VIVE.

on the spot. See SPOT.

open sesame. See SESAME.

open shop. See SHOP.

opportunity knocks but once. See TAKE TIME BY THE FORELOCK.

orange. See DOLLARS TO DOUGHNUTS.

Order of the Garter. See GARTER.

osculate. See BUSS.

ostracize. See COVENTRY.

ounce. See LEOPARD.

out loud. See CRYING OUT LOUD.

out of circulation. See HOCK.

out of kilter. See KILTER.

out of sorts. See SORTS.

out of the red. See RED.

overboard. See STARBOARD.

over the broomstick. See JUMP.

over the coals. See HAUL OVER THE COALS.

over the left (shoulder). See DEXTEROUS.

oyster. While it is true that the closed season for native oysters, in England, includes the months of May, June, July, and August, the old rule about not eating an oyster except in the "r" months is kept alive chiefly for the convenience of the oyster farmers. The Encyclopedia Britannica says that a clean fat oyster can be eaten with impunity at any time of the year. An early explanation of the prejudice was that oysters had been found to be "venerious" in the summer; but the oyster has long been famed as an aphrodisiac (from Aphrodite, goddess of love and beauty) at any season. The point is that during the summer months the growers would rather attend to the spawning and spatting than the harvesting. Not that the newlywed bivalves tend to ruin their constitutions by petty quarrels. "Spatting" is the process of settling down, when the swimming larva hooks up to something permanent, like a rock. The other *spat* is apparently related to *slap*, while a third *spat* is short for *spatterdash*—and logically, too, as the absurd little ankle-blankets are abbreviated from the knee-length gaiter of the longer name.

oyster. See COVENTRY.

Oz. See LAND OF NOD.

P

pack-staff. See PLAIN AS A PIKE-STAFF.

pad. See FOOTPAD.

paint the town red. Since about 1880, this has meant "to make *whoopee*" (q.v.) but the reason is not immediately clear. At one time "to paint" meant to drink; and of course the effect of drink on the complexion, particularly the nose, is well authenticated. Then, too, when celebrating alcoholically, folks sometimes reach the point where it seems to them a good idea to light bonfires.

pal. In almost any gypsy tongue, this means an accomplice or a brother. It comes from *pral* or *bhratr*, defined as brother.

palaver. Listed as modern slang, this goes back at least to the nineties, and even, in the form of the Spanish *palabras*, to Shakespeare (*Much Ado About Nothing*). The Portuguese name for a council of African chiefs was a *palavra*. The word is cognate with *parable*. A cant expression in England for "Shut up" (B. & L., 1897) was "Nantee palaver"—*nantee* standing for Italian *niente*, nothing.

pale. See BEYOND THE PALE.

palm. See GREASE.

palooka. As this word for a "dumb cluck" crept up from hoboland to the prize ring and thus into society, it was natural to look for its origin in the Southwest, especially as it resembled *gazabo* in general appearance and respectability. When I found *peluca*, a severe reproof, in a Spanish dictionary, I felt confident it was the source of *palooka*, though I have not seen this suggestion elsewhere, except that Mathews (1951) quotes, without comment, Mencken's statement that "Holt suggests . . . Spanish *peluca*" (Sup. II, *American Language*, 1948). The Spanish word is cognate with English *peruke*.

palpably ben trovato. See BEFORE YOU CAN SAY JACK ROBINSON.

pan. See DEAD PAN. FLASH IN THE PAN.

Panama hat. In South America such hats are given the name of the plant from which they are made (it is also the name of the town in Ecuador where the industry started)—*jipijapa* (pronounced "heepy-hoppa"). Knowing that they were not manufactured in Panama, scholars tried to derive our name for the hat from *palmata*; but now Webster returns to Panama, on the ground that it was the chief center of distribution.

panhandler. Usually when a part of a state resembles, on the map, a pan handle, that area is affectionately known by that name; the best-known are in Texas, West Virginia, and Idaho. This widespread distribution has made it an excellent opener for the confidence man, and this I believe to be the source of "panhandler" as beggar: "I'm from the old Panhandle—don't you remember me?" The scalawag has at least three chances of hitting the state right. Others derive the expression more prosaically, from the pan held out for alms, but I have yet to see a genuine panhandler with a pan.

pannier. See CODGER.

pansy. I see nothing effeminate in the quaint square face of a pansy. If the fragility of a flower accounts for the modern sense of a pervert or weakling, I feel that almost any other flower would be more appropriate than a pansy as a symbol of this—unless the Pansy Books, by Mrs. Isabella Alden (born in 1841), can be given the credit. They were a series of religious stories for young people, and were at one time very popular.

The word itself has an interesting origin: from French *herbe de la pensée*, translated (freely) by Shakespeare when he said "That's for thoughts." *Pensive* comes from the same root.

pantaloon. Originally meaning "all lion," this became a familiar baptismal name among Venetians, in honor of their patron saint,

Pantaleone. Thus there were eventually so many men of that name wearing the "breeches and stockings all of a piece" that were characteristically Venetian, that the name soon was applied to the costume. When the Italian pantomime (Harlequin and Columbine routine) chose the name for the emaciated old clown in slippers, "covetous and yet amorous old dotard" (Skeat), its fame was established. In *The Merchant of Venice*, Shakespeare uses it in reference to the "sixth age" of man.

There was great opposition in England to the wearing of pantaloons; in 1794 the Cambridge chancellor led a campaign to prohibit them. Similarly there is now British opposition to the American abbreviation, "pants," and, I suppose, "panties."

paper. See SCRAP OF PAPER.

parable. See PALAVER.

pard. See LEOPARD.

park. In the sense of "park" a car or the multitude of uses which grew out of this, as "park" a suitcase or "park" yourself (the origin, of course, of the punning "Greek" name, Parkyakakas), this verb is quite recent. It probably came from the military term, to "park" artillery or wagons in a specified location.

Most states label those wide places in the road (equipped with a rustic table and a trash can) with attractive if sometimes misleading monikers (q.v.) such as "Wayside Rest," "Picnic Area," etc., while New York State says coldly and bluntly just "Parking." To most people that suggests one of two things: either a place to leave your car, or a place to pet. Can't New York do better than that?

Perhaps at this point we can drag in the wry comment of President Clark Kerr (University of California) on three of America's supreme preoccupations. In his immortal words, delivered at the University of Washington (*Time*, Nov. 17, 1958), "the three major administrative problems on a campus are: sex for the students, athletics for the alumni, and parking for the faculty."

pasha. See BASHAW.

pass. See MAKE.

passed master. See JOURNEYMAN.

pass in the night. See SHIP.

pass in your checks. See CHECK.

pass the buck. See BUCK.

pat. See FOOTPAD.

patches. See PURPLE PATCHES.

Paternoster Row. The usual explanation that links this with *Amen Corner* (q.v.) does not apparently satisfy Webster. He points out that this street, long the headquarters of the book trade, took its name from the fact that the makers of rosaries and prayer books were formerly concentrated there.

A somewhat flippant application of "paternoster" is to a fishing line equipped with a series of hooks and sinkers.

patter. B. & L., who have a bit of a gypsy complex, are not entirely satisfied with the usual *paternoster* explanation, and suggest that a gypsy word derived from the Hindu *bat*, "slang" or "cant," may have combined with the idea of rattling off the Lord's Prayer in Latin, to give the modern sense of a rapid line of talk such as a circus barker uses.

Paul. See ROB PETER TO PAY PAUL.

paved with good intentions. See HELL IS PAVED WITH GOOD INTENTIONS.

pawnbroker. See BALLS. UP (the spout).

pay. "The devil to pay" is the short form of an ejaculation which went on thus: "and no pitch hot"—showing that this word "pay" was from the Latin *picare*, "to make waterproof with pitch," via Old French, *peier*.

"Pay-dirt," on the other hand, is probably just what it seems to be, dirt with a profitable amount of gold dust in it, though B. & L. thought it might be from the Chinese, I suppose through the Cantonese *pei*, "to give."

payola. This light-hearted word for bribery in the disc-jockey racket (payments made by record companies to insure that their discs were "aired") appears to have been spawned recently (1959) out of *pay* and the *-ola* of Victrola or Motorola. Maybe related to *moolah*, money.

pay through the nose. Many conjectures have been offered as to the derivation of this somewhat gruesome figure for "paying till it hurts." The most plausible is perhaps that the Swedish poll-tax was once called a "nose-tax." However, the very fact that the process of delivering up tribute money via the passages of the nose would be uncomfortable and indeed impossible makes the expression the more vigorous.

pease. See CHERRY.

pecker. See KEEP.

peek-a-boo. See BO-PEEP.

peeler. See BOBBY.

pen. See BULL PEN.

penguin. See GULL.

pensive. See PANSY.

pentagon. See PUNCH.

perish forbid. This delightful collision-form of "perish the thought!" and "God forbid!" was, I believe, first popularized, over the air, by Ed Gardner of Duffy's Tavern.

pert. See CHIP.

pet. See NECK.

petard. See HOIST WITH HIS OWN PETARD.

Peter to pay Paul. See ROB PETER TO PAY PAUL.

petitio principii. See BEG THE QUESTION.

petrel. See MOTHER CAREY'S CHICKENS.

phenagler. See FINAGLER.

Philip drunk. See APPEAL FROM PHILIP DRUNK TO PHILIP SOBER.

phlegmatic. See HUMOR.

phoney, phony. Meaning "fake," "not genuine," this term may, in my opinion, be a corruption of the old cant name for the "phoney ring" trick, the "fawney rig"—"fawney" being British slang for a valueless ring. The old game was, usually, to plant an imitation ring, watch someone pick it up, and then frighten or persuade him into paying you a round sum for your share in the find. The word "fawney," from the Irish, did not originally connote fraudulence at all, but was simply a ring.

Mencken looks with disfavor on "phone" as a source, and with doubt on "funny"; his contribution is that there was once a manufacturer of cheap jewelry named Forney. Webster implies a possible connection with "funny" (as in "funny business").

picayune. A picayune was an old Piedmont coin, and "not worth a picayune" was roughly equivalent to our "not worth a nickel." In Louisiana it was the regular name for a coin that, previous to 1857, was known as a "fippenny bit" or "fip" in Pennsylvania and Virginia, as "fourpence hapenny" or "fourpence" in New England, and as "sixpence" in New York.

pickle. See ROD IN PICKLE.

pick-up. See CHIP.

Pickwickian sense. When Mr. Pickwick was called a "humbug" by a fellow club-member, and resented this as a vile calumny, bloodshed appeared imminent, but was happily avoided by the decision that the remarks of both sides were to be taken "in the Pickwickian sense." Laboring to make this difficult conception clear in as simple terms as possible, Webster calls it a sense that is "esoteric, constructive, recondite, or parliamentary," to which OED adds "conveniently idiosyncratic." On the other hand, the scholarly Brewer describes it as "a whitewashed insult," for it developed that each party to the quarrel had the highest regard and esteem for the other.

pie. See HUMBLE PIE.

piffle. Webster thinks this may be the offspring of a marriage between *piddle* and *trifle*, while OED guesses that it is "onomatopœic with a diminutive ending." While guesses are still in order, I propose that this is a slightly eroded pronunciation of "pitiful." A piffling shot on the tennis court is precisely "pitiful." In literary circles, "piffle" means nonsense, trash.

pig. See GUINEA PIG.

pigeon. See STOOL PIGEON.

pig in a poke. *Poke* is a pocket or bag. The phrase is related to "letting the cat out of the bag"; i.e., to the whole process of inducing a bumpkin to purchase a pig, sight unseen, and get nothing but a mangy cat.

pig iron. Since 1576, as an N. & Q. correspondent has pointed out, the name "sow" or "pig" has been applied to "certeine rude lumps" of cast iron. Technically, today, the *sow* is the main channel of the gridiron of sand into which the molten metal is poured, while the *pigs* are the ingots of iron formed in the short connecting channels of specified length. The family relationship here between *sow* and *pig* is clear enough, but perhaps all that can be said about the original choice of swine to mean iron is that mechanical devices (e.g., crane and monkey wrench) have frequently been given the names of animals they resembled.

pig's whisper. Dickens lovers recognize Mr. Jingle in this item. The American equivalent of it was "pig's whistle," which B. & L. say, with a believe-it-or-not air, is from *pigen waeshael*, Hail to the Virgin, transmitted and popularized through the tavern sign, The Pig and Whistle. A slightly less satisfactory explanation (that is to say, none at all) has been offered for the origin of "pig's whisper," in the sense of "a brief moment."

piker. Some "poor whites" migrated to California in the early days, and made so unfavorable an impression that the section from which they came, Pike County, Missouri, received an undeserved stigma it may never live down. One reason "piker" caught on so powerfully as meaning a poor sport, a cheap skate, a chicken-feed gambler, was that a merger was soon consummated with an older English word, "pike," derived from "turnpike" and meaning tramp or vagrant. OED has an 1838 date for the last-named, an 1856 for the Pike County pioneers, and a 1901 for the "poor sport" sense.

pike-staff. See PLAIN AS A PIKE-STAFF.

pile of jack. See JACK.

pillar to post. Though this may be connected with certain maneuvers in early riding academies, it seems to have been used even earlier in descriptions of tennis, a very ancient game.

The present idiomatic use of it is in the sense of going fruitlessly or monotonously just from one thing to another.

pink. From Shakespeare's "pink of courtesy" through Goldsmith's "pink of perfection" to the modern (1905) "pink of condition" is an easy transition, and "in the pink" is a picturesque abbreviation. As for the thought back of it, Brewer experiments with a Welsh word for "point" and with the slang verb *pink*, to stab; OED thinks the originator had the specific flower in mind, making the phrase equivalent to "in flower"; but it seems equally likely that it refers to the healthy pink of firm flesh.

pin-money. Nowadays, fifty cents would keep a wife in pins for a long long time; but when the expression originated, in the 14th century, pin-money was a real item in the budget. Usually on the first or second of January the husband presented his duly impressed wife with money enough to buy all her pins for a year. We later husbands, rather graciously pretending not to know that quantity production has played hob with the high price of pins, continue to speak of our wives' large personal allowance in medieval terms.

pipe down. Nautical slang for "shut up," this useful command gained widespread distribution during and after World War I, owing to the increased supply of sailors and semi-sailors. The origin is the "tattoo" signal that precedes "taps" and that indicates it is time to quiet down. While bugles are now to be found on men-of-war, the original "pipe" was the boatswain's whistle. Perhaps the primitive hornpipe was danced to the music of a similar instrument.

pipe of peace. See BURY THE HATCHET.

place in the sun. In 1911, Kaiser Wilhelm II used this phrase (found in Pascal's *Pensées* 200 years earlier) in reference to the German occupation of Kiaochou, and it was even more appropriately applied to Prussian aspirations of 1914. Like some other saber-rattlers who have demanded a place in the sun, he found it, but was not entirely pleased to discover that it was equipped with sunlight and nothing else.

plain as a pike-staff. While this is now the accepted form, Svartengren says that "pack-staff" was about twenty years earlier, though both go far back into the 16th century. There was little to choose between the expressions, both being alliterative, and both staves (the peddler's and the pilgrim's) being alike smooth and unornamented.

play ducks and drakes. See DUCKS AND DRAKES.

play hookey. See HOOKEY.

pleonastic. See MOB.

pluck. In Sir Walter Scott's time, only "blackguards" used this indelicate word for courage, derived from the tradition that the heart and liver were the seat of heroism (compare "lily-livered"). In 1864, however, even the ladies were toying with the forbidden word, and in recent years it has been completely outmoded by the equivalent "guts," which was at first so improper for drawing-room conversation that it had to be translated by "intestinal fortitude." According to Tom Burns Haber of Ohio State, this was originated in about 1915 by, of all people, a football coach! Dr. John W. Wilce, on coming to Ohio State as head coach, invented and used it as a protest against the lurid language of gridiron and locker room. After painstaking investigation over several years, Professor Haber still (1960) claims that my use of it in the 1936 *Phrase Origins* was the earliest in print. In poultry circles, of course, pluck is still used in its original sense of "entrails."

A special British use of it, which is well understood in the U.S. Navy, through "plucking board" (committee in charge of the retiring of officers), derives from the ancient practice of permitting tradespeople to attend the graduation exercises of English universities, and to *pluck* the gown of the Proctor or Vice Chancellor when the name of any candidate was read who had neglected to straighten up any little financial matters. Thus to be plucked meant about the same as to fail.

pluck a crow with you. See CROW.

plum-duff. See DUFFER.

plump. In such an expression as "the district plumped for Baldwin," this is British slang for "decided in favour of," and seems to have arisen in the same way as American "fall for." The word is imitative, and carries the idea of thumping down heavily or suddenly.

plus fours. See KNICKERBOCKER.

Pluto. See HADES.

point. See FORLORN HOPE.

poke. See MAKE. PIG IN A POKE.

poker. America first became poker-conscious as a result of the fondness of the gold-digging forty-niners for the game. Webster and B. & L. agree that the name may derive from that of a somewhat similar German game, *pochspiel*, from *pochen*, to brag. B. & L. say further that "*Ich poche*," "I pass," is commonly heard in the course of the German game. There is a Yiddish word *pochger* which suggests the concealing of winnings and losses (a sense clearly kept in our "poker-face"), but there is something slightly fantastic in the picture of a Jew introducing this cut-throat game to a saloon-full of bearded prospectors.

police. See KITCHEN POLICE.

politics. See MACHINE POLITICS.

poltroon. The guess that this was from *pollice truncus*, cut-off thumb, has long been discredited. "Laziness" is the basic idea. (See BOLSTER.)

pompadour. Men who still affect the bristly hedge of hair rising from the forehead may be surprised to know that the style owes its name to the Marquise de Pompadour, mistress of Louis XV.

poney up. American slang (since 1824) for "pay up," this may come, according to B. & L., from German *poniren*, to pay. Another possibility is the legal Latin *pone*, pronounced "pony," meaning "Place thou," and used in connection with writs for attaching the goods of people who don't "pay up." The word "pontoon," used in the game of vingt-et-un, has the same root meaning (this is not the same word as that for a float, from Latin *pons*, bridge). The fact that in English racing circles a "pony" is understood to mean £25 seems to lead us nowhere in particular. A "pony" is also a small chorus girl.

pooped. Meaning "exhausted," this apt-sounding word cannot claim any very convincing ancestry, though Partridge (1937) lists a couple of indelicate possibilities. In the sense of "out of breath," it may be related to "pumped." Or perhaps the nautical disaster of being boarded by a following sea, technically known as being "pooped" in the days when ships held their rears high, somehow linked itself, centuries later, with a disaster equally terrifying to a college track man. A variant of *poop* is "poo out"—easily explained on the ground that the victim is too tired even to negotiate that final *p*.

poor as Job's turkey. There is a play on *poor*, here, as the bird was thin and weak—so weak that it had to lean against a fence to gobble—while the expression is usually taken to refer to lack of money. This fowl seems to have been some sort of relative of Ludlam's dog, who was so lazy that he always lay down to bark. As *turkey* is, paradoxically, an American by origin, it seems illogical to associate this Job with the ancient Hebrew, but is probably correct.

poor cat 'i the adage. See CAT.

poor fish. See GAFF.

poor Nelly. See NELL.

poor whites. See PIKER.

Pope Joan. In this old card game, similar to the French *nain jaune*, yellow dwarf (from which the English name may somehow have been concocted), one card, the eight of diamonds, was left out. The fact that one card was omitted may have been associated with the historical fact that there never was a Pope Joan; the legend was, it may be remembered, that in the ninth century a handsome young woman got herself elected pope, only to have her secret discovered when she was so incautious as to have a baby.

Conceivably as a slap at England's enemy, Joan of Arc, the name Joan was for many years proverbially that of a "female rustic" (OED). Who in America, in relating one of the adventures of the travelling salesman and the farmer's daughter, would give her the heroic and rather gorgeous name of Joan?

popgun is a popgun. See CRACK.

poppycock. This word for ridiculous nonsense has recently been discovered by Webster to come from Dutch *pappekak*, soft dung. I suspect a relationship to *cucking-stool* (q.v.). Also see BOOSHWAH.

pork chops will hang high. See GOOSE.

port. See STARBOARD.

porterhouse steak. A substantial cut served in saloons where porters gathered and where the strong brew of that name was a specialty.

portmanteau word. Meaning "a word like a valise" (from the French for "clothes-carrier"), this was invented by the author of *Alice in Wonderland* to cover such coinages as *chortle* (q.v.) and *slithy* (slimy + lithe). Lewis Carroll was not, however, the first to use *slithy*; it appears in Bunyan's *Life and Death of Mr. Badman.* Several people think "torrible zone" the best of these inventions, but I favor *insinuendo* on the ground that you and I both thought it was in the dictionary.

possession. Possibly with a jury in mind, our ancestors spoke of possession as being "eleven points of the law." Later, thinking of ten as a complete kind of number, they made the phrase "nine points." If you consider 100 as the perfect number, you should say "ninety-nine points" (it not being necessary to keep the percentages exact). In other words, the law will usually, but not always, uphold the "haves" in any contest with the "have-nots."

An entertaining old list of the nine things necessary for success in a law-suit begins with "a good deal of money" and ends with "good luck."

post. See PILLAR TO POST.

pot. Authorities are in surprising agreement that "go to pot," in the sense of "be ruined," derives from the chopping up of meat for a stew. When in that condition, you are, obviously, "all cut up about it." The Elizabethans sometimes spoke of "going to pot."

A "potboiler" is a book or picture produced less for glory than for the money on which to keep alive; usually, therefore, hasty and not up to a high artistic standard. It is chiefly a nineteenth century word, the idea supplanting to a large extent that contained in *Grub Street* (q.v.). (See MELTING POT.)

pot calls the kettle black. See PUNIC FAITH.

pot luck. Weseen says that a cowboy invitation to a pot luck meal means that each guest contributes his share of the food. (I doubt this. He must have been thinking of "covered-dish supper.") In origin, however, it is probably connected with French *pot au feu*, the ordinary family dinner, nothing fancy, no extras. You take a chance that the contents of the pot will be edible and will go round.

pot valor. A temporary and reckless courage derived from alcoholic liquor (1627). (See DUTCH.) The British spell this *valor* with a *u*, and have another word *valor* that means "assessment value."

powwow. Largely through the antiquarians of Tammany Hall, with their wigwams and warriors, this Indian word meaning "he dreams," hence a ceremony featuring the medicine-man, hence any conference, has been preserved to posterity.

P.P.C. This does not stand for "paying party call," and does not mean that. It is for French *pour prendre congé*, "for taking leave," and signifies, when written on a calling card, that you have come around to say goodby and found nobody at home.

practise what you preach. Our minister confessed the other day that he was surprised to discover this in the Bible (Matthew 23:3). I was too. I hurried home and looked it up in Bartlett. Lo, the quotation book gave the credit to one Rowland Howard (c. 1876) and to Logan Pearsall Smith, and did not even include Matthew 23:3 in its New Testament compilation. I soon found why: the King James version and the 1901 Nelson had translated the phrase as "they say and do not"; Moffatt, as "they talk but they do not act"; Weymouth, as "though they tell others what to do, they do not do it themselves." Not till I got to the new Revised Standard (1946) and Phillips, did I find "they preach but do not practise." This, I submit, is a beautiful illustration of circular source. Christ said a tremendous thing in Aramaic. People translated it in various ways. The most striking version became proverbial (made its appearance in *Old Curiosity Shop* in 1848, for instance) and eventually got into the Bible by the back door.

praiseless and blameless dead. See LIMBO.

preposterous. See CART BEFORE THE HORSE.

pretty kettle of fish. See FISH.

prevaricate. See FENCE.

price. Even the cynical Robert Walpole probably did not say "Every man has his price"; nor did he add (though he would doubtless have been glad to, had he thought of it) "and every woman her figure" (a modern variant). What Sir Robert said was apparently, "All *those* men have their price"—which is quite different. He was referring, of course, to a singularly corrupt Parliament.

prince. See HEFT.

printer's devil. See DEVIL.

prism. See PRUNES.

proud as Lucifer. See LUCIFER.

proves the rule. See EXCEPTION THAT PROVES THE RULE.

prunella. Pope's "leather and prunella," in the famous "Worth makes the man" couplet, is more likely derived from French *prunelle*, small prune, as applied to a plum-colored heavy cloth formerly used for shoe uppers, than from Italian *prunello*, little plum. The implication in Pope's phrase is probably that a worthy man is as different from an unworthy one as real leather is from cloth used as a leather substitute. Another theory is that leather symbolizes the cobbler, prunella the "cloth" of the clergy. This reverses the order of the couplet, however, unless the intention was to make the cobbler the worthy one, the clergyman the "fellow":

> Worth makes the man, and want of it the fellow;
> The rest is all but leather or prunella.

prunes. "Full of prunes" is explained by Weseen as frisky or spirited. But to many the association with the wizened and mournful appearing fruit, as well as with its well-known therapeutic effect, makes "You're full of prunes" a term of high reproach intimating that your logic is lame and your reactions altogether sluggish.

The famous "prunes and prism," as calculated to give the lips a perfectly chaperoned shape, is of course from *Little Dorrit*, succeeding the earlier "niminypiminy."

p's and q's. See MIND YOUR P'S AND Q'S.

Puck. See BOGEY. HOBGOBLIN.

pu'd the gowans fine. See GOWANS.

pull a fast one. See FAST ONE.

pull bacon. See THUMB THE NOSE.

pull devil, pull baker. Popularized in 1933 as the title of a book, this phrase has occasioned much speculation. It may be from the legend of the tug-of-war held between the devil and a baker on the edge of a volcano; or from the crude "movie" contrived by pulling back and forth, past the lens of a magic lantern, a slide depicting the same sort of contest, with first the devil, then the baker, victorious.

pull the wool over his eyes. See WOOL.

pull your leg. See LEG.

pun. According to Weekley, this is short for *pundigrion*. But the origin of the latter is uncertain. Perhaps it is related to the Italian *puntiglio*, a quibble, or fine point (a *punctilio*).

punch. Webster admits the possibility that this originally Anglo-Indian word for a usually alcoholic beverage may come from Sanskrit *panca*, five (the same as in *Punjab*, five rivers, and cognate with the Greek word familiar to all in *pentagon*), the theory being that there were five ingredients. But OED, better acquainted, perhaps, with the subject in its purest form, is doubtful, because of pronunciation difficulties, and because the five essentials have been so "very variously specified." The only other possibility seems to lie in the rum *puncheons* of the India-bound vessels.

Why did Dickens put "punch" in quotation marks, in *Pickwick Papers*, in reference to a blow with the fist? Both Byron and Scott had been using it as a fully naturalized word.

"Cowpuncher" originated in the goading of reluctant cows with sticks of some sort.

Punch's advice. In 1845 the British magazine perpetrated what is said to be its most famous joke. It announced that it would send advice to those about to marry. The advice was, "Don't." A similar hoax was carried out in this country, when a publisher advertised a book entitled *What Every Young Wife Should Know*; he received a flood of orders, paid in advance, of course, and thus sold thousands of cook-books.

Advising people not to marry has been a favorite indoor sport for centuries, to which nobody has ever, I believe, paid the slightest attention. Samples: "A young man should not marry yet, an old man not at all" (1540); "Advise none to marry or go to war" (1640).

punctilio. See PUN.

Punic faith. One of the wholesome and invigorating things about war is the impetus it gives to the associating of the enemy's name with everything hateful and dishonorable. In Carthage vs. Rome, Punic faith and Roman faith meant one and the same thing—treachery—just as a venereal disease was, to the English, "the French disease," or as "Dutch" was attached to disorderly or ignoble practices. In almost every case, the performance smells suspiciously like a pot calling a kettle black.

purple patches. In the sense of brilliant passages that stand out conspicuously from the rest of a book, this phrase has been traced to Horace's *Ars Poetica*. Smart translated it as "purple patchwork," but other scholars have pointed out that "bright" would have expressed the sense of *purpureus* more accurately. Macaulay popularized the expression, in certain references to his history.

purse. See SILK PURSE OUT OF A SOW'S EAR.

put across. See GET.

put a spoke in his wheel. See SPOKE.

put in big licks. See LICKETY SPLIT.

put it down. See CUFF.

put on the dog. "To put on" has long meant, in itself, to pretend, as one who puts on a disguise of some sort. Just why "dog," so often used in a derogatory connection (as "a dog's life") should be added to the phrase to convey the idea of showing off, of being "high-hat," is not clear. One writer has linked "put on side" with "put on dog," asserting that dogs often show off by arching out one side while performing highly intricate maneuvers with the feet.

In explanation of *side*, it has been suggested that the billiard-table term, to put on side (i.e., "to put English on the ball") has possibilities. But the sounder authorities refer us only to an old English adjective *side*, meaning (in 1508) haughty or proud.

After this, "put on the ritz" is easy. Webster cites the Ritz of London and the Ritz-Carlton of New York (not there any more, try Atlantic City) as being "ultrafashionable" hotels.

put the kibosh on. See KIBOSH.

put your foot in it. See FOOT.

Pyrrhic victory. See CADMEAN VICTORY.

Q

Q.T. Stevenson has traced "on the Q.T." (meaning "on the quiet," "off the record") to a broadside ballad of 1870, "The Talkative Man from Poplar," but it is not known whether its author was the first to use the mystic initials Q.T. for "quiet."

Quaker. Without questioning the honesty of founder George Fox, who says it derives from his having bidden Justice Bennet to "quake and tremble at the word of the Lord," scholars point out that the judge was probably already familiar with the name Quaker as applied derisively to a somewhat similar earlier sect. It may be, too, that people noticed primitive Friends (the official name) actually trembling under the stress of religious emotion.

quality. See KICKSHAWS.

quarantine. No longer to be taken literally, this word for the isolation of contagious disease is from French *quarante* (Italian *quaranta*). It was applied first to the regulation forbidding communication between ship and shore when there was danger of spreading an epidemic. The old belief was that forty days of this isolation was long enough. There is a poetic possibility that the biblical "forty days and forty nights" of flood may have had some occult influence on the choice of that particular number. (See COVENTRY.)

quartered. See DRAWN.

quelque chose. See KICKSHAWS.

question. See BEG THE QUESTION.

queue. See CURLICUE.

quiet life. See ANYTHING FOR A QUIET LIFE.

qui vive. The equivalent of our "Who goes there?" this looks to the beginner like "Who lives?" It is the subjunctive, however, and could be translated, in our idiom, "Who you for?" In other words, "Do you say *Vive la France*, or *vive* what?"

"On the *qui vive*" means on the alert.

quiz. It's probably a fable, but the story goes that an Irish theater-manager once bet that he could coin a word which would become the talk of all Dublin within twenty-four hours; he then hired small boys to write the word *quiz* on walls and fences throughout the city. Naturally thinking the word was indecent, everybody got excited about it—and the manager won his bet. Hence, it may be, the original meaning of *quiz* as a practical joke. More than one quiz, in the later sense of test or examination, has looked to the unprepared student like a practical joke of the cruelest sort.

R

rabbit. Just as somebody with an imagination christened sturgeon "Albany beef," the cheese-on-toast dish of Wales came to be called, about 1725, a *Welsh rabbit*. *Rarebit* was later, a well-meaning attempt to spoil one of those little jokes that help to take the sting out of life.

racket. In the sense of a lawless, get-rich-quick activity, this is not a new word. It was known in England as early as 1812 as a shady line of business. Such a thing as fortune-telling, for instance, has long been a "racket," having usually, as Webster says, "the outward consent of the victims." But OED recognizes that since 1928 the word has been in constant use to describe the criminal activities of gangsters, particularly in Chicago and New York, in controlling by violence such dissimilar features of our daily life as laundry and artichokes. One guess as to its source is that it was the name of an ancient game played with dice. Another is that those who do not meekly pay the tribute money will be persuaded in a noisy way. Racketeers have been known to use bombs and machine guns. (See GRAFT.)

radical. See GRASS ROOTS.

rag. See CHEW THE RAG. KEEP YOUR SHIRT ON.

ragman's roll. See RIGMAROLE.

rain cats and dogs. Many conjectures, far-fetched and otherwise, decorate the history of this metaphor. Some invoke a Greek expression, similar in sound, which means "contrary to all reason and experience." Others have turned up a nugget in the shape of a rare French word, *catadoupe*, waterfall. I prefer the more literal interpretation, based on the fact that after a cloudburst in seventeenth, and even eighteenth, century England, the gutters would rage with a filthy torrent not unlikely to include dead cats and dogs. The supporters of this theory find ammunition in the concluding verses of Swift's "City Shower" (though Stevenson lists an earlier use of the figure). In any case, the exaggeration is sufficiently robust and unpleasant to appeal to our modern taste for realism.

raise the wind. See FLY A KITE.

rake. This word for a dissipated, swaggering man-about-town was, to begin with, an abbreviation of *rake-hell*. The idea was that you could hardly find such another if you were to rake hell with a fine-tooth comb.

Rake-off derives also from the garden rake, but by way of the gaming table, from which one rakes one's profits. It usually means a commission, a share of the proceeds of a deal.

ramp. In the modern sense of an inclined plane by means of which vehicles reach higher levels on their own power, this goes back to a French verb *ramper*, to creep or climb (used especially of plants when first adopted into English). The "lion rampant" of heraldry is a relative.

rap. The mad quest for proof that a *damn* of the twopenny or continental or tinker's variety was not a *damn* at all but a small coin or counterfeit of some kind was spurred on, no doubt, by the discovery that "not worth a rap" meant not worth a bogus halfpenny. The little coin circulated in Ireland about 1800, and the phrase has been extant since 1820.

The verb *rap*, to criticize, is one of the leaders among journalism's pygmy shock-troops, the headline words. Another use of *rap* is the gangster's stolid "I'll take the rap," meaning the punishment.

rarebit. See RABBIT.

raspberry. See RAZZ.

rat. See ROSTRUM. SMELL.

razor. See ROSTRUM.

razz. Though "give him the razz" has been superseded by "the berry," "the bird," and "the Bronx cheer," it will make a good enough text for a dissertation on derision.

The word is doubtless short for *raspberry*, the scornful sense of which is perhaps connected with dialect *rasp*, to belch. Such use of the delightful raspberry is of venerable antiquity; B. & L. (1897) quote this description of a derisive noise particularly popular with coachmen (appropriately enough): "The tongue is forced through the lips, producing a peculiarly squashy noise that is extremely irritating. It is termed, I believe, a raspberry . . . and is regarded rather as an expression of contempt than of admiration." B. & L. go on to say (mistakenly, however) that it is a grating noise like that produced by rasping. It is clearly the same as the Rabelaisian "Bronx cheer," a noise of an elementary, not to say alimentary, nature. Weseen describes it, mildly, (under *bird*) as "a lip noise indicating dissatisfaction."

In this sense, *bird* probably derives from the old-fashioned *hiss*, as of a goose, for the theaters have long known the term, "to get the big bird," in this sense. The American audience's equivalent for the European hiss is still the boo (for which I have seen no derivation); if there must be some method of expressing corporate displeasure, it is to be hoped that the sonorous boo will not be supplanted by the spluttering and dirty "Bronx cheer"—which, presumably, was popularized in this country by some of the less delicate denizens of Jafsie Condon's "most beautiful borough in the world" (Lindbergh case, 1932).

Paradoxically, "the berry" connotes scorn, while "the berries" is still understood as high praise.

read. See RUN.

real McCoy. See MCCOY.

re-appraisal, agonizing. See BRINKMANSHIP.

reason. See RHYME NOR REASON.

record. See HEART.

red. "Red tape" has been a symbol for government procrastination for a century, and will probably continue to be as long as there are bureaucracies. The usage derives, obviously, from the red tape with which lawyers did up their bundles of documents. Lytton, Irving,

Dickens, and Carlyle all had a hand in popularizing the new insult. One wonders how the world had previously got along without it.

"Red letter days" were, simply and literally, saints' days and holidays that were marked in red on the calendars. Now they are, more broadly, days on which something pleasantly memorable has happened.

America's equivalent for "not a brass farthing" is "not a red cent," or even more laconically, "not a red." OED accounts for the expression on the ground that the cent "was formerly made of copper," implying that our penny is no longer red. Most observers, however, feel that it is still reddish and still copperish enough (95%) to justify the expression.

"Out of the red" is our joyful way of saying that our account books no longer show a preponderance of red ink (i.e., debits as opposed to credits).

When one politician accuses another of attempting "to drag a red herring across the trail," he is referring to the traditional use of a particularly strong-smelling smoked fish to throw the dogs off the scent. Red herring were sometimes used in the training of hounds. The figurative use implies evading of the issue, dragging in something irrelevant, especially a personal insult fired at the other man to cover your retreat from a bad hole.

In "neither fish, nor flesh, nor good red herring," the notion is that of being nothing in particular—food neither for monks, for ordinary people, nor for paupers. The expression is Elizabethan.

red. See PAINT THE TOWN RED.

red line of heroes. See THIN RED LINE OF 'EROES.

redundant. See MOB.

renege. Connected with *renegade*, this means (in cards) to revoke, to fail to follow suit when able to. (See FINAGLER.)

resurrection-man. See ODOR OF SANCTITY.

retaliation, massive. See BRINKMANSHIP.

revamp. See VAMP.

reverse English. A backward spin given a billiard ball by striking it "below the belt" with the cue. I have no explanation to offer as to why we say "English" where the British say "side."

rhyme nor reason. Bacon gives the witty Sir Thomas More the credit for originating the "neither rhyme nor reason" phrase. The story is that after a friend of his had versified an indifferent book, More exclaimed, "That's better! It's rhyme now, anyway. Before, it was neither rhyme nor reason." The French have a corresponding expression which originated also about 1500.

riata. See LARIAT.

rice Christian. In India and China, ever since 1816, one whose conversion has been motivated by a desire for material rather than for spiritual benefits has been thus nicknamed. In 1897 such a person was known in this country (at least on the Bowery) as a "souper," a tramp who gets religion in order to get soup-tickets.

riches grow in hell. See ADMIRE.

ride. To "take someone for a ride" has a sinister meaning and a facetious one. The former was the gunman's offhand way of describing a gangland execution: the victim was enticed or forced into a car; he was taken to some lonely place, dispatched, and dumped out. The second sense is synonymous with "to kid," "to pull one's leg," to make fun of. Inasmuch as most people like to be taken for a ride in the dear old literal way, it may be that this "kidding" sense, inasmuch as it is never particularly pleasant for the victim, derives from the cold-blooded brutality of the underworld.

ride off in all directions. See JEHU.

right as a trivet. See TRIVET.

right away. John Bull and Uncle Sam have enjoyed a good many chuckles over this American synonym for immediately. Dickens hadn't the slightest idea what the waiter meant by asking him if he wanted his dinner "right away" (*American Notes*, Chapter II). Since then, several earnest English folk have asserted that the American usage is common in the old country too. For instance, writes one to N. & Q., "It rained right away till tea-time"; for another, "She has been crying right away." If those things mean anything at all to an American, they do not mean "directly." Another idea is that when a Yorkshire railroad man uses "Right away!" to mean "All aboard!" or "Highball!" he is speaking the purest American. The only railroad use resembling that, in this country, is "right o' way," which may be either the prior right of a fast train to a clear track, or simply the strip of land owned by the railroad.

right of kings. See DIVINE RIGHT OF KINGS.

right of way. See RIGHT AWAY.

right rudder. See STARBOARD.

rigmarole. (Commonly pronounced, more rhythmically, "rigga-marole.") In the late 13th century, many Scots signed an oath of allegiance to Edward I. This list of names was known as the "ragman's roll"; and eventually any list monotonously reeled off was nicknamed "rigmarole."

Riley. See LIFE OF RILEY.

ring a bell. In the sense of "click" (q.v.), i.e., succeed, strike home, make an impression, I believe this derives from the well-known carnival device rather than from a target with a bell in its center. I refer to the spring-action contrivance that you hit with a sledge hammer in an effort to send a small weight up a slide to a bell at the top. No doubt the best ones are equipped with an ingenious braking arrangement by which action can be slowed up if some Hercules threatens to carry off all the profits.

A *ringer*, in sporting parlance, is an outsider, often a professional masquerading as an amateur. The term, Webster says, is from the bell-ringer's expression, "ring in," to work a certain bell into the performance.

The old telephone term, "ring off," is still heard, though we now simply "hang up" rather than wind a little crank to show we are through talking.

Ringgold. See GRINGO.

rip. OED reports "Let 'er rip!" as early as 1853. This quotation's coming from St. Louis strengthens the belief that the engine of a steamboat, or the boat herself, was the female who was to be encouraged to "rip" along at her topmost speed. Perhaps the ever imminent danger of being ripped open by a sunken tree added to the appropriateness of the cry; but it is unlikely that the R.I.P. found on tombstones played any important part in its history, except as a crack for comedians. The phrase does not necessarily imply full speed ahead; it may be simply "Let's go!"

ritz. See PUT ON THE DOG.

river. See SWAP HORSES IN THE MIDDLE OF THE STREAM. WATER.

road to hell. See HELL IS PAVED WITH GOOD INTENTIONS.

roast. See RULE THE ROAST.

Robin Goodfellow. See HOBGOBLIN.

Robinson. See BEFORE YOU CAN SAY JACK ROBINSON.

rob Peter to pay Paul. There has been no satisfactory origin for this, since chronology disproved the statement that the phrase was first used in connection with the diversion of funds from St. Peter's church, in London, for the repair of St. Paul's.

rod. See SPARE THE ROD AND SPOIL THE CHILD.

rod in pickle. Though there is no apparent connection with the proverb about "spoiling the child," it is amusing that it is the *rod* that has been "salted away" to keep it from spoiling before the time for beating the culprit arrives. In the earliest appearance of the phrase, and also in Mandeville (1714), *pickle* is replaced by a short and salty substitute that likewise begins with a *p*.

Roger. See JOLLY ROGER.

rolphing. See LYNCH LAW.

Roman Empire. See HOLY ROMAN EMPIRE.

Roman faith. See PUNIC FAITH.

Romany rye. Before looking it up, I was firmly convinced that this meant a kind of whisky drunk by the gypsies of Romany, a country down near Czechoslovakia. Unfortunately there is no such country. *Romany* is from gypsy *rom*, man or husband, and a *Romany rye* is a gentleman who can talk their language and associate with them as a friend. The word *Romany*, incidentally, rhymes with *hominy*.

Rome. "When at Rome do as the Romans do," advised St. Ambrose when St. Augustine consulted him as to the proper day of the week on which to fast, inasmuch as usage was different in Milan and in Rome. Unfortunately, the maxim has been taken to be justification for drifting with the stream. Bernard Shaw says drily that at any rate it is "the surest road to success."

roof. See BRING DOWN THE HOUSE.

room to swing a cat. Authorities speak of the old "sport" of swinging a cat by the tail, but it seems equally likely that "cat" is here the sailor's abbreviation for "cat o' nine tails," a whip. Smollett was one of the first to speak of "no room to swing a cat," and he was no landlubber. The most recent advocate of the "cat o' nine tails" theory is Sir Philip Gibbs, in *England Speaks*.

roost. See RULE THE ROAST.

root. B. & L. suggest the slang verb "to root," meaning to kick from behind, as an origin for this word descriptive of people who cheer for a team or something. Webster and OED, more scientific, derive it from good old Anglo-Saxon stock—live-stock, we might say; the former mentions *rout*, to shout or roar (secondary pronunciation the same as *root*); the latter, with a patronizing nod at *rout*, favors the verb *root*, especially as applied to swine digging with their snouts.

The expression "root, hog, or die," goes back to about 1830; it simply conveys, "If you don't work, you don't eat." (See GRASS ROOTS.)

root of all evil. See MONEY.

ropes. See LEARN THE ROPES.

rose. See SUB ROSA.

rostrum. Strictly, we should say "The speaker mounted the *rostra*," because that is how the famous trophy-decorated platform in Rome was referred to; the rostra were the beaks of captured Carthaginian ships. The word, surprisingly enough, is akin to *razor* and *rat*, through *rodere*, to gnaw; the notion being that a bird gnaws, after a fashion, with its beak.

rosy cheek. See DAMASK CHEEK.

rotten in the state of Denmark. See ANCIENT AND FISH-LIKE SMELL.

roué. This is not the French version of "rounder," though there is a similarity in meaning; by origin, a *roué* is a man who deserves to be "broken on the wheel" for his wickedness.

roughneck. See RUFFIAN.

rounder. See ROUÉ.

rout. See ROOT.

row. See KICK.

rubber check. See FLY A KITE.

rube. See GRANGER. JOSH.

Rubicon. See DIE IS CAST.

rub out. Used by gangsters as a pleasantly indirect way of saying "kill," this is not, however, their invention. OED has quotations for it dated 1848 and 1890, both Western in origin.

rubric. What might be called the stage directions in the Prayer Book always used to be, and still frequently are, printed in *red*, which is what *rubric* indicates (cf. *ruby*). Before the 16th century it was generally spelled "rubrish," but this was altered, perhaps because of a certain similarity to "rubbish."

ruffian. This is closely connected with modern "roughneck," as both suggest "uncouth of hair." The former, however, meant at first a pimp or procurer. Its gradual evolution to its present ferociousness would seem to indicate that men in that humble walk of life were not always perfect gentlemen.

rug. See SNUG AS A BUG IN A RUG.

rule. See EXCEPTION THAT PROVES THE RULE.

rule the roast. OED does not recognize our American "roost" at all, and Webster says it is erroneous. It means the master of the feast and not of the chicken coop. But Mathews found *roost* in Heywood (c. 1545), rhyming, unfortunately for our side, with *boast*. He thinks our American "rule the roost" may have been an attempt at rationalization, to which I say "Amen."

rum. Both the drink and the adjective meaning queer are believed by Webster to derive from gypsy *rom*, man (see ROMANY RYE). Rumbullion was the early and unabridged name for the drink, and apparently meant something uproariously good. Perhaps it was this drink that brought the shift in meaning, in the adjective *rum*, from "excellent" to "queer."

rumble seat. See DICKEY.

rum card. See CARD.

ruminate. See CHEW THE RAG.

rumor. See GRAPEVINE ROUTE.

run. Habakkuk's reference to a message's being written so clearly that "he may run that readeth it" was popularized by Cowper and Scott in the inverted form, "he who runs may read." The difference is hardly worth disputing about, though many have; while we ordinarily visualize, in this connection, a huge billboard that we can read out of the corner of one eye at forty miles an hour, it is unlikely that the Hebrew prophet's notion was anything so utterly different as "that he may dash off as messenger of the vision that he has seen." The Hebrew words suggest merely "that he may read on fluently without stumbling." (See CUT AND RUN.)

run amuck. See AMUCK.

run the gantlet. See GANTLET.

run with the hounds. See HOLD WITH THE HARE.

rustler. In some parts of the Southwest, though not all, a cattle rustler is a thief. On Texas ranches, according to Weseen, the rustler is simply the wrangler who tends the horses. The word is probably a collision form of *rush* and *hustle*, the idea being similar to *hustler*.

rye. See ROMANY RYE.

S

saber-rattlers. See PLACE IN THE SUN.

sack. There is a story that this was the last word uttered at the Tower of Babel before the languages were scrambled—because so many of these languages retain it or a strikingly similar form. Brewer lists a dozen of these.

"To get the sack," meaning to be dismissed, has been explained by reference to: the old Turkish custom of dumping a bagged lover into the Bosphorus; the Spanish verb, *sacar*, to dismiss; the handing of an empty sack to a departing workman, rather than one containing some work to do overnight; or the furnishing him with a bag of provisions, on his final departure. The simplest explanation, however, is that a workman used to carry his own bag of tools; to "fire" a man, an employer would need only to hand the unsatisfactory workman his personal equipment.

sack. See GUNNY SACK.

saddle. See BOOTS AND SADDLES.

safe as a dog in a rug. See SNUG AS A BUG IN A RUG.

Saint Anselm. See SAINT ELMO'S FIRE.

Saint Audrey. See TAWDRY.

Saint Elmo's fire. There are plenty of names for this striking display of static electricity from the tips of masts and yard-arms: St. Anselm's fire; corposant (from the Portuguese for "holy body"); Helena (sister of the twins Castor and Pollux). As there is no such saint in the calendar as Elmo, the source is generally found in Italian *Sant Ermo*, a corruption of St. Erasmus, patron saint of Mediterranean sailors.

Saint Swithin. If it rains on July 15—or July 4, or June 8, or June 19, or April 3, or December 2 (all of these subject to variation, as the calendar was changed subsequent to the birth of the multiple proverb)—it will rain for the next forty days. And yet somehow tennis continues to be played from year to year. Perhaps it is because St. Swithin was not a real saint. The legend is that when this good man (who was never formally canonized) died, he left instructions that he should not be buried in a place of honor inside the church, but outside, under the eaves. Later admirers, obstinately wishing to honor him, planned to remove his remains to a better place, but were prevented by forty successive days of rain. The figure "forty" may however have been arrived at through association with Noah's flood.

salad days. The greenness and coolness of a salad led to Shakespeare's metaphorical use of it, in reference to a young person, in *Antony and Cleopatra*. The thought is that the blood is still cool and the judgment somewhat unripe. *Salad*, incidentally, is related to *salt*, *sausage*, and *silt*. (See FLAMING YOUTH.)

Sally in Our Alley. See NAMBY PAMBY.

salt. See GRAIN OF SALT. SALAD DAYS.

salt away. See ROD IN PICKLE.

Sam. "To stand Sam" can be derived from Uncle Sam, if you accept the capital *S*—the idea being perhaps that the generous and idealistic old uncle "stands treat" for other nations, especially those who wish money to fight a war. Another expression of it was Will Rogers's assertion that "the United States never lost a war or won a conference."

The only other explanations are that *sam* is an old English word meaning "to collect things" (cognate with German *sammeln*), and that a Swedish word for money, *samla*, may have had something to do with it. (See also UNCLE SAM.)

sambo. Commonly used as a nickname for a negro (a step lower in the social scale than "George" for a Pullman porter), this is believed by Webster to go back, through Spanish *zambo*, bowlegged, to Kongo *nzambu*, monkey. Slightly more charitable, OED suggests another possibility, that of Foulah *sambo*, uncle. Be that as it may, Zamboanga, in the Philippines, is of Spanish derivation—and if you didn't hear Wallace Beery sing "The monkeys have no tails in Zamboanga," you missed something.

same a hundred years from now. See FIRST HUNDRED YEARS ARE THE HARDEST.

Sam Hill. Though there is in OED a word *sam-hale*, meaning, literally, "half-whole, in poor health," it does not illuminate the obscurity surrounding "go like Sam Hill," because "poor health" has nothing to do with the case. It is also true that there was on exhibition at the Century of Progress exposition an engine named the Sam Hill, and solemnly purporting to be the source of the expression; clearly enough, it was simply an accessory-after-the-fact—it was named that because it ran like that. Possibly a biblical demon named Samuel was a factor. All that is certain is that our Puritan ancestors found the expression a convenient euphemism for "go like hell."

Sam Patch. See BEFORE YOU CAN SAY JACK ROBINSON.

sanctity. See ODOR OF SANCTITY.

sand. Meaning courage, this is probably a short form of "sand in his craw" (found in *Huckleberry Finn*, 1884), from the notion that a chicken that eats some sand will have more endurance than one that does not. An equivalent term is *grit*.

The *sandman*, who is supposed to cause you to rub your eyes, in the morning, by having deposited sand in them while you are asleep, is also called the *dustman* in England. Which you might think would be unfortunate when you realize that the prosaic British dustman (as in *Our Mutual Friend*) collects ashes and rubbish, and must connote, to the British child, dirt and noise rather than drowsiness. "Sand-blind," an old term for half-blind, was not from this kind of sand, but from either *semi*, half, or a German word meaning "virtually." Shakespeare was familiar with "sand" in the sleepy-time sense; he has Launcelot Gobbo connect it ludicrously with "gravel," in *The Merchant of Venice*.

sand. See FAN MY BROW.

sandwich. The fourth Earl of Sandwich is believed to have been so devout an attendant at the gambling table that he invented this convenient and painless way of eating lunch without taking time out. The wits used to say that he had given his name to half a dinner just as Spencer had given his to half a coat (a short jacket).

Dickens apparently furnished the idea for "sandwich-man" when he dubbed one of the men who parade the streets, bearing advertising boards fore and aft, "an animated sandwich."

sans culottes. This French term for "without breeches" was practically English by the time Carlyle got through with it. He certainly rang all the changes there were on "sansculottism" in his great symphonic history of *The French Revolution.* All it means is that the proletariat wore *pantaloons* (q.v.) instead of knee-breeches.

sausage. See SALAD DAYS.

save face. See LOSE FACE.

sawney. Here we have a slang word meaning three distinct things, with apparently no provable connection between them. First, it is short for Alexander (i.e., a corruption of Sandy). Second, it means silly or indecisive, perhaps through association with *zany.* Third, it is occasionally heard to mean bacon or pork; B. & L., as usual, have a gypsy origin for it, *sani.*

say Jack Robinson. See BEFORE YOU CAN SAY JACK ROBINSON.

scallion. Walter Winchell popularized this as a sort of opposite to *orchid*; i.e., something that you send to people whom you actively dislike. It derives from the Palestine seaport town of Ascalon, and is actually a sort of diseased onion.

scene that beggars description. See BEGGAR DESCRIPTION.

scheme. See HECTIC.

schooner. The Scotch dialect *scoon*, from a Teutonic root meaning "hasten," means to skip a pebble over the water (see DUCKS AND DRAKES). When a newly designed sailboat appeared to "scoon" over the water, at Gloucester (Mass.), the name "schooner" was born. Dutch influence is credited with the insertion of the superfluous *h.*

Scott. See GREAT SCOTT.

scram. This raucous little brother to "skiddoo" and "beat it" is no doubt short for *scramble.* Who fathered (or mothered) it is so far unknown. My guess is that it was first popularized by the early "talkies" (around 1930).

scrap of paper. Like Voltaire's God, this is one of those happy phrases that it would have been necessary for a British propagandist to invent, if a high German official had not obliged by actually saying it himself. At least, Stevenson is very positive that Bethman-Hollweg, German Foreign Minister, in a conversation with Sir Edward Goschen, British Ambassador, which was reported to the British Foreign Office on August 4, 1914, referred to England's treaty with Belgium as "a scrap of paper."

seamy side of life. The wrong or "shady" side of life, the side that shows the crude seams. In *Othello*, Iago's wife suggests that, when one is jealous without cause, his wits have been turned with the seamy side out.

second-string. See TWO STRINGS TO HIS BOW.

sedan. See COACH.

see you coming. See LET.

Seine. See THAMES.

send to Coventry. See COVENTRY.

sense. See PICKWICKIAN SENSE.

sesame. One or two reference books say that this is an oily seed used as a food and a laxative. If this last were one of its qualities, there would be particular point in a punning password, "Open sesame." However, medical dictionaries stress only its value as a demulcent, a soothing agent in cases of dysentery. In any case, it was a fairly familiar plant in the country of the Forty Thieves. Its oil can be used for cooking, but is largely made into soap.

sesquipedalian. See INNOCUOUS DESUETUDE.

set her cap at him. See CAP.

set the Thames on fire. See THAMES.

seven. See NINE DAYS' WONDER. SIXES AND SEVENS.

sex for the students. See PARK.

Shah. See CHECK.

shake a leg. See LEG.

shank's mare. "To go by shank's nag" or "shank's mare" (*shanks* being about equivalent to legs), or "by marrow-bone stage" (a play on Marylebone stage, pronounced nearly the same), or "by Walker's bus"—all mean that you are a little embarrassed about having to walk places.

share. See LION'S SHARE.

she can be had. See HAD.

she is no better than she should be. See NO BETTER THAN SHE SHOULD BE.

Shelta. See MIZZLE.

sheriff. See BUM.

shibboleth. Meaning a test or password, and then extended to signify something that is repeated until it has lost its usefulness, this Hebrew word for "stream in flood" was used to pick out the sons of Ephraim (who could not pronounce the "sh" but had to say "s") from the members of other tribes. It was a little as if Missouri were to close its borders to all Easterners, and to admit only people who could say "Mizoora" without feeling self-conscious.

shill, schill. As the sense in which this is most familiar today is that of accomplice in the art of luring "suckers" into rubberneck buses, it is barely possible that there may be a connection with old British slang for omnibus, *shillibeer* (from the name of a bus magnate who died in

1866). *Shill* does seem to be short for *shillaber*, as the words are used interchangeably for the sort of people who are hired to sit in parked buses all day ("Yes, ma'am, going right out, ma'am"), or who lead the way to the circus ticket office, or who start the buying from the gyp artist on the curbstone, or who help along the bidding at an auction. Other possible sources to consider are: an American humorist ("Mrs. Partington") bore the name of B. P. Shillaber; there may be a tenuous relationship between "suckers" and German *Schill*, the giant pike perch; or between Anglo-Saxon *scyl*, sonorous, and the remarkable noises produced by the sideshow barker.

shilling. See BIT.

shimmy. See BRAWL.

shindig. See SHINNY.

shingle. See HANG OUT.

shinny. The informal small brother—and, no doubt, ancestor—of hockey is known as shinny. Its characteristic cry, "Shinny on your own side!" is translated by B. & L. as "Attend to your own personal interest," but means simply, "You are off-side (i.e., ahead of the puck) and the penalty for that is to be rapped across the shins." This I believe to be the origin of the name "shinny," though some dictionaries refer us to "shindy" and "shindig," of uncertain origin but probably connected either with Gaelic *sinteag*, meaning skip or jump, or with a gypsy word meaning *quarrel*. The expression "monkey-shines" may be a relative of *shindig*, but not, I think, of *shinny*.

ship. The editors of N. & Q. once descended from Olympus to reveal that the source of the quotation, "ships that pass in the night," is requested with "irritating persistency." It is from Longfellow's "Elizabeth," in *Tales of a Wayside Inn*; it was also the title of a novel in 1893. *The Literary Digest* for years used "Slips That Pass in the Night" as the title for its department of amusing misprints, but later had to change "Night" to "Type," inasmuch as some of the best mistakes have appeared in afternoon papers.

The figure, "ship of state," has been traced to Machiavelli's *Prince* (1675). Longfellow and Whitman both used it effectively.

ship comes in. See COW.

shirt. See KEEP.

shivaree. This is an American corruption of French *charivari*, which goes back to the 14th century. The derivation is unknown. One work defines it as a "callithumpian concert," a ridiculous coinage suggesting a beautiful thumping. The German equivalent for this highly obnoxious mock serenade for newlyweds is *Katzenmusik*, cat-music. There is an Australian word, *corroboree*, meaning a wild dance, but it is altogether unlikely that there is any connection between it and *charivari*, though the similarity is striking.

shoot the bull. To shoot, or sling, the bull is an outmoded but still understandable way of saying to deliver a considerable volume of talk, "hot air," always fluent but not always sincere. The only connection that I see with the animal, unless it be in the notion of "puffed up" which is inherent in *bull* and *ball*, lies in its bellowing. But "bull" and its successor "boloney," which owed much of its vogue to its similarity with "bull," are often suave and persuasive. (See BOOSHWAH.)

A "bull session" is an educational institution of an informal character; meeting in a student's room, the group generally opens with a discussion of sex, gets into politics, and touches on God and the United Nations before returning to sex.

An Irish bull ("It's grand to be alone, especially if your swateheart is wid you") has no connection with a Papal bull. The latter derives from the *bulla* or seal which makes it official. The source of "Irish bull" is not clear, unless the basic idea be the same as in "a bull in a china shop."

shop. I have not been able to find a satisfactory explanation of *closed shop* or *open shop* in OED, perhaps because the British are to a large extent unfamiliar with our use of shop to mean a place for manufacturing and repair as well as (increasingly in America) for retail selling. The word *shop* was first created in English to fill a terrific need: *gazophylacium*, the treasury of the temple, had to be translated into Anglo-Saxon.

A closed shop is one in which the employer agrees to employ no non-union labor. An open shop is one in which no discrimination is made against any worker because of membership or non-membership in a union. Obviously, the laborers in a closed shop have far more power when they come to bargain collectively for bigger wages or shorter hours. Webster says that the two expressions are occasionally, and incorrectly, reversed, I suppose in order to take from *closed shop* the stigma of a cramping restraint that interferes with a man's personal liberty.

A *union shop* is almost indistinguishable from a *closed shop*: a new employee *must* become a union member within a specified time.

shopkeepers. See NATION OF SHOPKEEPERS.

short hairs. OED rather innocently, I think, lists "to have someone by the short hairs" as an equivalent of "to have someone by the hip"; i.e., at a disadvantage; and explains that the hair of the head is referred to. But anyone who has tried to get a firm grip on a Prussian haircut (also known as a "crew-cut") will suspect that the curly pubic hair must be what is meant. I have always assumed that the expression was a coarse one. Kipling and Galsworthy both used it—unquestionably without meaning to be vulgar—but I think they would have been hard put to it to explain the thing in any other way.

shot-gun wedding. See NELL.

shot his bolt. See BOLT.

shoulder. See CHIP.

show me. See MISSOURI.

show the door. See GATE.

shut up. See PIPE DOWN.

side. See PUT ON THE DOG. SEAMY SIDE OF LIFE.

sieve. See GARBLE. THAMES.

silent upon a peak in Darien. See STOUT CORTEZ.

silk purse out of a sow's ear. Though this business of not being able to make a silk purse out of a sow's ear is included in Swift's *Polite Conversation*, indicating that it was then trite (1738), few early instances of it have been found in print. The source recorded in Brewer and Hyamson is Peter Pindar, date about 1800. OED says that, with the substitution of "luggs" for "ear," this proverb was already current in Scotland in 1700. It has had many relatives in foreign lands, such as: you'll never make a good coat out of poor cloth (Spanish); a shaft (or arrow) of a pig's tail (Portuguese); a hunting horn of a pig's tail (Danish); a sieve of an ass's tail (Greek). English variants are: velvet of a sow's ear; an archbishop of a rogue; a hawk of a buzzard.

silly. Cognate with German *selig*, blessed, this adjective originally meant happy or good. To Shakespeare it meant rustic or plain. From the idea of harmless, innocent, it came to mean weak or dumb, presumably because holy people get taken in more than others. However, as Professor Billy Phelps once said, those of us who are frequently taken in at least get to see the inside of things. (See DUFFER.)

silt. See SALAD DAYS.

silver spoon in his mouth. According to Wilson's *Noctes Ambrosianae*, the advantage of being born in this remarkable condition was proverbial in Scotland before 1830—the opposite predicament being the possession of a wooden ladle; but OED intimates that American children were arriving thus equipped before 1800. Which does not prove that it was not ultimately Scotch in origin. The source idea seems to be simply that the lucky child of wealth does not even have to wait for his first meal with a silver spoon—he comes completely assembled and ready for anything in the way of luxury.

simian. See MONIKER.

simply true. See CONSISTENCY IS A JEWEL.

sincere. Most scholars are skeptical about the derivation that would occur to almost any first-year student of Latin: *sine cera*, "without wax." If *sincerus* did have some such meaning, it probably referred to honey free from beeswax. Weekley says that the second element may have been cognate with *caries*, decay.

sin eaters. Probably from the Hebrew scapegoat idea, but perhaps from an ancient heathen rite, the practice of hiring people to eat food that had been placed on or near a corpse persisted into the 17th century. Somehow the sins of the deceased were thus transferred to the more or less hardened conscience of the hireling, and the recently departed soul was spared a few years of his purgatory sentence. It is not impossible that the hearty eating and drinking at Irish wakes may be traced to the conviction that the guests were doing the dead host a favor. A story by Fiona Macleod, *The Sin Eater*, appeared in 1895.

single-track mind. See BEE IN HIS BONNET.

sinister. See DEXTEROUS.

sit on the fence. See FENCE.

sixes and sevens. A bit of mystery here, why these numbers should be chosen as symbolic of disorder. Originally they may have been "fives and sixes," the two highest counts on the dice; "set on sinque and sice" referred apparently to a move in the game of hazard. Originally, perhaps, a joking shift from "five and six" to the impossible "six and seven," the latter phrase may have caught the imagination because it added up to the unlucky thirteen. According to Stevenson, it goes clear back to 1340.

sixpence. See PICAYUNE.

sixth age. See PANTALOON.

sixty. According to Wesley Stout, "he ran like sixty" did not refer to the breathtaking speed of sixty miles an hour, but rather to a terrible drought in the Missouri and Arkansas valleys that ended after Lincoln's election in 1860. The memory of the drought was so vivid that people began linking "sixty" with an extreme of any kind.

skate. See BLATHERSKITE.

skedaddle. See TWENTY-THREE SKIDDOO.

skeleton at the feast. See EAT, DRINK, AND BE MERRY.

skeleton in the closet. It seems unnecessary to try to trace this phrase to some specific horror-story, such as that of the wife forced by her revengeful husband to kiss every night the skeleton of her lover, whom the husband had killed. The figure is a very obvious one to represent a shameful secret which a family tries to hide. An early variant of it is "a black man in the closet," which is of course reminiscent of "a nigger in the woodpile."

skiddoo. See TWENTY-THREE SKIDDOO.

skin flint. See FLINT.

skip it. This admonition to drop a matter is a practically perfect, though often unkind and abrupt, equivalent for the older "forget it," even to the note of impertinence or "freshness" that is seldom missing.

sleeper. See COACH.

sleep like a top. See TOP.

sleeveless errand. Popularized by being the title of a 1929 novel, this phrase has aroused much comment. It comes from an Anglo-Saxon word meaning "having no sleeve"—but from there back its history (in Bartlett's words) "has defied the most careful research." Brewer suggests the spelling "sleave," representing the ravelled thread on the edge of a piece of silk, but that hardly accounts for the sense of "useless" in "sleeveless." Others have found that the French have used their word for sleeve, *manche*, to mean a tip, just as the expression "a pair of gloves" has been (this is supported by an Italian equivalent for *pourboire*, *mancia*, "a penny for drink") or that a Teutonic root for "sleeve" meant dull, inactive, blunt. The most plausible explanation I have seen is that envoys used to wear sleeves on their helmets, just as knights often wore similar tokens in honor of their girl-friends. An envoy without an identifying sleeve, his "credentials," was likely to be turned back with his errand unaccomplished. E.P.'s first quotation is dated 1546.

slide. See HIT THE DIRT.

slide, Kelly, slide. Stevenson found the source of this baseball expression to be an 1889 song about Michael Kelly, Chicago and Boston ballplayer. It is therefore not necessary to mention that *kelly* is also the top-soil that must be removed in order to get at the clay used in making bricks.

sling the bull. See SHOOT THE BULL.

slips that pass in the type. See SHIP.

slithy. See PORTMANTEAU WORD.

small beer. See CHRONICLE SMALL BEER.

smell. To "smell a rat," meaning "suspect something," was familiar in the middle of the 16th century. A famous Irish bull was born when Sir Boyle Roche, it is alleged, forgot that he was dealing with metaphors in exclaiming: "I smell a rat; I see him forming in the air and darkening the sky; but I'll nip him in the bud." There have been some painstaking but not authentic improvements on this, such as "I see it *brewing* in the air." (See GREEK and UP.)

"Your work smells of the lamp," we are told by Plutarch, was said by Pytheas to Demosthenes, who had been preparing his orations in an underground cave. Though Demosthenes made a brilliant and caustic retort—"Your lamp and mine do not witness the same labors"—Pytheas's criticism is still employed of writing that, possessing substance, lacks sparkle; as if the pick-ax work had taken too many chips off the writer's *joie de vivre.*

smell. See ANCIENT AND FISH-LIKE SMELL.

Smith, Al. See BOLONEY.

smoke-filled room. See AMEN CORNER.

smoothy. See MANGLE.

sneeze. See GOD BLESS YOU.

sniff. See UP.

snuff. See UP.

snug as a bug in a rug. Though E.P.'s earliest example is 1769, an early (1798) form of this has *safe* in place of *snug*; the latter is clearly much better, because of the rhyme factor. Why the British, notoriously squeamish about the word *bug* (q.v.), should have kept it in this deliciously cozy expression, unless purely for the rhyme, is not known. It has been conjectured that in Shakespeare's time, "dog" was used instead of "bug." A 1603 variant was "as snug as pigs in pease-straw." Which reminds me of "happy as a dead pig in the sunshine"—North Carolina expression that I recently heard used casually by a Georgia girl in Florida.

sober as a judge. Fielding seems to have invented this, for his *Don Quixote in England.* Lamb also used it. (See APPEAL FROM PHILIP DRUNK TO PHILIP SOBER, for a possible source.)

soccer. This is explained as a British corruption of "Association," the rules of the game having been compiled by the "London Football Association." The process, it seems to me, illustrates the characteristic British formation of a nickname; the Englishman sees the SOC in the word, pronounces it "sock," and likes it. The American would hear the soft and slushy sound of that "soshy," in the middle of "association," and probably never think of calling the game "soccer." Similarly, seeing the initials NIRA, the Englishman immediately pronounces it "Nira," whereas the American, finding Miss Nira somehow kittenish, desperately throws away the *I* and calls the thing NRA.

soft underbelly of Europe. An invention of Sir Winston Churchill's? Not so, says *Time* (Dec. 7, 1959). It was the brilliant Sir Geoffrey Crowther, editor of the London *Economist* from 1938 to 1956.

so long. OED's first reference is to F. H. Nixon's *Legends and Lays of Peter Perfume*, Melbourne, 1865—which indicates clearly that the phrase has no claim to be called exclusively American. On the other hand, the Shorter OED gives 1834 as its earliest date; as the editors are unable, "except at great expense," to supply me with information as to the country of origin, we have the right to guess the 1834 quotation was American, especially since Craigie dates his first quotation 1860 (the same Whitman passage dated by OED as 1868, evidently a later edition). In meaning, the expression is similar to *au revoir*, *auf wiedersehen*, *hasta la vista*, etc.; perhaps originally a gesture accompanied it, playfully indicating with the hands that only *this* much time will elapse before we see each other again. It was a favorite with sailors, which accounts for its widespread distribution.

something on the ball. See BALL.

song. See WINE, WOMEN, AND SONG.

son of a biscuit-eater. See CRYING OUT LOUD.

sorts. While it is likely that "out of sorts," meaning depressed, disgusted about something, derives from the printing plant, where the letters in a font of type are known as "sorts," it is still a fact that the phrase in that sense preceded the appearance in print of the word "sorts" alone by some sixty years (back in the 17th century).

so's your old man. See MANGLE.

soul. See IRON.

soup and fish. This slang term (probably ephemeral but still in 1951 Webster) for dinner coat or white-tie-and-tails can best be accounted for by the fact that only at a formal dinner would an American expect to have separate soup and fish courses preceding the *pièce de résistance*.

souper. See RICE CHRISTIAN.

South Sea Bubble. See BULLS AND BEARS.

sow. See PIG IRON. SILK PURSE OUT OF A SOW'S EAR.

Spain. See CASTLE IN SPAIN.

Spanish fan. See THUMB THE NOSE.

span-new. See SPICK AND SPAN.

spare the rod and spoil the child. This old proverb (back to the year 1000, in English) does not appear in the Bible in this precise form, but in substance can be found six distinct times in the book of Proverbs. The nearest is this (13:24): "He that spareth his rod hateth his son." (Moffatt: "He hates his son who fails to ply the rod.")

sparrow-grass. See ASPARAGUS.

spat, spatterdash. See OYSTER.

speak their language. See LIMEHOUSE.

speed. See WITH ALL DELIBERATE SPEED.

spencer. See SANDWICH.

spheres. See MUSIC OF THE SPHERES.

spick and span. Though it is great fun to dally with the notion that this might be from an Italian bootblack's proud boast, *spiccata della spanna*, snatched from the hand (equivalent to "fresh from the mint," or "brand new"), it is more likely that both are ancient English words, the first meaning "spike" and the second "chip," being related to "spoon"—as the earliest spoons were, naturally, chips. This derivation is borne out by "span-new," new as a chip (a Middle English expression), and German *spanneu* and *splinterneu*, also meaning new as a chip. I have not seen any full explanation of why "spike and chip new" should come to mean "in perfect order." It suggests, perhaps, that when your house or your boat has just been finished, spikes and chips are still lying about; but when the job is really finished, newness all but insures neatness. (See BRAND NEW.)

spieler. See BALLYHOO.

spike. See SPICK AND SPAN.

spinach. See GAMMON AND SPINACH.

spinning-jenny. See GIN.

spit and image. This form is considered better than "spittin' image," though it is no easier to explain. The French have exactly the same idea in saying, "*Il est son père tout craché*, "He is the very image of his father" (literally, "all spat"), while the Germans say, "as if cut out of the face." E.P. lists as an early proverb, "as like one as if he had been spit out of his mouth," finding the germ of this in about 1400.

spoils system. Andrew Jackson certainly did not invent this uncomplimentary name for the system of political appointments which he introduced in the early 1830's. Taking his cue perhaps from one J. S. Johnson, who, according to OED, made a pointed reference to "the spoils of war" in 1830, Senator W. L. Marcy arose in the Senate, two years later, to defend the appointment of a Minister to England, and in the course of his address reminded his hearers that "To the victors belong the spoils." This ill-chosen catch phrase has unquestionably done much to forward, against the heaviest odds, the development of the merit system, as in the gradual extension of the Civil Service.

spoil the child. See SPARE THE ROD AND SPOIL THE CHILD.

spoke. "Put a spoke in his wheel" has been used to mean both help and hinder, and the reason is the paradoxical one that historically this particular spoke helped by hindering; that is, it was inserted in such a way as to act as a brake and keep a heavy wagon from running away down a hill. The usually unromantic OED suggests that the phrase is possibly a mistranslation of Dutch *een spaak in't wiel steeken*, "stick a bar into the stave"—but this sounds to me as far-fetched as some of the inventions of P. B. Trovato (see BEFORE YOU CAN SAY JACK ROBINSON). Cobden made a delightful break when he announced that he would be glad "to put a spoke" in a friend's candidacy for office; meaning, apparently, to slow up his campaign for him.

sponger. See MOOCHER.

spoon. See SILVER SPOON IN HIS MOUTH. SPICK AND SPAN.

Spoonerism. The name is derived from that of an Oxford professor who had the same trouble Roy Atwell had. (See STOOGE.) Crowell's *Dictionary of English Grammar* mentions a number of Spoonerisms, the best of which are: "Is the bean dizzy?" "You have already tasted three worms here"; "Please sew me to another sheet—someone is occupewing my pie"; and "a well boiled icicle." Other good ones to juggle with are these: sporn rim hectacles; selling smalts; shoving leopard; kingkering congs; and perhaps the prize one—"When the boys come back from France, we'll have the *hags flung out.*"

sport your oak. In English college dormitories, the outer door of each room was usually of sturdier oak than the inner. When one was "not at home," for one reason or another, he would shut his outer door, i.e., "sport his oak."

spot. From the gunman's "on the spot" (slated to die), this has come to mean a difficult or dangerous position.

spotlight. "In the spotlight" and "in the limelight" developed their figurative use at about the same time, the early 1900's, though the form of lamp which burned lime with an oxy-hydrogen flame was known nearly a century earlier. The use of both expressions derives from the contrast with the stage flood-light, the spotlight being directed, as a small brilliant circle, on the player considered at the moment to be the headliner.

spots. See DANDER. KNOCK GALLEY WEST. LEOPARD.

spout. See UP.

spread-eagleism. See JINGOISM.

square. "Four-square" used to mean reliable, honest, as "a square-shooter." In bewilderment we ask why our teen-agers make it a term of contempt, like "flat tire." Is it because you bump on a flat tire? Is it related to "block-head"? Or is it simply because, by the law of opposites, when a beatnik (q.v.) says "cool" he means "hot"? (See BRICK.)

Evidently the slang word "square" means something different to almost everybody, running the gamut from Toots Shor's "A square don't know from nothin'" through Mencken's "stupid and tiresome person" all the way to "old-fashioned" and "respectable." The briefest, and just possibly the best, definition is: "A square ain't hep."

But—hold everything! Here comes the *Ladies' Home Journal* (Feb., 1960) shouting that not only is "hep" out—but "square" too! Seems that squares are squirrels now. Equally unexplainable.

square the circle. The realization of the impossibility of constructing a circle of the same area as a given square dates clear back to classical times (Horace and others). John Donne, in 1624, made perhaps the earliest reference to it in English. The reason why it cannot be done is that π, by which the area of a circle is determined, won't ever come out even but will always be 3.1416 *plus*; the question-mark may be infinitely small, but never disappears.

squeak. See BUBBLE-AND-SQUEAK.

S.R.O. See DRESS.

stacked. See WELL-STACKED.

stagnant. See TANK.

stake. See GRUB.

stammer. See LISP.

stand pat. See FOOTPAD.

stand Sam. See SAM.

stand the gaff. See GAFF.

starboard. Just as a canoe is usually steered by holding the stern paddle in the water a little to the right, Anglo-Saxon boats were steered with an oar—and the side on which the steering oar operated was the "steer-side" (*bord* meaning the side of the boat, the same as in *overboard*). The loading side was the "lade-bord," but this soon changed its *d* to *r* by assimilation to *starboard*, and became *larboard*. But this was an unfortunate move as it hastened its demise, it being felt that the two sounded dangerously alike. "Port" was adopted for the left side, possibly because the position of the steering oar on the right meant that the left side was always alongside the wharf while the ship was in harbor. Some years ago, however, the U.S. Navy ordered the use of *right* and *left* in all instructions to the steersman (while retaining the traditional *starboard* and *port* in describing parts of the ship, which the Air Force does, too, by the way). And the appalling *Mohawk* disaster (1935) doubtless had a hand in gradually introducing the same usage into our merchant marine, too, as it is believed that the confusion, on the *Mohawk*, as to whether "port" meant "turn the wheel to port" or "send the vessel in a port direction" could have been avoided had there been an iron-bound understanding that "left" meant "send the vessel to the left." (See U.S. Coast Guard Regulations, 78.20: "right rudder" or "left rudder" must be used; "right rudder" means that the top of the wheel, the rudder blade, and the head of the ship should all go to the right.)

Incidentally, the name of the large steering-oar on the right-hand side was the *lof*, akin to *aloof* ("steering away") and *luff* (steer up into the wind).

state. See SHIP.

steak. See PORTERHOUSE STEAK.

steal my thunder. About 1700, playwright Dennis complained that his rivals had stolen his invention of a machine to produce thunder off stage.

stereotype. See CLICHÉ.

Steven. See EVEN STEVEN.

stick. See DEAD STICK LANDING. JOY STICK.

stick in one's craw. This means two different things, depending on whether the direction is up or down. Theoretically, this craw is the crop of a fowl—a sort of preliminary stomach. You may then speak of something that "won't go down with you," something unacceptable, that you "can't swallow," as "sticking in your craw." On the other hand, thinking of the craw as vaguely equivalent to the throat, you may use it in connection with someone who is tongue-tied, whose words "stick in his craw." The former sense is the more usual.

sticks. As used by theatrical and baseball people, "the sticks" are the small towns, the rural districts. An American equivalent of the Roman "Thumbs down" is "Back to the tall timber!" It is likely that this indicates the meaning back of "the sticks."

"Cross as two sticks" is apparently just a play on words: two sticks that are crossed form a cross, and that's that. The adjective *cross*, meaning irritated, carries the same idea as the verb, in "Don't cross me"; i.e., "Don't thwart me"—and *thwart* itself means, by derivation, crosswise.

stick to your last. This proverb, which implies that a cobbler has a right to be consulted as an authority in his own field, but not outside it, doubtless originated in some tale about a cobbler who criticized the footgear represented in a painting, and then, emboldened, went on to attack some feature of the painting about which he could have no special knowledge. The word *last*, the pattern or model for a shoe, is from an Anglo-Saxon word meaning footstep. (See BALLAST.)

stiff upper lip. See KEEP.

stir. This cant word for jail is traced very circumstantially to the gypsy by B. & L. (a derivation supported by Partridge). But Webster austerely passes by on the other side, with an intimation that the term probably comes from Anglo-Saxon *steor*, *styr*, penalty. It was familiar in thief slang as early as 1851, and still is.

stone. See LEAVE NO STONE UNTURNED.

Stonewall Jackson. Whether General B. E. Bee said, at Bull Run, "See, there is Jackson, standing like a stone wall," or "Look at Jackson's men, they stand like a stone wall" is of no importance. The modest Jackson insisted that the reference was not to himself but to his men, as was of course the case. Anyway it made a superb nickname for a splendid man. And, speaking of nicknames, I find myself suddenly fascinated by the possibilities inherent in B. E. Bee. I wish I knew whether his men called him "Bee-bee," or "Baby," or "Honey," or "Busy."

stooge. If a Roy Atwell (see SPOONERISM) were to attempt to say "stage fool" he would sooner or later get around to "stooge fail." Can this be a clue to the origin of this theatrical term for either a "dumb cluck" comedian who gets battered about, or a "feeder" who assists a comedian by asking questions or "leading with his chin"? *Radio Guide* quoted Bottle (Phil Baker's British-speaking feeder) as unalterably opposed to being called a stooge. (See ZANY.)

stool pigeon. An old word (1841) for a low type of spy in the pay of the police, this apparently derives from the decoy pigeon attached to a stool to attract other pigeons into captivity. However, B. & L. list "carrier pigeon" as slang for a swindler, and "carrier" as meaning a tell-tale. These words may have influenced the development of "stool pigeon."

stools. See BETWEEN TWO STOOLS.

stout Cortez. Doing justice to Keats's gorgeous poetry by quoting "Silent upon a peak in Darien" in its article on Darien, the *Encyclopedia Britannica* is nevertheless true to its high mission in insisting that it wasn't Cortez but Balboa (in 1513). Tennyson called Palgrave's attention to the mistake, but no Keats fan seems to have cared a Darien dime! And both Bartlett and Stevenson quote the passage without correcting the error.

straw. See MAN OF STRAW.

street. See KEY OF THE STREET.

strike a bargain. See BARGAIN.

strike me pink. See FILLIP ME WITH A THREE-MAN BEETLE.

string. See GEE-STRING.

strong. See DRAW.

strut your stuff. See CAKE.

study. See BROWN.

stunt. It has been suggested that a trick done by a stunted acrobat may have appeared more sensational, i.e., "more of a stunt," than one done by a full-sized man. However, Webster and OED see greater possibilities in *stint*, a task, and German *Stunde*, an hour or period of time. In 1895 the word was still American college slang. (See AEROBATICS.)

sub rosa. The rose being the symbol of silence, consecrated roses are sometimes carved above the Roman Catholic confessional. In German dining rooms, the presence of roses suggests silence, not with special reference to soup, but rather to the principle that "nothing said here shall go beyond these walls." The English, "under the rose," is often used instead of the Latin equivalent.

suck about. See CURRY FAVOR.

sucker. Illinois is the Sucker State. And in the absence of any authoritative reason, we may follow Walsh and others in the theory that the Illinoisans who worked in the lead mines of southern Wisconsin except during the winter were wont to return to work there every spring just about the time the suckers (fish) began to run in the streams. Hence, "Here come the suckers again" was the glad cry with which the Wisconsin Badgers hailed the spring. OED's first quotation hints at all this, but seems vague about whether suckers run in the spring or the fall. (See SHILL.)

sulfite. See BROMIDE.

summer. See INDIAN.

sun. See PLACE IN THE SUN.

sure. See COCK-SURE.

sur le tapis. See CARPET.

susceptible. See HEFT.

suspicion. See CÆSAR'S WIFE MUST BE ABOVE SUSPICION.

swallow. See GULL. STICK IN ONE'S CRAW.

swap horses in the middle of the stream. An excellently documented story attributes the saying to Abraham Lincoln, though the wording vibrates around quite a little, what with honest differences of opinion as to whether he said it as above or spoke of "while crossing the river." In accepting renomination for the Presidency, he modestly waved aside the honor as having anything personal about it, explaining simply that the Republicans had concluded that it was "not best to swap horses while crossing the river." It need hardly be said that the "river" was the Civil War.

sweat. See LATHER.

sweetness and light. The interesting thing about this phrase of Swift's, taken up by Matthew Arnold, is that the figure is taken with striking literalness from the bee hive; the honey, as Swift points out, furnishing the sweetness, and the wax the light. (See EUPHUISM.)

swim. While it may seem cynical to say that "in the swim" means acting like all the other poor fish, the figure is certainly "piscatorial," as OED says. The "swim" is the fashionable gathering-place of the fish; and to be in it is, figuratively, to be in style or popular.

swing a cat. See ROOM TO SWING A CAT.

T

taboo, tabu. This Polynesian word for a "sacred interdiction" like Greek *anathema* and Latin *sacer*, has the double meaning of "sacred" and "cursed." Captain Cook, by having his men raid a native temple for firewood, became taboo and had to be liquidated. In 1920, I noticed that dead-end streets in Honolulu, instead of being posted as "No Thoroughfare," bore the sign "Tapu."

tack. See BRASS TACKS. HARD TACK.

tackle. See HARD TACK.

tail between his legs. See COWARD.

tailor's goose. See GOOSE.

tails. See HARP.

take a flyer. See ANGEL. FLY.

take an ell. See ELL.

take a poke. See MAKE.

take for a ride. See RIDE.

take French leave. See FRENCH LEAVE.

take it. In "He can't take it," the understood antecedent of *it* is something like "punishment" or "kidding." When phrase-tracers exultantly report that they have found "take it" in this sense in Mark Twain or even Chaucer, look narrowly at the passage and the chances are that you will discover an *expressed* antecedent. The beauty of our present-day use is the unexpectedness of that "it." If there is a logical antecedent within harpooning distance, there is nothing original or slangy about being able to "take it."

take it and like it. See LUMP.

take it or leave it. See HOBNOB.

take pains. See GENIUS.

take the cake. See CAKE.

take the count. See DOWN FOR THE COUNT.

take the rap. See RAP.

take time by the forelock. Of all the writers, ancient, Elizabethan, classicist, romanticist, who have been fascinated by the fable that Old

Man Opportunity has his pig-tail in front but is bald behind, Heywood and Swift came nearest to expressing it in the epigrammatic form given above. The idea is similar, of course, to that of "Opportunity knocks but once,"—you can't catch him after he's gone by.

talent. See GENIUS.

talk like a Dutch uncle. See DUTCH.

talk turkey. The Librarian of Congress has kindly transcribed for me this paragraph from a report issued by the U.S. Engineer Department in 1848: "Today I heard an anecdote that accounts for one of our common sayings. It is related that a white man and an Indian went hunting; and afterwards, when they came to divide the spoils, the white man said, 'You may take the buzzard and I will take the turkey, or, I will take the turkey and you may take the buzzard.' The Indian replied, 'You never once said turkey to me.'"

This tale has been repeated, with variations, a number of times. Mathews found it first in 1830, and has again come across the phrase "talk turkey" as recently as 1950, in a Florida publication. The surprising persistency of this in the sense of "getting down to brass tacks," of "talking business," would seem to indicate that this is the historically correct interpretation. It means something more tangible than "saying pleasant things" to someone, as Hyamson and OED seem to think. Yet Webster's emphasis on bluntness, on willingness to air the unpleasant aspects of a subject, seems to go too far in the other direction. OED says the latter concept is expressed by "talk cold turkey," and further that one who "doesn't say pea-turkey" is one who doesn't say anything at all. But neither of these glamorous emendations is at present familiar in America.

Tammany. Saint Tammanend (or Tamendy, or Tammenund) was a Delaware chieftain who lived up to his name (meaning "affable") by his friendliness to the white men. The colonists canonized him, unofficially, and later the Democrats adopted him as their tutelary saint, along with the Indian expressions still associated with the New York Democratic machine, *wigwam* and *sachem.* The earliest reference to St. Tammany listed in OED is 1771.

tank. One of the great triumphs of the British War Department was the secrecy with which the tanks (armored caterpillar tractors) were manufactured. The name tank was adopted, not because it was the name of Thomas Tank Burall, a designer of tractors, but because it made excellent camouflage. OED implies a negative value, the name being so "undescriptive"; Webster goes farther, stating that the reason these queer-looking contraptions were called tanks was that they were destined, everybody thought, to haul water in Mesopotamia. This had quite a little to do with the stunning surprise that the British were able to spring on the Germans, in 1918.

The old word *tank*, meaning a cistern, was an Anglo-Indian contribution, related to Portuguese *tanque*, pool or cistern, and Latin *stagnum*, ancestor of *stagnant*. Provincial English *stank* (no relative of the verb *stink*) has retained the sense of pool or pond which *tank* has lost, except in references to indoor swimming pools.

tantrabogus. See BOGUS.

tantrum. See DOLDRUMS.

tape. See RED.

tapestry. See CARPET.

Tartar. See CATCH A TARTAR.

tawdry. In *The Winter's Tale* Shakespeare used this in a sense quite different from the one we are accustomed to: "Come, you promised me a tawdry lace, and a pair of sweet gloves." It comes from *St. Audrey*, the story being that before she was converted one of her vices was a passion for laces and trinkets. Such things were sold at her fair, on St. Audrey's Day, but unfortunately they became more and more showy and cheap until *tawdry* came to be the word for that sort of thing.

taxi. From the Latin word meaning "to touch sharply," this is an abbreviation of taximeter-cab. A taxi dance is one at which there are salaried "hostesses" and the men pay by the dance. At an airport, to taxi is to behave like a taxicab; i.e., maneuver along the ground. Do not apply to the coasting after a landing.

tea. See DISH OF TEA. HOT CHA.

tear off. See NAB.

tears. See CROCODILE TEARS.

tear your hair. See DANDER.

tease. See HECKLE.

teeth. See ARMED TO THE TEETH.

teetotaller. In the sense of "total abstainer from intoxicants," this word was probably first used in England about 1830, perhaps by one Richard Turner, whose proud claim to be its originator has been carved on his gravestone. The adverb *teetotally* was in use in America at about the same time, but not with reference to liquor. Evidence is lacking that "teetotal" was first used in America on a list of converts to the cause of temperance, "O.P." representing those who took the "old pledge" and "T." those who promised total abstinence. It is likely that the initial "T" of "total" had a hand in the formation of the emphatic new word, though the fact that "tea" played an important role at temperance meetings doubtless added to the popularity of *teetotal*.

Weekley's theory that the "teetotum" (a top, used in games of chance, bearing a "T" on one side to signify *totum*, "all") might have fathered "teetotaller" is disregarded by both Webster and OED.

telegraph. See GRAPEVINE ROUTE.

tell it to the marines. See MARINES.

tennis. This is one of the words of which the new Webster is particularly proud. Brushing aside the old allusions to a conjectured "Tenez!" ("Hold!" in the sense of "Ready!" or "Service!") Webster announces without a quiver that the early balls were made of light cloth produced at Tinnis, a medieval town in lower Egypt that was famous for its cloth.

tenor. The best-known uses of this word in the sense of smooth course or progress are in Gray's *Elegy*, "the noiseless tenor of their way" (often misquoted as "even tenor") and in Hawthorne's *The Great Stone Face*, "tested by the tenor of a life." Any attempt to connect this word with the fluty notes of the higher male voices runs up against the characterization of *this* tenor as noiseless, an invention yet to be perfected in the field of music, though long devoutly desired in some quarters. However, the "holding on" quality of the tenor voices in the days when they usually "held" the air may have had something to do with the "even tenor" idea.

terminological inexactitude. See INNOCUOUS DESUETUDE.

Thames. In spite of valiant attempts to rationalize the old exaggeration, "He'll never set the Thames on fire," it is now pretty well agreed that this characterization of a somewhat dull and indolent person means about what it says. A rough equivalent is our "He is no ball of fire." A minor fault in the explanation that *temse*, sieve, was originally meant is that it is obviously nearly as hard to set fire to the iron rim of a sieve by too vigorous operation as to burn up a river; but the chief trouble is that the idea is very old and that in whatever language it is found the name of some river is invariably introduced. In origin, of course, it may have been associated in people's minds with some memorable occasion on which oil or a chemical has spread on the surface of a river, and caught fire. It is possible too that the similarity in sound between *Thames* and *temse* may have added piquancy to the proverb. And it strikes me as more than a coincidence that in the French form of it *Seine* is used, which means also "drag-net," and that in Lancashire and Yorkshire the Ribble is the river—and Ribble sounds a good deal like *riddle*, a sieve for grain.

thatch. See THUG.

there, but for the grace of God. See GRACE OF GOD.

thinking cap. See CAP.

thin red line of 'eroes. The credit for this exact wording goes to Kipling's *Tommy*, who also remarked "We aren't no thin red 'eroes." But the source of the immensely popular notion at which Tommy was scoffing was a news letter by W. H. Russell from the Crimea to the London *Times*, in which he spoke of the "thin red line tipped with steel." Another writer of about the same time kept the ball rolling with "slender red line."

thirteen. See BAKER'S DOZEN. SIXES AND SEVENS.

thirty. See TWENTY-THREE SKIDDOO.

thousand of bricks. See BRICK.

three bites of a cherry. See CHERRY.

three golden balls. See BALLS.

three-man beetle. See FILLIP ME WITH A THREE-MAN BEETLE.

threepence. See THRIP.

threesheet. This modern slang term for "boast" seems to have no connection with "three sheets in the wind," old phrase for "drunk" (which goes back at least to Dana's *Two Years Before the Mast*, 1840); the latter expression probably refers to what happens to a sail when three of the ropes ("sheets") which hold it in position are allowed to run loose. Inasmuch as "loose" would be contradictory of "tight" in the sense of "drunk," perhaps the notion is that the ship would stagger, with "three sheets in the wind."

A threesheet was a large notice that would fill most of the permanent billboard in front of a theater, to the exclusion of the displays advertising other acts. This, Chester Cook wrote me, gave rise to the complaint, "He's threesheeting himself all over the place."

three-tailed bashaw. See BASHAW.

thrip. Weseen says this is understood in some sections of this country to be a nickel. It is, of course, a British abbreviation (like "threpps") for threepence. OED Supplement says that a thrip was formerly an American coin between a nickel and a dime (1834–1848).

throttle. See GUN.

through the nose. See PAY THROUGH THE NOSE.

throw down the gauntlet. See GANTLET.

thug. Much older than most people dream. The organization of professional stranglers, in India, from whose name the modern "thug" was derived, was suppressed by the British before 1840. The Sanskrit word was related to our word "thatch," in the sense of dishonestly concealing something, the name of the strangling robbers having signified "cheaters."

Thule. See ULTIMA THULE.

thumb. As motorists hope the practice will become obsolete, the term had better be explained for posterity. Used as a verb it means to appeal for a lift to the passing motorist. It is the badge of the hitch-hiker. A more effective method (adjusting her garter) was used by Claudette Colbert in *It Happened One Night*.

The proverbial "miller's golden thumb" may have implied the profitable if not strictly honest practice of including the thumb on the flour side of the weighing balance. More complimentary to the much maligned miller is the explanation that the successful mill operator could test the efficiency of his machine by rubbing the meal between his thumb and fingers.

"Thumbs down" should, more correctly, be "thumbs out," in translation of *verso pollice*, the Roman term for signal of condemnation to death of the defeated gladiator. By concealing their thumbs inside their fists, the Roman crowds could show mercy.

The fact that the disreputable old gesture of thumbing the nose is popularly said to be an invitation to kiss one's posterior checks with the alleged origin of the Franco-Italian insult of biting the thumb-nail or of inserting the thumb between the two middle fingers: namely, that Frederick Barbarossa avenged a bit of Italian barbarism to his wife by forcing the guilty parties, on pain of death, to remove with their teeth a fig (*fico*) from the rear end of a mule. This does not explain the terms "pull bacon" or "take a sight," for thumbing the nose; the latter, however, is clearly from the similarity in appearance to the operation of sighting the sun with a navigation instrument. Rabelais knew this immemorial, if not immoral, gesture as the "Spanish fan"; and the god Thor is believed to be using it on an ancient Danish coin.

thunder. See STEAL MY THUNDER.

thunder-bolt. See BOLT.

Thursday. See MAUNDY THURSDAY.

tiffin. When this word for mid-day meal got back from India, people didn't recognize it. It is not Anglo-Indian at all, but derived from an English dialect word meaning to eat or drink between meals.

tight. See THREESHEET.

Tillie the Toiler. See MOOCHER.

till my ship comes in. See COW.

till the cows come home. See COW.

time. See BIG TIME. NICK OF TIME. TAKE TIME BY THE FORELOCK.

tin ear. Weseen lists this as about the same as "cauliflower ear" (q.v.). It usually occurs, however, in the phrase, "on his tin ear," an apparently meaningless intensive of "on his ear," upset, irritated. The latter goes back to 1870, at least.

tinker's damn. In *The Literary Digest* of Nov. 9, 1935, it was categorically stated that this expression refers to the small dam of dough or putty erected by a plumber to keep molten solder from spreading. This, says OED, is "an ingenious but baseless conjecture." If, as is likely, it is not from *dam*, the practically worthless Hindu coin, it is probably exactly what it purports to be, an idle curse made ineffective by much repetition.

Tinker, by the way, is apparently derived from "tink," the noise of a hammer on metal, rather than from "tin."

Tinker to Evers to Chance. Having been a Cub fan ever since Joe Tinker, at shortstop, Johnny Evers, at second, and Frank Chance, at first, began their astonishing series of double plays, I was pleased to find the resounding phrase in Stevenson's book of quotations. He does not, however, explain it, except to quote an F.P.A. lyric that only a baseball fan could possibly elucidate. If there be among my readers anyone who does not understand, I should say that, with a runner on first base, a ground ball is hit to Tinker, who tosses the ball to Evers, standing on second base, before the runner can reach the base; Evers then whips the ball to first base before the one who hit it can get there. These three famous infielders were members of the Chicago Cubs, National League team.

tip. The very obscurity that surrounds the origin of this word for a gratuity tempts one to connect it with *tipple*, drink, because so many similar words—drink-money, *Trinkgeld*, *pourboire*—have a beverage background. (See GREASE. SLEEVELESS ERRAND.)

tip-cat. See KIT-CAT.

tit-tat-to. See KIT-CAT.

toad-eater, toady. A conjuror's assistant would eat a toad (supposed to be poisonous) so that his master could demonstrate his magic powers of healing. Hence, a "yes-man," a sycophant, who will do any kind of dirty work for the boss.

toast. As applied to the drinking of healths, this use of toast originated in the custom of putting a piece of toast into the glass of wine. It was supposed to taste better or something. Dickens was in the habit of toasting, usually, with nothing but toast-and-water.

toe the mark. See UP.

Tom, Dick, and Harry. See HARRY.

Tommy Atkins. In 1815, the specimen blanks for British army paper-work were filled out with the fictitious name, Thomas Atkins (just as John Doe or Richard Roe was used in legal forms). It was perhaps not before 1883, however, that it came to be used figuratively for a private in Her Majesty's regular army. Then Kipling landed, like a whole regiment of marines, and Thomas Atkins soon had the situation well in hand.

tomorrow ye die. See EAT, DRINK, AND BE MERRY.

tomtit. See HOBGOBLIN.

ton of bricks. See BRICK.

too many irons in the fire. See IRON.

top. "To sleep like a top" is probably not borrowed from French *taupe*, a mole. The French also say *dormir comme un sabot*, to sleep like a wooden shoe—and the interesting thing is that *sabot* can mean also a wooden top and the phrase can refer to the apparent motionlessness of a top spinning at high speed. A correspondent of N. & Q. complains that this makes too good sense—that a figure of speech should be a little far-fetched in order to attract attention; however, it may be pointed out that an ordinary top sleeps for only a fleeting instant before it begins to wabble.

torch singer. Webster's suggestion that the idea of unrequited love is inherent in the "torch" or "blues" song is borne out by the participation of at least two such singers in sensational mystery killings. It is said that Libby Holman's throat operation made inevitable the erotic and emotional gurglings with which she captivated Broadway (see *The Kablegram*, for March, 1934) and that "hot," in this sense, explains the connection with "torch." Note also "carry a torch" for somebody. Rudy Vallee reports that the expression was originally started by a Broadway nightclub singer named Tommy Lyman.

torrible. See PORTMANTEAU WORD.

tote. Lumbermen still speak of the "tote road," over which supplies are drawn. In use as long ago as 1676, it has been conjectured to be (1) from Latin *tollit*, (2) of African origin, (3) from Anglo-Saxon *teohan*, carry or draw, (4) connected with Dutch *tot*, the preposition "to." But OED demolishes everything, and Webster says laconically, "Origin uncertain."

to the dogs. See GO TO THE DOGS.

to the nines. See NINE.

to the victors belong the spoils. See SPOILS SYSTEM.

touch and go. Derived from a coach-driving expression for a narrow escape or brief encounter (the wheels touch but both vehicles are able to proceed), this has been applied to a time of crisis, to a hasty temper, and to an impulsive or careless action. Anyone who has skidded and scraped fenders with another car can recognize the presence of all these elements.

tough. "Tough going" and "tough customer" are not as recent concoctions as some may think. In the sense of "You make it tough for me" and "a tough piece of work," the date 1297 is given by OED. Meaning "vicious" or just "unfortunate," the usage is American, but the phrase "tough customer" was British enough to get into *Barnaby Rudge*.

tough hombre. See HOMBRE.

tough luck. See HARD LINES.

tough-minded. See EXCEPTION THAT PROVES THE RULE.

tout. As a tipster, or one who seeks customers or votes, this is an old expression of uncertain origin. In the sense of "spy," it may go back to Anglo-Saxon *toten*, to peep or look. Brewer repeats a circumstantial but not too authentic account of how some "Toots" from Tooting used to stand at a fork in the road and urge people to go to Tooting instead of to Epsom.

tout battant neuf. See BRAND NEW.

town. See PAINT THE TOWN RED.

transcendent capacity. See GENIUS.

treat. See DUTCH.

tree's inclined. See CHILD IS FATHER OF THE MAN.

tribute. See MILLIONS FOR DEFENSE.

trimming. See DRESS. HEDGE.

trivet. When you stop to think of it, you realize that a three-legged stool or a tripod easily adapts itself to an uneven surface. This is probably the origin of "right as a trivet," though Truefits, a wig manufacturer, and an Admiral Trivet, who escaped from a sea disaster, have been summoned to the breach, without conspicuous success. It is doubtful whether the saying goes back much beyond 1800. *Pickwick Papers* has it.

trouble. See GENIUS.

troubled waters. See OIL ON TROUBLED WATERS.

truth. See NAKED TRUTH.

tuck. See NIP AND TUCK.

tuft-hunter. British slang for a toady or parasite, this began to be obsolescent when the gold tassels once worn by undergraduate noblemen, to distinguish them from ordinary people, were ridiculed out of existence. It means about the same as "hand-shaker" or social climber.

tug-of-war. See GREEK.

tumbler. See HEEL-TAPS.

turkey. See POOR AS JOB'S TURKEY. TALK TURKEY.

turn a hair. See HAIR.

turncoat. Found in English as early as 1557, the term may still, chronologically, derive from the popular story of a certain Duke of Saxony who occupied a "spot" (q.v.) between Spanish and French possessions, so he had a coat made that was blue (for Spain) on the outside and white (for France) on the inside—or vice versa, depending on which army appeared the more menacing at the time.

turn tail. See COWARD.

twenty-three skiddoo. This pre-war predecessor of "scram" and "beat it" has, I believe, a most interesting origin. While the first element may be just a meaningless code number used by telegraphers (like *thirty*, signifying the end of a message or article), it has never been proved that it does not owe its existence to the fact that the most gripping and thrilling word in *A Tale of Two Cities* is "twenty-three." Sidney Carton was the twenty-third to be guillotined that day.

The second half may be just a short-cut for the older "skedaddle"; or, less likely, a corruption of "at the first go-to," which has also appeared as "kittoo."

twig is bent. See CHILD IS FATHER OF THE MAN.

two-dollar bills. See DEUCE.

two-faced. See TWO-TIMER.

twopenny (tuppenny) damn. A number of dear old ladies who idolized the Duke of Wellington found real comfort in the theory that the Duke's favorite curse derived from Hindu *dam* (q.v.). OED admits the ingenuity of it but says it is baseless. An interesting parallel was the French nickname for Marshal Foch, "General Deux-sous," based on his frequent mention of the fact that he didn't "care two sous" about something or other. (See TINKER'S DAMN.)

two strings to his bow. The Elizabethans were very fond of this old archery figure for having something in reserve in case of accident. It is not so often heard today, but its two children, first-string and second-string, are well known on every athletic field, though almost nobody thinks to pay homage to their sturdy old father. The Latin form of the idiom used two anchors instead of two bow-strings.

two-timer. Meaning "double-crosser" (q.v.), this conceivably owes its origin to fraudulent timing of a horse race. There is also, of course, the basic idea that we have in "two-faced" and "lead a double life." Do not confuse the verb "two-time" with the American infantry "double-time," a sort of dog-trot supposed to be just twice as fast as a walk.

U

ulna. See ELL.

Ultima Thule. A classical way of indicating the extreme limits of the world, this has been variously taken to mean the Shetlands, Norway, Denmark, and Iceland. Explorer Nansen translated it by "Farthest North" and used it as the title of his 1897 book. Poe's musical ear caught the cold and sinister ring of the Latin, and rendered it unerringly as "ultimate dim Thule." In 1929 *Ultima Thule* was used as the title of a novel, the third of Henry Handel Richardson's memorable trilogy.

For many years there was an Eskimo village named Thule on the northwest coast of Greenland, but only since September of 1952 has the press been free to mention the construction of the huge NATO airbase near it.

umble pie. See HUMBLE PIE.

uncle. As a euphemism for a pawnbroker, the phrase "at my uncle's" probably arose naturally, without any assistance from the fact that an *uncus* or hook was used to handle the pawned articles before the spout was adopted. The French sometimes use *chez ma tante*, "at my aunt's," or *ma tante Dumont*, from the French and Italian name for certain large money-lending establishments, "Mounts of Piety." The use of uncle and aunt in this sense may derive from the common fiction that one has been left some money by a rich relative. (See also DUTCH.)

Uncle Sam. Two things about the origin of this name for the collective citizens of the United States have been established: that it arose in the neighborhood of Troy, N.Y., about 1812; and that it is no coincidence that Uncle Sam's initials are U.S., letters that were especially familiar in those days to army men and those that sold them supplies. Whether Sam Wilson, uncle of Elbert Anderson, inspector of supplies, was the first "Uncle Sam," will probably never be certainly known. Visitors to Catskill, N.Y., may assure me that it must be true as they saw it posted at the south end of the big bridge there.

under the rose. See SUB ROSA.

under the table. See KNOCK.

under the weather. Though Robert Louis Stevenson uses the expression in a nautical sense in *The Wrecker*, OED and Mencken insist that this is originally American slang, when taken to mean ill, indisposed, financially embarrassed, and, eventually, drunk. In fact, Mencken has high praise for it as a local invention that is "terse, eloquent, picturesque." The first quotation in OED is from "Ik Marvel" (pen-name of D. G. Mitchell), dated 1850. The phrase was almost ruined at one time by being recommended in several books as a convenient euphemism for the discomfort accompanying menstruation.

under way. The spelling "weigh" has a certain elaborate plausibility about it, but is wrong. The phrase "under way" has no connection with weighing the anchor; it is the *way* which appears in *headway*. And as for this *weighing* of the anchor, I was surprised to learn that one of the root meanings of *weigh* is to lift up, to carry.

unextinguishable. See HOMERIC LAUGHTER.

unfriendly act. See INNOCUOUS DESUETUDE.

union shop. See SHOP.

unturned. See LEAVE NO STONE UNTURNED.

up. "Come up to scratch" is virtually the same thing as "toe the mark." In the early days of prize-fighting, a bout used to last nearly all day and there was a refreshing absence of rules. But when it was found that battered hulks unable to stand were being trundled up to the center of the ring by their seconds, and that the death toll was rapidly mounting, it was decided there had to be a rule. So it came about that no one was allowed to continue fighting who could not "toe the mark" under his own steam. The figurative use of both expressions is to be on the starting line and ready to go.

"Up to snuff" conveys, rather, a keen alertness to what is going on about you. *Snuff*, the tobacco preparation, and *sniff* are both from a Teutonic root meaning "smell," and the figure is similar to that in "smell a rat." A person is "up to snuff" who is wise enough to sense that there is "something rotten in the state of Denmark."

The reason why things are sometimes said to have gone "up the spout" is that pawnbrokers developed a sort of spout up which they poked newly received articles, and down which these came again if they were by some remote chance redeemed. The figurative use, implying collapse or even death, dates back to 1812 at least.

up against it. See WEAKEST GOES TO THE WALL.

upper lip. See KEEP.

upset the apple cart. There seems to be no particular reason why this should have meant, ever since 1796 or thereabouts, to spoil or ruin a project. Skeat says that it may have originated as a provincial or childish reference to the human body, somewhat similar to "bread-basket" for stomach; at least, he remembered hearing it as a joking remark to a child who had fallen down: "Now you have upset your apple cart." But Stevenson shows that the idea was familiar even in classical Latin. The most recent prominent use of it was in George Bernard Shaw's play, *The Apple Cart.*

utilitarian. See FUTILITARIAN.

V

valet. See HERO.

valor. See POT VALOR.

vamoose. From the Spanish *vamos*, "let's go." Webster suggests that slang *mosey*, to go, may be akin.

vamp. The shoemaker's term, used by most of us in the word *revamp*, is from French *avant-pied*, the front part of the foot. The same idea is perhaps responsible for the musical expression, "vamp until ready," signifying that the accompanist is to improvise, or to play repeatedly an introduction, until the singer is ready to begin. The provincial English "vamp-horn," a sort of loud speaker used by village choirs of the last century, probably has nothing to do with the case.

The slang word meaning allure or attract is of course short for *vampire*, a bloodsucking ghost.

varlet, vassal. See HERO.

viscous. See BIRD-LIME.

vliet. See GRAMERCY PARK.

vociferous. See HALCYON DAYS.

Voltaire's God. See SCRAP OF PAPER.

voodoo. See HOODOO.

W

wagon. See CART BEFORE THE HORSE.

wait. See GEEZER.

walk. See COCK OF THE WALK.

Walker. See HOOKEY.

Walker's bus. See SHANK'S MARE.

wall. See WEAKEST GOES TO THE WALL.

wallflower. These flowers, known as "bloody warriors" in Devon, are fragrant and decorative. But don't tell your girl she is like a wall-flower. It means, as everybody knows, a girl who sits out dances because nobody will dance with her.

ward-heeler. See HEELED.

water. A diamond "of the first water" is not any longer, technically, the very best. Built on the same analogy, *river* and *extra river* are now used of the finer specimens. While "water," as signifying the transparency of a diamond, may be from an equivalent Arabic word for "luster," it is clear enough that the fundamental factor in the development of the word was the shining limpidity of water.

waters. See OIL ON TROUBLED WATERS.

way. See UNDER WAY.

weak as dishwater. See EYEWASH.

weakest goes to the wall. As you will discover if you try to keep to the right, going west along the south wall of Central Park (N.Y.C.), there are still people who have some sort of superstitious veneration for "keeping the wall." Originally, no doubt, it was cleaner or safer to stay as far as possible from the muddy road; and this accounts for the rule still in effect that a gentleman walking with a lady keeps the outside, or he may hear the venerable chant, "Girl for sale." The curious thing is that to be forced to the wall through weakness is considered highly undesirable. Already in the 16th century, "to go to the wall" meant to be "up against it," to be bankrupt or put on the shelf.

weasel words. This was Theodore Roosevelt's pungent description of a statement from which the original meaning has been sucked; i.e., a retraction, an explanation that the offending remarks should have been taken in the *Pickwickian sense* (q.v.). Weasels are able to suck eggs without breaking them.

weather. See UNDER THE WEATHER.

wedlock. See HOLY DEADLOCK.

weigh. See UNDER WAY.

well-heeled. See HEELED.

well met. See HAIL FELLOW WELL MET.

well-stacked. When I first encountered this picturesque equivalent for "well-built," there was a distinct mammary flavor about it, but later "research" has convinced me that it can now be used in medium-polite society. Yet the fact that "Dear Abby" (see *Reader's Digest*, Dec., 1959) contrasts a "stacked" girl with one "from Flatsville" is significant if not ominous.

Welsh rabbit. See RABBIT.

wet your whistle. The traditional British inability, or unwillingness, to make any distinction in sound between *wet* and *whet* led to a belief that *whet* might be the answer to the etymologist's prayer, in the search for a fitting explanation of this invitation to drink; but OED declares this erroneous. The dictionaries also disregard the ingenious tankard that would whistle for more when it was empty; evidently the originator of this theory thought of "wetting the whistle" as meaning the pouring in of liquor to stop the insistent whistling. An opposite conception is that a little moistening of the mouth and lips greatly improves the quality of your whistle. Anyone who has tried the children's game of filling the mouth with soda crackers and then trying to whistle *The Star Spangled Banner*, can vouch for the truth of this. Yet the authorities solemnly fall back on *whistle* as ancient slang for the mouth or throat.

we who are about to die salute thee. See MORITURI SALUTAMUS.

we won't get home until morning. See HOME.

whack. See BUSHWHACKER.

what cheer. See CHEER.

what every young wife should know. See PUNCH'S ADVICE.

what's right. "Not who's right, but what's right." Moral Re-Armament, through steelworker John Riffe, apparently originated this fine slogan (see *Wall Street Journal*, Oct. 15, 1959, p. 13). It was used to good effect in the negotiations that led to the settlement of the 1952 steel strike.

what the dickens. See DICKENS.

What will Mrs. Grundy say? See GRUNDY.

What, you egg! See EGG.

wheel. See CHUKKER. SPOKE.

when at Rome, do as the Romans do. See ROME.

when Greek meets Greek. See GREEK.

whet. See WET YOUR WHISTLE.

while crossing the river. See SWAP HORSES IN THE MIDDLE OF THE STREAM.

whisper. See PIG'S WHISPER.

whisky. Like *aquavitae*, this word for an intoxicant means, by derivation, "water of life" (Irish *uisgebeatha*).

whistle. "As clean as a whistle" may originally have been "as a whittle" and thus related to "white." Or the swish of a sword-blade may be somehow connected, as in the fairy-tale cliché, "He cut off the giant's head as clean as a whistle." Before 1800 the idea was already a common one. If it can be proved that the secret of making willow whistles was known to 18th century boys, too, then the slippery smoothness of the denuded stick might certainly have suggested "clean as a whistle." (See PIG'S WHISPER. WET YOUR WHISTLE.)

white feather. The story about the Quaker feeding the horde of savages is now definitely out of date. It has been established that the expression, as in the case of "crest-fallen," is a legacy from the cock-fighting ring. If the game bird had a white feather in his tail, it showed him to be of impure strain and therefore, presumably, less game than a thoroughbred.

Whittington's cat. See CAT.

whole hog. See HOG.

whole works. See WORKS.

whoopee. "To make whoopee" was popularized by Walter Winchell as much as by anybody, but he does not, I believe, claim to have invented it. It means, in the scholarly words of the Oxford Dictionary, "to go on the razzle-dazzle"; i.e., to be simply whooping with hilarity. "Whoopee water," for hard liquor, is a picturesque derivative. Sir William Craigie has pointed out that the ejaculation "Whoopee!" was familiar to Britons 300 years ago.

widow. See GRASS WIDOW.

wife. See CÆSAR'S WIFE MUST BE ABOVE SUSPICION. HUSSY.

wild and woolly. Alliteration had something to do with the popularity of this term describing our frontier West. OED quotes an 1891 writer who felt that the woolliness was in allusion to the shagginess of a really untamed sheepskin coat. Perhaps the notion of "courage" in "good-wooled" helped things along.

willies. There seems to be no very good reason why this should mean "the creeps," "nervous fears." A "Willy-boy" or "little Willy" is not, of course, perceptibly a he-man. Perhaps the notion of contempt that clings to the name Willy has been helped along by Leacock's "Willie is no good, I'll sell him." Then, too, there was silly Willy Stevens, of the Hall-Mills case (1926).

Wilson, Woodrow. See O.K.

wind. See GOD TEMPERS THE WIND TO THE SHORN LAMB.

wind blew great guns. See BLOW.

wine, women, and song. With his tongue in his cheek, probably, Thackeray ascribed this famous phrase to "Dr. Luther." An adherent of Luther's, having heard, long before Thackeray, this wicked libel, and fearing it was true, changed *Weiber*, women, to *Weib*, wife. Bartlett says the rhyme was composed by J. H. Voss in about 1775. The columnist, F. P. A., no doubt with "Sweet Adeline" in mind, remarked that these three are "the hardest to control, in the order named."

Wisconsin. See BADGER.

wise-crack. As long ago as 1903, a cutting remark was known as a "crack." Earlier still, to "crack a wheeze" meant to say something clever, or something that once was clever. Farther back still, in Shakespeare, we find "wise-acre" and "a college of wit-crackers." All of these, well scrambled, seem to furnish a good foundation for "wise-cracker" as a peddler of "smart Alecky" remarks.

Returning to "wise-acre" for a moment, we find considerable doubt as to why *acre* should have been dragged in at all. Probably Old High

German *wizzago* (*wicega*), prophet, was the source, though we are conscientiously warned not to associate this *zago* with German *sagen*, to say. As with *Gothamite* (q.v.), the history of this word teaches us the valuable lesson that he who pretends to know it all is soon recognized as a showy fool.

witches' Sabbath. See BAKER'S DOZEN. JUMP.

wit-cracker. See WISECRACK.

with all deliberate speed. Tom Burns Haber asks how these memorable words got from the English Court of Chancery (does anybody remember Chancery's "deliberate speed" in *Bleak House*?) where they were commonly used, into the mind of Francis Thompson and "The Hound of Heaven." It was apparently by way of Oliver Wendell Holmes (1912) that the phrase seeped into the Supreme Court's 1954 verdict on desegregation.

Wobblies. This nickname for the notoriously radical "I.W.W." ("I Won't Work") centered chiefly on the Pacific Coast is said to have been the distressing result of a Chinese attempt to pronounce two successive "double-yous." Other possibilities are very slim, such as *wobbler* for "infantryman" and the old *nobbler* for a "pickpocket" or "thimble-rigger." Surely "wobbly" does not describe the characteristic "Industrial Worker of the World," who is considered rather stubborn than otherwise.

womanly. See GENTLEMAN.

women. See WINE, WOMEN, AND SONG.

women who love their lords. One of Dickens's favorite euphemisms for pregnancy (see *Nicholas Nickleby*, chapter xxiii) was borrowed by him from a poem by John Home:

> . . . . I found myself
> As women wish to be who love their lords.

wonder. See NINE DAYS' WONDER.

woodchuck. This is a good illustration of a type of word coinage. Three Indian tribes, Cree, Algonquin, and Ojibway, had somewhat similar sounding names for a little frequenter of their woods and streams: *otchock*, *otchig*, *otchek*, *wuchak*, *wejack*. Obviously the chucking of wood has nothing to do with our present name for him, but the sound of it had everything to do with its formation. (See GROUND-HOG DAY.)

Wooden Horse. See GREEK.

woodpile. See NIGGER IN THE WOODPILE.

woods are full. See DRUG ON THE MARKET.

wool. A subject of long and acrimonious controversy in N. & Q., "wool-gathering," signifying unprofitable meditation, appears in the end to come from exactly what it says it does; namely, wool-gathering, by children, from hedges and bushes which have pulled shreds of wool from passing sheep. It was notorious as an occupation that brought very small immediate returns and had practically no future.

Though there was a word "to wool," meaning to get the better of, the picture envisaged in "pull the wool over his eyes" is probably just that of keeping a person from seeing what is going on, by covering his eyes with wool.

woolly. See WILD AND WOOLLY.

woozy. In the sense of dizzy, confused, or intoxicated, this word can as yet claim no formal etymology. Webster sees some possibilities in "oozy." I think "boozy" a more promising lead.

work. See BUCKLE DOWN TO WORK.

work oneself into a lather. See LATHER.

works. "Give him the works," or more accurately "woiks," has been sufficiently exploited in gangster pictures to make it hardly necessary to explain that it means to erase, to liquidate, to kill. It probably comes from "Give him the whole works," i.e., go the limit. In this sense "works" is perhaps from the word for factory, as in "Down by the vinegar works." In the case of a large factory or plant, "the whole works" would be, in today's laconic phrase, "something."

work smells of the lamp. See SMELL.

world. See ALL'S RIGHT WITH THE WORLD.

worse to the worst. "If the *worst* comes to the *worst*"—what sense does that make? Why not say, with Robinson Crusoe, "If the *worse comes to the worst*"?

worth a rap. See RAP.

worth makes the man. See PRUNELLA.

worth the candle. See CANDLE.

wrangler. See DUDE WRANGLER.

wrench. See MONKEY.

wrong side of the blanket. See BLANKET.

Y

Yankee. The once popular "Yengees" derivation (mispronunciation of "English") has been largely discarded in favor of the Dutch diminutive for John, *Janke*, used by the New Yorkers in derision of the New Englanders. At one time it was argued that it derived from the

Scotch *yankie*, "a gigantic falsehood"; at another early date, it was ascribed to the Yankow Indians, but unfortunately the tribe disappeared before it could be interviewed.

yen. No connection with the Japanese equivalent of our dollar. To have a yen for something is to crave it the way an opium fiend craves his narcotic. Literally, *yen* is nothing but "smoke," to "eat smoke" being the usual way to express the smoking of opium, in Chinese.

yes-man. See TOAD-EATER.

yoke. See CONJUGAL. JOY STICK.

young. See GOOD DIE YOUNG.

you're the doctor. See DOCTOR.

youse. See GUY.

youth. See FLAMING YOUTH.

yo-yo. See BANJO.

Yule. Rescued from oblivion by headline writers, this convenient little word for Christmas is believed now to be from an Old Norse word for one of the winter months. It is akin to *jolly*.

Z

zany. Our nearest equivalent for this Italian word (*zanni*, diminutive of *Giovanni*, John) is *stooge* (q.v.). Boastful and cowardly, he imitated the clown and served as the "goat" or butt of his practical jokes. Originally he was, Weekley says, a conjuror's assistant. Now we use *zany* to mean any awkward fool or "dumb cluck." (See SAWNEY.)

zed. See IZZARD.

zwieback. See BISCUIT.

&. See AMPERSAND.

BIBLIOGRAPHY

Barrère and Leland: *Dictionary of Slang*; London, 1897.

Bartlett, John: *Dictionary of Americanisms*; Boston, 1877. *Familiar Quotations* (latest editions).

Benham, W. G.: *New Book of Quotations*; New York, 1929.

Bombaugh, C. C.: *Facts and Fancies for the Curious*; Phila., 1905.

Brand-Ellis: *Popular Antiquities of Great Britain*; London, 1905.

Brewer, E. Cobham: *Dictionary of Phrase and Fable*; Phila., 1923.

Craigie, Sir William: *Dictionary of American English*; Chicago, 1944.

Crowell: *Dictionary of Business and Finance*; New York, 1930.

Dixon, J. M.: *Dictionary of Idiomatic English Phrases*; New York, 1891.

Edwards, Eliezer: *Words, Facts, and Phrases*; London, 1911.

Gerwig, Henrietta: *Crowell's Handbook for Readers and Writers*; New York, 1925.

Horwill, H. W.: *Modern American Usage*; Oxford, 1935.

Hotten, J. C.: *Dictionary of Modern Slang . . .*; London, 1867.

Hyamson, A. M.: *Dictionary of English Phrases*; New York, 1922.

Jamieson, John: *Dictionary of the Scottish Language*; London, 1877.

Kastner and Marks: *Glossary of Colloquial and Popular French*; London, 1929.

Mathews, Mitford M.: *Dictionary of Americanisms*; Chicago, 1951.

Mencken, H. L.: *The American Language*, Sup. II; New York, 1948.

Oxford Dictionary of English Proverbs; Oxford, 1935.

Oxford English Dictionary (through Supplement); Oxford, 1933.

Partridge, Eric: *Slang, Today and Yesterday*; London, 1933. *Dictionary of Slang*; New York, 1937. *Dictionary of the Underworld*; New York, 1950.

Pearson, Hesketh: *Common Misquotations*; London, 1934.

Read, A. W.; *Lexical Evidence from Folk Epigraphy*; Paris, 1935.

Serjeantson, Mary S.: *History of Foreign Words in English*; London, 1935.

Skeat, W. W.: *Etymological Dictionary of the English Language*; Oxford, 1910.

Stevenson, Burton: *Home Book of Quotations*; New York (latest editions).

Svartengren, T. Helding: *Intensifying Similes in English*; Lund, 1918.

Thornton, R. H.: *An American Glossary*; Phila., 1912.

Tucker, G. M.: *American English*; New York, 1921.

Vizetelly and de Bekker: *Desk Book of Idioms . . .*; New York, 1923.

Walsh, W. S.: *Handbook of Literary Curiosities*; Phila., 1892.

Webster's New International Dictionary; Springfield (latest editions).

Weekley, Ernest: *Etymological Dictionary of Modern English*; New York, 1921. *The Romance of Words*; New York, 1934. *Something about Words*; New York, 1935.

Weseen, M. H.: *Dictionary of American Slang*; New York, 1934. *Dictionary of English Grammar*; New York, 1928.
Wesleyan University: *Familiar Quotations*; Middletown, 1935.
Wright, Joseph: *English Dialect Dictionary*; New York, 1900.
Yule-Burnell: *Hobson-Jobson*; London, 1903.

A CATALOG OF SELECTED

DOVER BOOKS

IN ALL FIELDS OF INTEREST

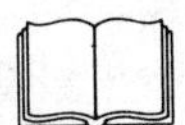

A CATALOG OF SELECTED DOVER BOOKS IN ALL FIELDS OF INTEREST

DRAWINGS OF REMBRANDT, edited by Seymour Slive. Updated Lippmann, Hofstede de Groot edition, with definitive scholarly apparatus. All portraits, biblical sketches, landscapes, nudes. Oriental figures, classical studies, together with selection of work by followers. 550 illustrations. Total of 630pp. 9⅛ × 12¼.
21485-0, 21486-9 Pa., Two-vol. set $25.00

GHOST AND HORROR STORIES OF AMBROSE BIERCE, Ambrose Bierce. 24 tales vividly imagined, strangely prophetic, and decades ahead of their time in technical skill: "The Damned Thing," "An Inhabitant of Carcosa," "The Eyes of the Panther," "Moxon's Master," and 20 more. 199pp. 5⅜ × 8½. 20767-6 Pa. $3.95

ETHICAL WRITINGS OF MAIMONIDES, Maimonides. Most significant ethical works of great medieval sage, newly translated for utmost precision, readability. Laws Concerning Character Traits, Eight Chapters, more. 192pp. 5⅜ × 8½.
24522-5 Pa. $4.50

THE EXPLORATION OF THE COLORADO RIVER AND ITS CANYONS, J. W. Powell. Full text of Powell's 1,000-mile expedition down the fabled Colorado in 1869. Superb account of terrain, geology, vegetation, Indians, famine, mutiny, treacherous rapids, mighty canyons, during exploration of last unknown part of continental U.S. 400pp. 5⅜ × 8½. 20094-9 Pa. $6.95

HISTORY OF PHILOSOPHY, Julián Marías. Clearest one-volume history on the market. Every major philosopher and dozens of others, to Existentialism and later. 505pp. 5⅜ × 8½. 21739-6 Pa. $8.50

ALL ABOUT LIGHTNING, Martin A. Uman. Highly readable non-technical survey of nature and causes of lightning, thunderstorms, ball lightning, St. Elmo's Fire, much more. Illustrated. 192pp. 5⅜ × 8½. 25237-X Pa. $5.95

SAILING ALONE AROUND THE WORLD, Captain Joshua Slocum. First man to sail around the world, alone, in small boat. One of great feats of seamanship told in delightful manner. 67 illustrations. 294pp. 5⅜ × 8½. 20326-3 Pa. $4.50

LETTERS AND NOTES ON THE MANNERS, CUSTOMS AND CONDITIONS OF THE NORTH AMERICAN INDIANS, George Catlin. Classic account of life among Plains Indians: ceremonies, hunt, warfare, etc. 312 plates. 572pp. of text. 6⅛ × 9¼. 22118-0, 22119-9 Pa. Two-vol. set $15.90

ALASKA: The Harriman Expedition, 1899, John Burroughs, John Muir, et al. Informative, engrossing accounts of two-month, 9,000-mile expedition. Native peoples, wildlife, forests, geography, salmon industry, glaciers, more. Profusely illustrated. 240 black-and-white line drawings. 124 black-and-white photographs. 3 maps. Index. 576pp. 5⅜ × 8½. 25109-8 Pa. $11.95

THE BOOK OF BEASTS: Being a Translation from a Latin Bestiary of the Twelfth Century, T. H. White. Wonderful catalog real and fanciful beasts: manticore, griffin, phoenix, amphivius, jaculus, many more. White's witty erudite commentary on scientific, historical aspects. Fascinating glimpse of medieval mind. Illustrated. 296pp. 5⅜ × 8¼. (Available in U.S. only) 24609-4 Pa. $5.95

FRANK LLOYD WRIGHT: ARCHITECTURE AND NATURE With 160 Illustrations, Donald Hoffmann. Profusely illustrated study of influence of nature—especially prairie—on Wright's designs for Fallingwater, Robie House, Guggenheim Museum, other masterpieces. 96pp. 9¼ × 10¾. 25098-9 Pa. $7.95

FRANK LLOYD WRIGHT'S FALLINGWATER, Donald Hoffmann. Wright's famous waterfall house: planning and construction of organic idea. History of site, owners, Wright's personal involvement. Photographs of various stages of building. Preface by Edgar Kaufmann, Jr. 100 illustrations. 112pp. 9¼ × 10.
23671-4 Pa. $7.95

YEARS WITH FRANK LLOYD WRIGHT: Apprentice to Genius, Edgar Tafel. Insightful memoir by a former apprentice presents a revealing portrait of Wright the man, the inspired teacher, the greatest American architect. 372 black-and-white illustrations. Preface. Index. vi + 228pp. 8¼ × 11. 24801-1 Pa. $9.95

THE STORY OF KING ARTHUR AND HIS KNIGHTS, Howard Pyle. Enchanting version of King Arthur fable has delighted generations with imaginative narratives of exciting adventures and unforgettable illustrations by the author. 41 illustrations. xviii + 313pp. 6⅛ × 9¼. 21445-1 Pa. $5.95

THE GODS OF THE EGYPTIANS, E. A. Wallis Budge. Thorough coverage of numerous gods of ancient Egypt by foremost Egyptologist. Information on evolution of cults, rites and gods; the cult of Osiris; the Book of the Dead and its rites; the sacred animals and birds; Heaven and Hell; and more. 956pp. 6⅛ × 9¼.
22055-9, 22056-7 Pa., Two-vol. set $20.00

A THEOLOGICO-POLITICAL TREATISE, Benedict Spinoza. Also contains unfinished *Political Treatise*. Great classic on religious liberty, theory of government on common consent. R. Elwes translation. Total of 421pp. 5⅜ × 8½.
20249-6 Pa. $6.95

INCIDENTS OF TRAVEL IN CENTRAL AMERICA, CHIAPAS, AND YUCATAN, John L. Stephens. Almost single-handed discovery of Maya culture; exploration of ruined cities, monuments, temples; customs of Indians. 115 drawings. 892pp. 5⅜ × 8½. 22404-X, 22405-8 Pa., Two-vol. set $15.90

LOS CAPRICHOS, Francisco Goya. 80 plates of wild, grotesque monsters and caricatures. Prado manuscript included. 183pp. 6⅜ × 9⅜. 22384-1 Pa. $4.95

AUTOBIOGRAPHY: The Story of My Experiments with Truth, Mohandas K. Gandhi. Not hagiography, but Gandhi in his own words. Boyhood, legal studies, purification, the growth of the Satyagraha (nonviolent protest) movement. Critical, inspiring work of the man who freed India. 480pp. 5⅜ × 8½. (Available in U.S. only)
24593-4 Pa. $6.95

HOW TO WRITE, Gertrude Stein. Gertrude Stein claimed anyone could understand her unconventional writing—here are clues to help. Fascinating improvisations, language experiments, explanations illuminate Stein's craft and the art of writing. Total of 414pp. 4⅝ × 6⅝. 23144-5 Pa. $5.95

ADVENTURES AT SEA IN THE GREAT AGE OF SAIL: Five Firsthand Narratives, edited by Elliot Snow. Rare true accounts of exploration, whaling, shipwreck, fierce natives, trade, shipboard life, more. 33 illustrations. Introduction. 353pp. 5⅜ × 8½. 25177-2 Pa. $7.95

THE HERBAL OR GENERAL HISTORY OF PLANTS, John Gerard. Classic descriptions of about 2,850 plants—with over 2,700 illustrations—includes Latin and English names, physical descriptions, varieties, time and place of growth, more. 2,706 illustrations. xlv + 1,678pp. 8½ × 12¼. 23147-X Cloth. $75.00

DOROTHY AND THE WIZARD IN OZ, L. Frank Baum. Dorothy and the Wizard visit the center of the Earth, where people are vegetables, glass houses grow and Oz characters reappear. Classic sequel to *Wizard of Oz*. 256pp. 5⅜ × 8. 24714-7 Pa. $4.95

SONGS OF EXPERIENCE: Facsimile Reproduction with 26 Plates in Full Color, William Blake. This facsimile of Blake's original "Illuminated Book" reproduces 26 full-color plates from a rare 1826 edition. Includes "The Tyger," "London," "Holy Thursday," and other immortal poems. 26 color plates. Printed text of poems. 48pp. 5¼ × 7. 24636-1 Pa. $3.50

SONGS OF INNOCENCE, William Blake. The first and most popular of Blake's famous "Illuminated Books," in a facsimile edition reproducing all 31 brightly colored plates. Additional printed text of each poem. 64pp. 5¼ × 7. 22764-2 Pa. $3.50

PRECIOUS STONES, Max Bauer. Classic, thorough study of diamonds, rubies, emeralds, garnets, etc.: physical character, occurrence, properties, use, similar topics. 20 plates, 8 in color. 94 figures. 659pp. 6⅛ × 9¼. 21910-0, 21911-9 Pa., Two-vol. set $14.90

ENCYCLOPEDIA OF VICTORIAN NEEDLEWORK, S. F. A. Caulfeild and Blanche Saward. Full, precise descriptions of stitches, techniques for dozens of needlecrafts—most exhaustive reference of its kind. Over 800 figures. Total of 679pp. 8⅛ × 11. Two volumes. Vol. 1 22800-2 Pa. $10.95
Vol. 2 22801-0 Pa. $10.95

THE MARVELOUS LAND OF OZ, L. Frank Baum. Second Oz book, the Scarecrow and Tin Woodman are back with hero named Tip, Oz magic. 136 illustrations. 287pp. 5⅜ × 8½. 20692-0 Pa. $5.95

WILD FOWL DECOYS, Joel Barber. Basic book on the subject, by foremost authority and collector. Reveals history of decoy making and rigging, place in American culture, different kinds of decoys, how to make them, and how to use them. 140 plates. 156pp. 7⅞ × 10¾. 20011-6 Pa. $7.95

HISTORY OF LACE, Mrs. Bury Palliser. Definitive, profusely illustrated chronicle of lace from earliest times to late 19th century. Laces of Italy, Greece, England, France, Belgium, etc. Landmark of needlework scholarship. 266 illustrations. 672pp. 6⅛ × 9¼. 24742-2 Pa. $14.95

SUNDIALS, Albert Waugh. Far and away the best, most thorough coverage of ideas, mathematics concerned, types, construction, adjusting anywhere. Over 100 illustrations. 230pp. 5⅜ × 8½. 22947-5 Pa. $4.00

PICTURE HISTORY OF THE NORMANDIE: With 190 Illustrations, Frank O. Braynard. Full story of legendary French ocean liner: Art Deco interiors, design innovations, furnishings, celebrities, maiden voyage, tragic fire, much more. Extensive text. 144pp. 8⅞ × 11¾. 25257-4 Pa. $9.95

THE FIRST AMERICAN COOKBOOK: A Facsimile of "American Cookery," 1796, Amelia Simmons. Facsimile of the first American-written cookbook published in the United States contains authentic recipes for colonial favorites—pumpkin pudding, winter squash pudding, spruce beer, Indian slapjacks, and more. Introductory Essay and Glossary of colonial cooking terms. 80pp. 5⅜ × 8½. 24710-4 Pa. $3.50

101 PUZZLES IN THOUGHT AND LOGIC, C. R. Wylie, Jr. Solve murders and robberies, find out which fishermen are liars, how a blind man could possibly identify a color—purely by your own reasoning! 107pp. 5⅜ × 8½. 20367-0 Pa. $2.00

THE BOOK OF WORLD-FAMOUS MUSIC—CLASSICAL, POPULAR AND FOLK, James J. Fuld. Revised and enlarged republication of landmark work in musico-bibliography. Full information about nearly 1,000 songs and compositions including first lines of music and lyrics. New supplement. Index. 800pp. 5⅜ × 8¼. 24857-7 Pa. $14.95

ANTHROPOLOGY AND MODERN LIFE, Franz Boas. Great anthropologist's classic treatise on race and culture. Introduction by Ruth Bunzel. Only inexpensive paperback edition. 255pp. 5⅜ × 8½. 25245-0 Pa. $5.95

THE TALE OF PETER RABBIT, Beatrix Potter. The inimitable Peter's terrifying adventure in Mr. McGregor's garden, with all 27 wonderful, full-color Potter illustrations. 55pp. 4¼ × 5½. (Available in U.S. only) 22827-4 Pa. $1.75

THREE PROPHETIC SCIENCE FICTION NOVELS, H. G. Wells. *When the Sleeper Wakes, A Story of the Days to Come* and *The Time Machine* (full version). 335pp. 5⅜ × 8½. (Available in U.S. only) 20605-X Pa. $5.95

APICIUS COOKERY AND DINING IN IMPERIAL ROME, edited and translated by Joseph Dommers Vehling. Oldest known cookbook in existence offers readers a clear picture of what foods Romans ate, how they prepared them, etc. 49 illustrations. 301pp. 6⅛ × 9¼. 23563-7 Pa. $6.00

SHAKESPEARE LEXICON AND QUOTATION DICTIONARY, Alexander Schmidt. Full definitions, locations, shades of meaning of every word in plays and poems. More than 50,000 exact quotations. 1,485pp. 6½ × 9¼. 22726-X, 22727-8 Pa., Two-vol. set $27.90

THE WORLD'S GREAT SPEECHES, edited by Lewis Copeland and Lawrence W. Lamm. Vast collection of 278 speeches from Greeks to 1970. Powerful and effective models; unique look at history. 842pp. 5⅜ × 8½. 20468-5 Pa. $10.95

THE BLUE FAIRY BOOK, Andrew Lang. The first, most famous collection, with many familiar tales: Little Red Riding Hood, Aladdin and the Wonderful Lamp, Puss in Boots, Sleeping Beauty, Hansel and Gretel, Rumpelstiltskin; 37 in all. 138 illustrations. 390pp. 5⅜ × 8½. 21437-0 Pa. $5.95

THE STORY OF THE CHAMPIONS OF THE ROUND TABLE, Howard Pyle. Sir Launcelot, Sir Tristram and Sir Percival in spirited adventures of love and triumph retold in Pyle's inimitable style. 50 drawings, 31 full-page. xviii + 329pp. 6½ × 9¼. 21883-X Pa. $6.95

AUDUBON AND HIS JOURNALS, Maria Audubon. Unmatched two-volume portrait of the great artist, naturalist and author contains his journals, an excellent biography by his granddaughter, expert annotations by the noted ornithologist, Dr. Elliott Coues, and 37 superb illustrations. Total of 1,200pp. 5⅜ × 8.
Vol. I 25143-8 Pa. $8.95
Vol. II 25144-6 Pa. $8.95

GREAT DINOSAUR HUNTERS AND THEIR DISCOVERIES, Edwin H. Colbert. Fascinating, lavishly illustrated chronicle of dinosaur research, 1820's to 1960. Achievements of Cope, Marsh, Brown, Buckland, Mantell, Huxley, many others. 384pp. 5¼ × 8¼. 24701-5 Pa. $6.95

THE TASTEMAKERS, Russell Lynes. Informal, illustrated social history of American taste 1850's–1950's. First popularized categories Highbrow, Lowbrow, Middlebrow. 129 illustrations. New (1979) afterword. 384pp. 6 × 9.
23993-4 Pa. $6.95

DOUBLE CROSS PURPOSES, Ronald A. Knox. A treasure hunt in the Scottish Highlands, an old map, unidentified corpse, surprise discoveries keep reader guessing in this cleverly intricate tale of financial skullduggery. 2 black-and-white maps. 320pp. 5⅜ × 8½. (Available in U.S. only) 25032-6 Pa. $5.95

AUTHENTIC VICTORIAN DECORATION AND ORNAMENTATION IN FULL COLOR: 46 Plates from "Studies in Design," Christopher Dresser. Superb full-color lithographs reproduced from rare original portfolio of a major Victorian designer. 48pp. 9¼ × 12¼. 25083-0 Pa. $7.95

PRIMITIVE ART, Franz Boas. Remains the best text ever prepared on subject, thoroughly discussing Indian, African, Asian, Australian, and, especially, Northern American primitive art. Over 950 illustrations show ceramics, masks, totem poles, weapons, textiles, paintings, much more. 376pp. 5⅜ × 8. 20025-6 Pa. $6.95

SIDELIGHTS ON RELATIVITY, Albert Einstein. Unabridged republication of two lectures delivered by the great physicist in 1920–21. *Ether and Relativity* and *Geometry and Experience.* Elegant ideas in non-mathematical form, accessible to intelligent layman. vi + 56pp. 5⅜ × 8½. 24511-X Pa. $2.95

THE WIT AND HUMOR OF OSCAR WILDE, edited by Alvin Redman. More than 1,000 ripostes, paradoxes, wisecracks: Work is the curse of the drinking classes, I can resist everything except temptation, etc. 258pp. 5⅜ × 8½. 20602-5 Pa. $3.95

ADVENTURES WITH A MICROSCOPE, Richard Headstrom. 59 adventures with clothing fibers, protozoa, ferns and lichens, roots and leaves, much more. 142 illustrations. 232pp. 5⅜ × 8½. 23471-1 Pa. $3.95

PLANTS OF THE BIBLE, Harold N. Moldenke and Alma L. Moldenke. Standard reference to all 230 plants mentioned in Scriptures. Latin name, biblical reference, uses, modern identity, much more. Unsurpassed encyclopedic resource for scholars, botanists, nature lovers, students of Bible. Bibliography. Indexes. 123 black-and-white illustrations. 384pp. 6 × 9. 25069-5 Pa. $8.95

FAMOUS AMERICAN WOMEN: A Biographical Dictionary from Colonial Times to the Present, Robert McHenry, ed. From Pocahontas to Rosa Parks, 1,035 distinguished American women documented in separate biographical entries. Accurate, up-to-date data, numerous categories, spans 400 years. Indices. 493pp. 6½ × 9¼. 24523-3 Pa. $9.95

THE FABULOUS INTERIORS OF THE GREAT OCEAN LINERS IN HISTORIC PHOTOGRAPHS, William H. Miller, Jr. Some 200 superb photographs capture exquisite interiors of world's great "floating palaces"—1890's to 1980's: *Titanic, Ile de France, Queen Elizabeth, United States, Europa,* more. Approx. 200 black-and-white photographs. Captions. Text. Introduction. 160pp. 8⅞ × 11¾. 24756-2 Pa. $9.95

THE GREAT LUXURY LINERS, 1927-1954: A Photographic Record, William H. Miller, Jr. Nostalgic tribute to heyday of ocean liners. 186 photos of Ile de France, Normandie, Leviathan, Queen Elizabeth, United States, many others. Interior and exterior views. Introduction. Captions. 160pp. 9 × 12. 24056-8 Pa. $9.95

A NATURAL HISTORY OF THE DUCKS, John Charles Phillips. Great landmark of ornithology offers complete detailed coverage of nearly 200 species and subspecies of ducks: gadwall, sheldrake, merganser, pintail, many more. 74 full-color plates, 102 black-and-white. Bibliography. Total of 1,920pp. 8⅜ × 11¼. 25141-1, 25142-X Cloth. Two-vol. set $100.00

THE SEAWEED HANDBOOK: An Illustrated Guide to Seaweeds from North Carolina to Canada, Thomas F. Lee. Concise reference covers 78 species. Scientific and common names, habitat, distribution, more. Finding keys for easy identification. 224pp. 5⅜ × 8½. 25215-9 Pa. $5.95

THE TEN BOOKS OF ARCHITECTURE: The 1755 Leoni Edition, Leon Battista Alberti. Rare classic helped introduce the glories of ancient architecture to the Renaissance. 68 black-and-white plates. 336pp. 8⅜ × 11¼. 25239-6 Pa. $14.95

MISS MACKENZIE, Anthony Trollope. Minor masterpieces by Victorian master unmasks many truths about life in 19th-century England. First inexpensive edition in years. 392pp. 5⅜ × 8½. 25201-9 Pa. $7.95

THE RIME OF THE ANCIENT MARINER, Gustave Doré, Samuel Taylor Coleridge. Dramatic engravings considered by many to be his greatest work. The terrifying space of the open sea, the storms and whirlpools of an unknown ocean, the ice of Antarctica, more—all rendered in a powerful, chilling manner. Full text. 38 plates. 77pp. 9¼ × 12. 22305-1 Pa. $4.95

THE EXPEDITIONS OF ZEBULON MONTGOMERY PIKE, Zebulon Montgomery Pike. Fascinating first-hand accounts (1805-6) of exploration of Mississippi River, Indian wars, capture by Spanish dragoons, much more. 1,088pp. 5⅜ × 8½. 25254-X, 25255-8 Pa. Two-vol. set $23.90

A CONCISE HISTORY OF PHOTOGRAPHY: Third Revised Edition, Helmut Gernsheim. Best one-volume history—camera obscura, photochemistry, daguerreotypes, evolution of cameras, film, more. Also artistic aspects—landscape, portraits, fine art, etc. 281 black-and-white photographs. 26 in color. 176pp. 8⅜ × 11¼. 25128-4 Pa. $12.95

THE DORÉ BIBLE ILLUSTRATIONS, Gustave Doré. 241 detailed plates from the Bible: the Creation scenes, Adam and Eve, Flood, Babylon, battle sequences, life of Jesus, etc. Each plate is accompanied by the verses from the King James version of the Bible. 241pp. 9 × 12. 23004-X Pa. $8.95

HUGGER-MUGGER IN THE LOUVRE, Elliot Paul. Second Homer Evans mystery-comedy. Theft at the Louvre involves sleuth in hilarious, madcap caper. "A knockout."—Books. 336pp. 5⅜ × 8½. 25185-3 Pa. $5.95

FLATLAND, E. A. Abbott. Intriguing and enormously popular science-fiction classic explores the complexities of trying to survive as a two-dimensional being in a three-dimensional world. Amusingly illustrated by the author. 16 illustrations. 103pp. 5⅜ × 8½. 20001-9 Pa. $2.00

THE HISTORY OF THE LEWIS AND CLARK EXPEDITION, Meriwether Lewis and William Clark, edited by Elliott Coues. Classic edition of Lewis and Clark's day-by-day journals that later became the basis for U.S. claims to Oregon and the West. Accurate and invaluable geographical, botanical, biological, meteorological and anthropological material. Total of 1,508pp. 5⅜ × 8½.
21268-8, 21269-6, 21270-X Pa. Three-vol. set $25.50

LANGUAGE, TRUTH AND LOGIC, Alfred J. Ayer. Famous, clear introduction to Vienna, Cambridge schools of Logical Positivism. Role of philosophy, elimination of metaphysics, nature of analysis, etc. 160pp. 5⅜ × 8½. (Available in U.S. and Canada only) 20010-8 Pa. $2.95

MATHEMATICS FOR THE NONMATHEMATICIAN, Morris Kline. Detailed, college-level treatment of mathematics in cultural and historical context, with numerous exercises. For liberal arts students. Preface. Recommended Reading Lists. Tables. Index. Numerous black-and-white figures. xvi + 641pp. 5⅜ × 8½.
24823-2 Pa. $11.95

28 SCIENCE FICTION STORIES, H. G. Wells. Novels, *Star Begotten* and *Men Like Gods,* plus 26 short stories: "Empire of the Ants," "A Story of the Stone Age," "The Stolen Bacillus," "In the Abyss," etc. 915pp. 5⅜ × 8½. (Available in U.S. only)
20265-8 Cloth. $10.95

HANDBOOK OF PICTORIAL SYMBOLS, Rudolph Modley. 3,250 signs and symbols, many systems in full; official or heavy commercial use. Arranged by subject. Most in Pictorial Archive series. 143pp. 8⅛ × 11. 23357-X Pa. $5.95

INCIDENTS OF TRAVEL IN YUCATAN, John L. Stephens. Classic (1843) exploration of jungles of Yucatan, looking for evidences of Maya civilization. Travel adventures, Mexican and Indian culture, etc. Total of 669pp. 5⅜ × 8½.
20926-1, 20927-X Pa., Two-vol. set $9.90

DEGAS: An Intimate Portrait, Ambroise Vollard. Charming, anecdotal memoir by famous art dealer of one of the greatest 19th-century French painters. 14 black-and-white illustrations. Introduction by Harold L. Van Doren. 96pp. 5⅜ × 8½.
25131-4 Pa. $3.95

PERSONAL NARRATIVE OF A PILGRIMAGE TO ALMANDINAH AND MECCAH, Richard Burton. Great travel classic by remarkably colorful personality. Burton, disguised as a Moroccan, visited sacred shrines of Islam, narrowly escaping death. 47 illustrations. 959pp. 5⅜ × 8½. 21217-3, 21218-1 Pa., Two-vol. set $17.90

PHRASE AND WORD ORIGINS, A. H. Holt. Entertaining, reliable, modern study of more than 1,200 colorful words, phrases, origins and histories. Much unexpected information. 254pp. 5⅜ × 8½. 20758-7 Pa. $4.95

THE RED THUMB MARK, R. Austin Freeman. In this first Dr. Thorndyke case, the great scientific detective draws fascinating conclusions from the nature of a single fingerprint. Exciting story, authentic science. 320pp. 5⅜ × 8½. (Available in U.S. only) 25210-8 Pa. $5.95

AN EGYPTIAN HIEROGLYPHIC DICTIONARY, E. A. Wallis Budge. Monumental work containing about 25,000 words or terms that occur in texts ranging from 3000 B.C. to 600 A.D. Each entry consists of a transliteration of the word, the word in hieroglyphs, and the meaning in English. 1,314pp. 6⅞ × 10.
23615-3, 23616-1 Pa., Two-vol. set $27.90

THE COMPLEAT STRATEGYST: Being a Primer on the Theory of Games of Strategy, J. D. Williams. Highly entertaining classic describes, with many illustrated examples, how to select best strategies in conflict situations. Prefaces. Appendices. xvi + 268pp. 5⅜ × 8½. 25101-2 Pa. $5.95

THE ROAD TO OZ, L. Frank Baum. Dorothy meets the Shaggy Man, little Button-Bright and the Rainbow's beautiful daughter in this delightful trip to the magical Land of Oz. 272pp. 5⅜ × 8. 25208-6 Pa. $4.95

POINT AND LINE TO PLANE, Wassily Kandinsky. Seminal exposition of role of point, line, other elements in non-objective painting. Essential to understanding 20th-century art. 127 illustrations. 192pp. 6½ × 9¼. 23808-3 Pa. $4.50

LADY ANNA, Anthony Trollope. Moving chronicle of Countess Lovel's bitter struggle to win for herself and daughter Anna their rightful rank and fortune—perhaps at cost of sanity itself. 384pp. 5⅜ × 8½. 24669-8 Pa. $6.95

EGYPTIAN MAGIC, E. A. Wallis Budge. Sums up all that is known about magic in Ancient Egypt: the role of magic in controlling the gods, powerful amulets that warded off evil spirits, scarabs of immortality, use of wax images, formulas and spells, the secret name, much more. 253pp. 5⅜ × 8½. 22681-6 Pa. $4.00

THE DANCE OF SIVA, Ananda Coomaraswamy. Preeminent authority unfolds the vast metaphysic of India: the revelation of her art, conception of the universe, social organization, etc. 27 reproductions of art masterpieces. 192pp. 5⅜ × 8½.
24817-8 Pa. $5.95

CHRISTMAS CUSTOMS AND TRADITIONS, Clement A. Miles. Origin, evolution, significance of religious, secular practices. Caroling, gifts, yule logs, much more. Full, scholarly yet fascinating; non-sectarian. 400pp. 5⅜ × 8½.
23354-5 Pa. $6.50

THE HUMAN FIGURE IN MOTION, Eadweard Muybridge. More than 4,500 stopped-action photos, in action series, showing undraped men, women, children jumping, lying down, throwing, sitting, wrestling, carrying, etc. 390pp. 7⅞ × 10⅝.
20204-6 Cloth. $19.95

THE MAN WHO WAS THURSDAY, Gilbert Keith Chesterton. Witty, fast-paced novel about a club of anarchists in turn-of-the-century London. Brilliant social, religious, philosophical speculations. 128pp. 5⅜ × 8½. 25121-7 Pa. $3.95

A CEZANNE SKETCHBOOK: Figures, Portraits, Landscapes and Still Lifes, Paul Cezanne. Great artist experiments with tonal effects, light, mass, other qualities in over 100 drawings. A revealing view of developing master painter, precursor of Cubism. 102 black-and-white illustrations. 144pp. 8¾ × 6⅜. 24790-2 Pa. $5.95

AN ENCYCLOPEDIA OF BATTLES: Accounts of Over 1,560 Battles from 1479 B.C. to the Present, David Eggenberger. Presents essential details of every major battle in recorded history, from the first battle of Megiddo in 1479 B.C. to Grenada in 1984. List of Battle Maps. New Appendix covering the years 1967–1984. Index. 99 illustrations. 544pp. 6½ × 9¼. 24913-1 Pa. $14.95

AN ETYMOLOGICAL DICTIONARY OF MODERN ENGLISH, Ernest Weekley. Richest, fullest work, by foremost British lexicographer. Detailed word histories. Inexhaustible. Total of 856pp. 6½ × 9¼.
21873-2, 21874-0 Pa., Two-vol. set $17.00

WEBSTER'S AMERICAN MILITARY BIOGRAPHIES, edited by Robert McHenry. Over 1,000 figures who shaped 3 centuries of American military history. Detailed biographies of Nathan Hale, Douglas MacArthur, Mary Hallaren, others. Chronologies of engagements, more. Introduction. Addenda. 1,033 entries in alphabetical order. xi + 548pp. 6½ × 9¼. (Available in U.S. only)
24758-9 Pa. $11.95

LIFE IN ANCIENT EGYPT, Adolf Erman. Detailed older account, with much not in more recent books: domestic life, religion, magic, medicine, commerce, and whatever else needed for complete picture. Many illustrations. 597pp. 5⅜ × 8½.
22632-8 Pa. $8.50

HISTORIC COSTUME IN PICTURES, Braun & Schneider. Over 1,450 costumed figures shown, covering a wide variety of peoples: kings, emperors, nobles, priests, servants, soldiers, scholars, townsfolk, peasants, merchants, courtiers, cavaliers, and more. 256pp. 8⅜ × 11¼. 23150-X Pa. $7.95

THE NOTEBOOKS OF LEONARDO DA VINCI, edited by J. P. Richter. Extracts from manuscripts reveal great genius; on painting, sculpture, anatomy, sciences, geography, etc. Both Italian and English. 186 ms. pages reproduced, plus 500 additional drawings, including studies for *Last Supper, Sforza* monument, etc. 860pp. 7⅞ × 10¾. (Available in U.S. only) 22572-0, 22573-9 Pa., Two-vol. set $25.90

THE ART NOUVEAU STYLE BOOK OF ALPHONSE MUCHA: All 72 Plates from "Documents Decoratifs" in Original Color, Alphonse Mucha. Rare copyright-free design portfolio by high priest of Art Nouveau. Jewelry, wallpaper, stained glass, furniture, figure studies, plant and animal motifs, etc. Only complete one-volume edition. 80pp. 9⅜ × 12¼. 24044-4 Pa. $8.95

ANIMALS: 1,419 COPYRIGHT-FREE ILLUSTRATIONS OF MAMMALS, BIRDS, FISH, INSECTS, ETC., edited by Jim Harter. Clear wood engravings present, in extremely lifelike poses, over 1,000 species of animals. One of the most extensive pictorial sourcebooks of its kind. Captions. Index. 284pp. 9 × 12. 23766-4 Pa. $9.95

OBELISTS FLY HIGH, C. Daly King. Masterpiece of American detective fiction, long out of print, involves murder on a 1935 transcontinental flight—"a very thrilling story"—NY Times. Unabridged and unaltered republication of the edition published by William Collins Sons & Co. Ltd., London, 1935. 288pp. 5⅜ × 8½. (Available in U.S. only) 25036-9 Pa. $4.95

VICTORIAN AND EDWARDIAN FASHION: A Photographic Survey, Alison Gernsheim. First fashion history completely illustrated by contemporary photographs. Full text plus 235 photos, 1840–1914, in which many celebrities appear. 240pp. 6½ × 9¼. 24205-6 Pa. $6.00

THE ART OF THE FRENCH ILLUSTRATED BOOK, 1700–1914, Gordon N. Ray. Over 630 superb book illustrations by Fragonard, Delacroix, Daumier, Doré, Grandville, Manet, Mucha, Steinlen, Toulouse-Lautrec and many others. Preface. Introduction. 633 halftones. Indices of artists, authors & titles, binders and provenances. Appendices. Bibliography. 608pp. 8⅜ × 11¼. 25086-5 Pa. $24.95

THE WONDERFUL WIZARD OF OZ, L. Frank Baum. Facsimile in full color of America's finest children's classic. 143 illustrations by W. W. Denslow. 267pp. 5⅜ × 8½. 20691-2 Pa. $5.95

FRONTIERS OF MODERN PHYSICS: New Perspectives on Cosmology, Relativity, Black Holes and Extraterrestrial Intelligence, Tony Rothman, et al. For the intelligent layman. Subjects include: cosmological models of the universe; black holes; the neutrino; the search for extraterrestrial intelligence. Introduction. 46 black-and-white illustrations. 192pp. 5⅜ × 8½. 24587-X Pa. $6.95

THE FRIENDLY STARS, Martha Evans Martin & Donald Howard Menzel. Classic text marshalls the stars together in an engaging, non-technical survey, presenting them as sources of beauty in night sky. 23 illustrations. Foreword. 2 star charts. Index. 147pp. 5⅜ × 8½. 21099-5 Pa. $3.50

FADS AND FALLACIES IN THE NAME OF SCIENCE, Martin Gardner. Fair, witty appraisal of cranks, quacks, and quackeries of science and pseudoscience: hollow earth, Velikovsky, orgone energy, Dianetics, flying saucers, Bridey Murphy, food and medical fads, etc. Revised, expanded In the Name of Science. "A very able and even-tempered presentation."—The New Yorker. 363pp. 5⅜ × 8. 20394-8 Pa. $5.95

ANCIENT EGYPT: ITS CULTURE AND HISTORY, J. E Manchip White. From pre-dynastics through Ptolemies: society, history, political structure, religion, daily life, literature, cultural heritage. 48 plates. 217pp. 5⅜ × 8½. 22548-8 Pa. $4.95